Workers' Democracy in China's Transition from State Socialism

East Asia

History, Politics, Sociology, Culture

Workers' Democracy in China's Transition from State Socialism

Stephen E. Philion

Routledge
Taylor & Francis Group

NEW YORK AND LONDON

First published 2009
by Routledge
605 Third Avenue, New York, NY 10017

Simultaneously published in the UK
by Routledge
4 Park Square, Milton Park, Abingdon, Oxon OX14 4RN

Routledge is an imprint of the Taylor & Francis Group, an informa business

First issued in paperback 2012

© 2009 Taylor & Francis

Typeset in Sabon by IBT Global.

Library of Congress Cataloging in Publication Data

Philion, Stephen E.
   Workers' democracy in China's transition from state socialism / by Stephen E. Philion.
      p. cm.—(East Asia history, politics, sociology and culture)
   Includes bibliographical references and index.
   1. Labor—China.   2. Working class—China.   3. Management—Employee participation—China.   4. China—Economic policy.   I. Title.
   HD8736.5.P55 2009
   338.6'90951—dc22
   2008029453

ISBN13: 978-0-415-96206-3 (hbk)
ISBN13: 978-0-415-54257-9 (pbk)
ISBN13: 978-0-203-88397-6 (ebk)

I dedicate this book to my parents,
Richard and Patricia Philion.

Contents

Acknowledgments

This book grew out of my dissertation thesis, which was completed in 2004 at the University of Hawaii at Manoa. Thanks to a 'visiting foreign researcher' fellowship provided by the University of Hawaii at Manoa Center for Chinese Studies and Peking University, I was able to reside in Beijing for eight months and begin to make important acquaintances and friendships with Chinese scholars who studied and were sympathetic with the then increasingly active labor movement in China's state-owned enterprise (SOE) sector. I am especially grateful to Minqi Li for a heads up on potential and worthwhile contacts in Beijing, not least of whom was Zhang Yaozu. Mr. Zhang, then a graduate student at Peking University, was and remains a tireless activist with a dedication to the cause of helping China's workers fight for alternatives to surrendering to the forces of corporate globalization. Mr. Zhang and I engaged in endless discussions on the situation of China's working class and on the importance of the struggles that were occurring in the SOE sector, which few others in China's academy (or elsewhere) understood or appreciated at the time. He was especially supportive of my quest to meet with and interview workers who were resisting SOE privatization.

Zhang Yingsuo, a Korean scholar and labor activist who was finishing an MA at Peking University in 1999, also was a real asset as a sociologist who was collecting data on Chinese workers' conflicts and ideologies. He joined me on a trip to Zhengzhou to meet with protesting SOE workers and their supporters. In Zhengzhou, I had the unique opportunity to spend time with and interview leaders of protests against SOE privatization. Because some of the activists involved in these protests have been monitored and subjected to harassment by authorities as they endeavored to protect the assets of state workers against fraudulent 'investors,' I will not thank them in name. Suffice it to say, I perhaps owe them the greatest thanks for their help in gaining access to the SOE-based workers' movement in Zhengzhou in the first years of the new millennium.

In Beijing, as a graduate student, I had the good fortune of engaging in many fruitful and lively discussions with fellow international graduate students on the consequences and alternatives to China's transition from state socialism, including Joel Andreas, Saul Thomas, Jonathan Lassen, Viren Murthy, Gregory Chin, Christopher Swarat, Robert Cliver, and Michael Johnston. In Hawaii, I was especially fortunate to have a classmate of exceptional caliber in the form of Shijen He, whose theoretical level I was only too lucky to encounter and appreciate as I wrote both my dissertation and book.

Peter Manicas, my dissertation advisor, was endlessly supportive and patient as I worked on finishing my dissertation. The amount of time he puts into both academic writing and student advising has been a model for my own writing and teaching. At every step of revising the original dissertation into a book, Peter has encouraged me to stick with making arguments that I believe in, even when they run against established trends in the literature.

My other dissertation committee members, Hagen Koo, Oliver Lee, John Goldberg Hiller, and the late Herbert Barringer, also contributed numerous comments and criticisms, which later greatly contributed to revisions as I wrote this book. Colleagues from St. Cloud State University, including Jiping Zuo, Lindah Mhando, Robert Lavenda, Paul Greider, and Tom O'Toole, provided me with helpful advice on moving this project to completion in the last year. Conversations with colleagues from around the world, including Grant Arndt, Yiching Wu, Han Deqiang, Dai Jianzhong, Christopher Isett, Joel Andreas, Viren Murthy, Robert Cliver, Saul Thomas, Richard Smith, Anita Chan, Marc Blecher, Chen Hsin-Hsing, and Zheng Yiwen, all helped me with comments and critical suggestions as I thought about how to revise this dissertation into a book. Joel Andreas and Grant Arndt took time out of their own busy book projects to make extensive comments on several chapters of this book. Suffice it to say, only I am responsible for what flaws remain in the final outcome of that process.

Finally, I could never express enough appreciation to my family for their support as I completed this book. My wife, Chientzu Chou, and son, Langston, have both been forgiving of daddy as he spent innumerable hours in cafes and other makeshift 'offices' to write and edit this book.

My parents, Richard and Patricia Philion, have been a constant source of support and help with proofreading. So much of both this book and other life milestones are on account of their dedication and sacrifices; with this in mind, I dedicate this book to them.

1 Locating a Discourse in Transition

Workers' democracy as a discourse in China has comprised an ideological set of ideas, beliefs, and practices that has been deployed as a means to address contradictory patterns of social relations in China's state-owned enterprise (SOE) sector since the earliest days of the People's Republic of China. How and when the manifold concepts and practices that fall under the category of 'workers' democracy' in China were and are to this day deployed in the Chinese SOE, by whom and toward what ends are issues this book delineates and seeks to explicate. The answers help to address whether this idea has the potential to be deployed by China's state workers to challenge or even supersede the current set of social relations of coercion that characterize China's neoliberal turn since the 1990s.

In a nutshell, this book reviews this discourse of workers' democracy in China as one in transition. The periods covered are four in all: The People's Democracy Period from the later years of the Chinese Revolution and the first decade of Chinese socialism (the 1950s), the Cultural Revolution Period (mid-1960s to mid-1970s), the First Decade of Economic Restructuring Period (the 1980s), and the Period of Privatization (the 1990s to present).

WHY WORKERS' DEMOCRACY?

My interest in the role that discourses of workers' democracy played in China's transition from state socialism originated as I conducted field research in China from 1998 to 2000. As a researcher, I was critical of what Ching Kwan Lee aptly referred to as a reluctance on the part of mainstream sociology to critique the new forms of class inequality that post-Mao market restructuring has produced in China (Lee 2002). During the Maoist period (1949–1976), many prominent China-focused researchers overenthusiastically embraced the socioeconomic restructuring that took place in the Maoist period of Chinese state socialism (1949–1976). From the early 1980s, at times it appeared that 'institutionalist' China-focused researchers seemed to be almost bending over backwards to portray any moves that reshaped

China's social institutions away from the logic of Maoist collectivism to market-based competition as per se positive in the post-Maoist period (Cao and Nee 2000). However, as China experienced rapid and dramatic economic growth rates in the 1980s and 1990s, new forms of exploitation that emerged in private industry or the declining status and loss of social benefits of China's SOE workers received little careful attention or alarm. If anything, both were presumed to be the requisite price for new market-led institutions that would allow workers in both private and SOEs to experience more control over their destinies as the economy grew and political cadres no longer monopolized control over surplus distribution networks (Bian 1994; Nee 1996; Nee, Stark, and Selden 1989).

My study of trends in China's development led me to believe that, although for-profit-oriented market restructuring in China led to dramatic growth rates and the raising of living standards in just two generations, the types of injustice that workers in both SOE and private sectors of production experienced were ones that not only needed to be documented, but theorized as systemic features of China's transition from state socialism. It was important to look for openings, spaces, and mechanisms of resistance to the new forms of coercion that characterized social relationships in Chinese industry *and* to consider their role and significance as part of this transition from state socialism. That is to say, what did resistance and its attendant ideologies to these new forms of labor coercion in today's China tell us about the transition?

This issue of transition is not a simple one. Yet it is one that needs to be theorized and carefully. The matter of transition requires social science to ask 'transition from what to what?' Neither should be taken for granted. Transition is, like most social phenomena, a complex one. It is hardly evolutionary, although it is widely regarded as such by advocates and critics of China's transition from state socialism. Still, the complex character of transition from state socialism renders it something that need be theorized. This is the case even in this post-1989 period. Little remains of a socialist foundation to Chinese development and Sinology's mainstream wish for some happy admixture of socialism and capitalism in the form of 'market socialism' now finally appears less and less something that serious scholars spend much time contemplating (Greenfield and Leong 1997). However, it is hard to be half pregnant. There is a dynamic underlying the transition, and its endpoint remains an empirical question, one that I argue in this book is shaped by the kinds of struggles SOE workers have battled in response to privatization this last decade.

WORKERS' DEMOCRACY IN CHINA AS A CONTESTED DISCOURSE: A HISTORICAL AND CASE STUDY ANALYSIS

My field research on the eve of and in the first two years of the 21st century in China found a little explored feature of the process involved in

SOE reforms: the persistence of a discourse of workers' democracy that has been contested ideologically in the moment of Chinese transition from state socialism. By a discourse of workers' democracy, I refer to a frequently employed set of written or spoken concepts that broadly have as their reference the notion that workers should be directly involved and exercising one degree or another of participation in and control of the management of the SOEs.

The way that such a language took on the role of a discourse transpired on at least two levels. One, there are definitely real gaps between the rhetoric and the reality, as I discuss throughout this book in later chapters. At the same time, I would find in field interviews it was a language that Chinese workers could react to and themselves engage. I especially found evidence of this when I interviewed SOE workers and their leaders during and in the aftermath of protests against the price tag for privatization that they have been expected to pay. I focus on how this discourse has been shaped and constrained by the social relations of coercion that characterize China's political economy throughout the Maoist period and in the past two decades of transition from state socialism. Although I use the word 'discourse,' I do not spend much time doing a 'discourse analysis' as is the trend in certain poststructural camps of social science. I am interested, instead, at linking broad trends in this discourse with the shifting patterns of development in Chinese political economy and forms of consciousness that emerge in periods of systemic transition, such as China is undergoing at the moment. In this sense, the work is more dialectical in the sense that Harvey (1982),Ollman (1992), or Carchedi (1987) employ the term.

Although the concept of 'democratic management' (*minzhu guanli*) featured most prominently in this discourse, concepts as varied as 'enterprise transparency,' 'elections of managers,' 'shopfloor management committees,' 'workers representative congresses (WRC),' 'direct production control,' 'shareholder control,' and 'elimination of worker-cadre division of labor' have comprised part of this discourse of workers' democracy in Maoist and post-Maoist China. Initially framed during the later years of the Chinese Revolution, this discourse can be shown to be highly flexible and over the years of reform has been appropriated by various actors for contending objectives (Brugger 1976). Reform addresses the problem of transforming the social relations of production, something I argue cannot and should not be taken for granted in the moment of transition (whether it be from capitalism or state socialism). Conceptualizing ideology as the set of deeply held beliefs, not necessarily coherent, or articulated, or false or distorted, but that "inspire concrete attitudes and provide orientations for action (Bottomore 1983), in this context it is critical to consider workers' views regarding the changing social relations of SOE production. We can then also raise the question of how a discourse of workers' democracy, one that is employed by different Chinese social actors in contradictory ways, is engaged as a part of the transition from Chinese state socialism, at times enthusiastically at times perfunctorily. Likewise, how has workers' democracy developed as a phenomenon of ideological contestation in China in response to the process of state socialist transition—sometimes promoting certain kinds of change, but always with unintended consequences, including the potential to reproduce or supersede existing coercive social relations of production?

This book addresses itself specifically to the process through which a discourse such as workers' democracy has been appropriated by different social agents in China from 1949 to the present for multiple and contested ends. In this sense, the discourse of workers' democracy became, to borrow from Gramsci's conceptualization of ideology, "[a] terrain on which men move, acquire consciousness of their position, struggle, etc" (Gramsci 1971, 377). Although workers' democracy in China emerged as a transformative concept in the context of previous anticapitalist revolutions and its own revolution, from 1949 onward, it became an idea over which considerable struggles over interpretations would occur, both challenging and reproducing capitalist social relations. The net effect is that workers' democracy in China remains to date an idea that, among other ideas, has informed SOE workers' consciousness in the moment of transition from state socialism.

NOTICING A PHENOMENON OF TRANSITION

In 1999, while doing fieldwork on SOE workers' consciousness in China, I wondered whether there were any ideas or models of enterprise management that Chinese workers latched onto as alternatives to neoliberal strategies such as privatization as the panacea for failing SOEs. I especially began to take notice of a particular set of phrases that popped up frequently in *China Workers Daily* (*Gongren Rebao*). This Party-controlled newspaper is ostensibly aimed at China's working class, but actually is read primarily by cadres in the Chinese Communist Party (CCP)-controlled All China Federation of Trade Unions (ACFTU). Stories in *Workers' Daily* suggested that, in many instances, a new form of workers' democracy accompanied China's market restructuring. There were near daily stories of one or another factory that was transformed by 'transparency' (*changwu gonkai*), 'democratic management' (*minzhu guanli*), 'democratic selection of factory director' (*minzhu xuanze changzhang*), 'democratic election of factory directors' (*minxuan changzhang*), and, most radical of all, 'worker takeover to save the factory' (*shenchang zijiu*).

These stories were not only found in publications for ACFTU cadres. One could find such stories in national and local editions of the *Peoples' Daily*. These narratives were accessible and read, or at least seen, by almost anyone in China who purchased a newspaper. Furthermore, such stories appeared in TV news stories as well. Thus, they provided at least the semblance of a set of concepts, phrases, ideas, or a discourse in Chinese society that countered the (then widespread) enthusiasm toward complete privatization and augmenting managerial power in the SOE. This discourse of workers' democracy that I found in the official media suggested that China's rush to embrace capitalist markets was not so straightforward. Workers and managers in the SOE sector, even as it experienced widespread crises of debt and/or bankruptcy, both seemed to accept that, regardless of the changes in institutional form that were to take place through mergers, corporate stock-holding conversions, joint-venture arrangements, or outright privatization, Chinese workers would exercise forms of democratic participation in their enterprises that would protect their interests as state enterprise workers. Notably, these interests were typically defined in much the same manner as workers defined their interests during the Maoist period of state socialism: job security, steady wages, social benefits, and the principle that, market restructuring and all, China's state workers retained the status of 'masters of the house' (*zhurenwong*).

WORKERS' DEMOCRACY: JUST ANOTHER IDEOLOGY?

My initial reaction to this discourse of workers' democracy in China was natural sociological suspicion. The story line plainly did not conform to what is known about transitions toward markets and capitalism in other formerly state-socialist societies, much less privatization in countries that had no socialist past (Buraway and Vederey 1999; Clarke and Biziukov 1992; Kotz and Weir 1997a, 1997b). My familiarity with the role that ideas such as workers' democracy played historically to 'paint over' state socialism's actual conditions in its model enterprises and townships only exacerbated my sentiment that this discourse of workers' democracy in China's SOEs was suspect (Burawoy and Lukacs 1992; Filtzer 1994, 2002; Kaple 1994). Given the structure of China's political economy in 1998, how could ideas about workers' democracy in the state-owned media not but merely reproduce the power of China's ruling class—one enjoyed through access to the one-party state apparatus *and* enrichment through investment in for-profit market commodity production?

Most of sinology would argue that workers under Maoist state socialism were fed a daily dose of radical rhetoric that affirmed their vital and 'mass' activist role in the SOE, but in fact had little power or say in the administration of the enterprises (Cliver 2002; Lau 2001a, 2001b). SOE workers in China were dependent on powerful ministry bureaucrats who held the purses that determined which factories received which types of budgets for salaries, jobs, and, most critically, access to social (i.e., health, educational, pension, etc.) benefits that the enterprise alone provided (Walder 1986). The structure of state socialism in the Maoist Period required ideologies that rationalized the monopolistic and politically based power of Ministry bureaucrats, Party leaders, and factory directors (Harris 1978).

After Mao's death in 1976, China underwent a significant development, set in motion by Deng Xiaoping's call for employment of private market-oriented production in the rural economy as a means to boost economic productivity. The Party would no longer be the only institution that could generate and appropriate surpluses. However, this shift would not take place at the same pace in the (urban-based) industrial SOEs (Walder 1989). Although some experimentation would take place, overall the Party state's domination of industry remained for almost two more decades until the mid-1990s, when, in absolute figures at least, a huge number of (small- and medium-sized) SOEs were 'let go' by the state and left to fend for themselves (Lau 1999b).

The security that Chinese SOE workers long enjoyed was seriously threatened directly for the first time in the mid-1990s. As a result, the stage for a struggle between the Party and the 'masters of the house' in the SOEs was in clear motion by the end of the 1990s. Sure enough, by the start of the new millennium, China would distinguish itself as the new leader in worker-based collective forms of rebellion. It was during this time period that I was seeing on a daily basis narratives in the Party-controlled media about workers' democracy winning over workers to China's privatization policies in the SOE sector.

This paradox invariably moved me to go out 'into the field' and ask workers, managers, and Party cadres to find out just what role this discourse of workers' democracy played in their enterprises and, more generally, China's transition. I shared my fellow sociologists' skepticism toward this and other discourses that the Party prominently floated as a means to rationalize the new forms of coercion and inequality that accompanied ongoing for-profit market restructuring in Chinese society. I could see that all parties that deployed a discourse of workers' democracy in China have done so in frequently inconsistent and self-contradictory fashions. However, ideology, as Gramsci asserted with greatest clarity, is not merely ideas imposed on the masses to reproduce the power of the ruling class. Ideas can be believed, very much so and in ways unexpected and confused, especially in periods of transition from one set of social relations of coercion to new ones (Manicas 2007). The critical question is the direction of ideas in terms of *potential* outcomes. The making of ideology is then a process with varying possible consequences often shaped by real constraints of political-economic relations of power,[1] as opposed to simply a static indication of 'low' or 'high' degree of class consciousness.

METHODOLOGICAL PARAMETERS AND ISSUES

The methodology of this book diverges from what one finds in much of the literature focused on labor issues in China today. For starters, the focus of this work is China's SOE sector. Since the privatization thrust of the late

1990s, which subjected large numbers of small- and medium-sized Chinese enterprises to varying degrees of privatization, China-focused social science has regarded the importance of the SOE sector in China's economy as dwindling and increasingly marginal. Nonetheless, few would challenge the argument that the pace at which and what kinds of transformation occur in the SOE sector will continue to define the outcomes of China's future economic restructuring (Lo 2001).

This book also departs from a trend in the literature to dismiss the potential for the Chinese SOE worker to develop class consciousness. Even if the SOE sector is taken as yet viable and relevant to China's transitional outcomes, SOE workers are often regarded by labor researchers as too enmeshed in the 'past' values that valorized the SOE work unit as a 'collective' with social obligations to all its members. The concept of 'state owned' implied that the Party, by virtue of its control of the state, guaranteed and protected the interests of SOE workers. As a result, many researchers believe that SOE workers, unlike their counterparts in the private sector, do not have a sufficient sense of 'self' interests that are distinct from their administrators or their parents the Party state (Blecher 2005; Lee 2007; Tong 2005; Zhu and Chan 2005). The consensus in the literature follows that this identity with the state thereby limits SOE workers' capacity to develop a class consciousness that challenges managerial or state power. Although plainly this is one element of the SOE worker mindset, this book essays to show that, in some ways, the SOE workers possess ideas found in their own discourse of workers' democracy that significantly challenge the core social relations of neoliberalism that underlie China's transition from state socialism—in ways that private sector workers do not display.

THEORIZING CHINA'S TRANSITION
FROM STATE SOCIALISM

Chinese economic restructuring has taken on a form that has been unsystematic, careful, piecemeal, and opportunistic. China's efforts in this regard stand out as distinctly different from (and, in terms of standard economic growth indicators, far more successful than) its northern neighbor Russia (Burawoy 1996). Most notably, China has refused to accept wholeheartedly the Washington Consensus shock therapy program for 'reforming' state socialist economies. Instead, China has retained a much higher level of state involvement in the direction of capital flows within China, such that the SOEs continue to contribute demonstrable and significant value to Party coffers. State power remains inextricably tied in with the SOE, at least enough to frustrate politicians in Washington, DC, who would have China deregulate and privatize its economy immediately had they their druthers. Even when it appeared at times to some that China was on the verge of handing over the economy to a new capitalist class, the role of the

Party state in the Chinese political economy has (to date at least) remained intact (Lo 1999, 2001, 2002).

The response of Chinese workers to privatization in this sector is critical, and my study focuses on them. Because of the importance of the SOEs as the bedrock of state power in China, this book focuses on how Chinese economic restructuring impacted Chinese SOE workers. I proceed with a special emphasis on small- and medium-sized enterprises, where the greatest degree of SOE restructuring was transpiring as I conducted my field research in the late 1990s. The book's ultimate interest is in theorizing the resistance to privatization in the SOEs that I encountered in the field from the late 1990s to about 2002. By focusing on the SOE sector in China, in no sense should it be taken that I deny the importance of the expanded role of private (foreign and domestic) capitalist investors in China's economy. However, taking the political economy of Chinese transition as a systemic phenomenon, into the 1990s and at the start of the new millennium, it remained an empirical fact that competitive markets did not rule the economic heart of Chinese value production (i.e., the SOE sector) (Hassard et al. 2002; Liu and Link 1998; Lo 1999. 2001; Meng and Dollery 2006). Until such a sea change in the Chinese SOE is actualized, Chinese transition from state socialism to capitalism remains both uncertain and tenuous.

My contention is that those who assume that capitalism is the predestined (and/or already actualized, be it in a 'straight out' or 'mixed' capitalist) outcome of Chinese transition neglect the extent to which the battle over *whether* capitalist relations of production will systematically dominate the Chinese political economy has yet to be completed. This does not mean that China can be, in any serious sense of the word, characterized as 'socialist.' The only thing taken for granted in this book is that there is a transition from state socialism occurring in China today that is being contested with no definite end in terms of the relations of production in the heart of China's political economy.[2] Here plainly, attention to the efforts of SOE Chinese workers to resist, and the consequences of this resistance, will be critical. Accordingly, in addition to a clear understanding of the beliefs, attitudes, and rhetoric employed by SOE workers, enterprise administrators, Party cadres, and even intellectuals, we need an appreciation of the constraints imposed on their action by existing conditions, both local and global.

The analysis provided in this book leads to the conclusion that the Chinese future is problematic. What remains to be seen is how the playing out of the Chinese transition from state socialism will impact the level of contestation in the Chinese SOE (the focus of this book) and the Chinese working class in general. This invariably remains a matter of whether China's SOE workers are compelled to accept the logic of capitalist production as a system of class relations in China's future or encounter a stagnant but nonmarket type of coercive class relations that dominate the Chinese political economy, or reject both such outcomes as the path of transition from Chinese state socialism and battle for a new path that supersedes state socialist and capitalist relations of production. In this analysis, capitalism not only cannot be assumed to have arrived in China because of the existence of x, y, or z 'variable,' but whether its future arrival is desirable for China's workers remains a matter of ideological battles.

THEORIZING CLASS CONSCIOUSNESS IN TRANSITION

How will China's SOE workers challenge the coercive relations of transition in their workplaces? This is a question that was largely neglected by China-focused social science for the first two decades of economic restructuring in China. Today it interests researchers of the conditions of labor in China because China has been the site of perhaps the greatest amount of strikes, riots, factory occupations, and other types of rebellious activity. Certainly by the late 1990s and the first few years of the new millennium, the bulk of this activism was occurring in China's SOE sector (Chen 2006; Lee 2007). Nonetheless, researchers of China's labor issues did not have high expectations of SOE workers' consciousness, not to mention subjectivity.

A key premise of this book (already stated previously) is that, as a sector, the SOE remains critical for the direction of China's transition from state socialism. This is so not simply because that sector continues to provide a crucial economic basis for the one-party state's power (Hassard et al 2002, 2007; Lo 1999, 2002). Transition from state socialism has required attendant forms of consciousness geared toward market-based individualism and collectivism. It is in the SOE that the latter have been most strongly institutionalized and, it is safe to say, believed (Bian 1994; Korzec 1992; Saich 1984). Thus, the transition from state socialism in the SOE is not only a social phenomenon of economic significance, it is as much an ideological one.

Much of what I found in China would reflect what other sociologists have found already. With every passing day, faith in private markets as the means to cure the bottlenecks of SOE production in China seemed to be growing in the late 1990s. That entry into the World Trade Organization (WTO) would propel China into development, growth, and social progress appeared to be a given that required little serious debate. It seemed almost certain that not only was there no point to resist neoliberal ideology, but that there also was little likelihood of such resistance emerging that could challenge the terms of transition from state socialism in China on the eve of the new millennium.[3]

The specific set of ideas that I found and collapse under the concept workers' democracy ostensibly confirmed such sentiments. The claims that new forms of workers' democracy were emerging and transforming China's SOEs with an alternative way of thinking about and organizing enterprise production were plainly hyped. What was interesting, however, was that they were not only promoted by Party cadres who had an interest in rationalizing the new forms of competition and 'corporate' restructuring designed to submit small- and medium-sized SOEs to the logic of capitalist markets. Party cadres who criticized the Party's embrace of capitalist investment's expanded role in the Chinese economy and instead advocated maintaining the role of the SOE as a vital part of China's political economy *also* engaged the discourse of workers' democracy. Toward the end of my year-long research residence in Beijing in June 1999, I came upon a book written by Zhang Qinde, a Maoist CCP cadre in Beijing, which was a defense of the SOE as the basis of Chinese socialism (Zhang 1999). Zhang pointed to cases where SOEs had been revived to the benefit of China's economy and more generally China's workers. The SOEs, he contended, had been supplied with new motivational energy (*diaodong jijixin*) when SOE workers exercised democratic control over the production decisions and the hiring and firing of cadres (i.e., managers and factory directors). In every instance, the book claimed, where workers were able to experience greater control over the operation of the factory, there existed one form or another of *democratic management*, be it simply through increased enterprise transparency, elections of workers' representatives who could sit on enterprise boards and influence management decisions, direct elections of company director, or through outright worker takeover of the company to 'save the enterprise' (*shengchang zijiu*). This argument spoke directly to the issue of workers' consciousness and change in the Chinese SOE, highlighting workers' democracy as not only a practice, but as a counterintuitive (or even counterhegemonic) ideological concept in the context of growing calls for expanded use of capitalist markets to resolve the crisis of the SOE.

DISCOVERING THE LIMITS OF WORKERS' DEMOCRACY IN LUOYANG

One case that Zhang highlighted seemed especially worth visiting: The No. 1 Dyed Fabric Factory in Luoyang.[4] I visited it in early July 1999. I hopped on the next overnight train to Luoyang City and sought out the factory on my own. I basically showed up out of nowhere and approached the factory gates. It was easily accessible after a short bus ride from the town center because the spanking new housing complex that workers were said to have won as a result of their battle for the factory leaped out at the discerning eye. However, instead of a reinvigorated factory that the book advertised, the company grounds seemed to be deserted. I proceeded to the front office to see who I could find to ask about the enterprise's experience with workers' democracy. The union chief informed me that the enterprise had already stopped production for more than a year. When asked why, he stated that the East Asian Financial Crisis wiped out its customer base and the company was desperately looking for a new investor from Hong Kong. To make matters worse, the enterprise was compelled by the new environmental regulations to find an 'environmental cleanup loan.' Because the company was near bankruptcy, prospects for this were not terribly bright. Workers at the company lost their jobs, save for those who went to work in another privately owned textile company that absorbed a portion of the enterprise workforce.

During this field visit, I was able to interview several representatives of the workers' representative congress (WRC; *zhidaihui*) along with the union chief. I found that this discourse of workers' democracy in China's transition was deployed by both supporters and opponents of greater market involvement in the Chinese economy. Both employed it to fit their own ideological take on the significance of economic restructuring in China, contradictions that arose in the process, and what was needed for their resolution.

However, even if the Dyed Fabric story started out with such transformative potential, in reality it did not appear to be one that produced a consciousness on the part of workers that resisted the dominant ideologies of neoliberal restructuring or its consequences. The workers might have experienced a period of apparent radical orientation by taking over their factory and demanding new elections of their factory director and managers. However, this did not last terribly long. When faced with the same crisis of debt and loss of markets experienced across China during the East Asian Financial Crisis, the workers seemed unable to think of (much less demand) alternatives to layoffs. Rather, a *Waiting for Godot*-like state of hoping for a foreign investor to 'save' their 'worker controlled' factory ensued.

WORKERS' DEMOCRACY AND EMERGENT SOE REBELLIONS AGAINST PRIVATIZATION IN ZHENGZHOU

This led me to wonder about the increasingly frequent instances of workers involved in collective forms of activity to resist the terms of economic transition and its impact on the SOE sector and Chinese society in general. What did such SOE workers make of the discourse? Did they employ it themselves? In the process of using it, did SOE workers generate or create anew ideas that *challenged* the dominant ideology of neoliberalism that the discourse of workers' democracy in China seemed only able to sustain? As part of my attempt to answer these questions, I conducted a field visit to Zhengzhou, the capital of Henan Province, in October and November 2000. At this time in Zhengzhou, SOE workers had launched a spate of rebellious challenges against fraudulent privatizations and in many instances were demanding the right to take back control of their factories. In the case of the Zhengzhou Paper factory, workers had gone well beyond making appeals to city ministries for relief. Instead, they directly occupied their factory for almost two months before being forcibly removed by police on August 8, 2000. In almost every instance of workers' organization to defend their interests against fraudulent profiteers, workers turned to an organization that was showcased in the official narratives found in China's discourse of workers' democracy—namely, the WRC.[5] Not only were the workers' leaders utilizing this institution, but in interviews it became clear that they possessed ideas about what workers' democracy should look like that clearly diverged from and challenged the dominant neoliberal frame found in Chinese media, academic, business, and political circles. What forms of consciousness were revealed in these workers' discourse of workers' democracy, and what did it tell us about transition and ideology in China today?

This book moves across periods of changing discourses of workers' democracy in China since the late years of the Chinese Revolution. A shift in the discourse occurs most markedly in the 1990s, when, I argue, for the first time, the discourse is engaged at an official level to rationalize attempts to subject small- and medium-sized Chinese SOEs to the coercive forces of competition in capitalist markets. Other writers on this topic have lamented the way the expansion of capitalist modes of enterprise management have decreased the possibilities for workers' democracy in China. For them, the Party's use of repressive violence to deal with the role of workers in the Tiananmen Protests in 1989 combined with the Party's embrace of capitalist markets to effectively squelch any possible resurgence of workers' democracy's key institutions, most notably the WRC.

However, this overlooks the evidence that, starting in the early 1990s, the Party actually redeployed a discourse of workers' democracy in an even more aggressive fashion. This was significant in another manner as well; the discourses of workers' democracy that existed in previous periods (even during the 1980s' 'market socialism' years) were not officially deployed to rationalize ideologies of capitalist production. Given this change, it is easy to regard what remained of the discourse of workers' democracy as one that fed and reproduced new types of coercive relations of production in Chinese SOEs during the 1990s and the early years of the new millennium's first decade. After all, the pattern has the appearance of consistency. For the first four decades of Chinese state socialism, the discourse was used to reproduce the monopolistic power of Party cadres and enterprise administrators; for the most recent decade or two, it is now used to rationalize the right of the Party to monopolize state power and, more important, the right of an ascendant class of capitalist investors and managers to privately accumulate wealth and rule enterprises (even SOEs) as they see fit.

This book does not regard the discourse as one-sidedly ideological in such a top-down manner, whereby workers are fed ideas and passively assimilate them as the ruling class wishes. China's SOE workers have, at times, engaged in and reacted to this discourse in a manner that was hardly passive (Chen 2006; Unger and Chan 2004; Zhang 2001). Although the discourse has usually sprung from Party campaigns, these campaigns were often in response to collective forms of activity that reflected a consciousness on the part of Chinese workers that made the Party nervous in various manifestations. In part, rebellions of workers stemmed periodically from SOE workers' disappointments with the manifold campaigns to 'democratize' the enterprise (Sheehan 1998).

This book is sensitive to the role the discourse of workers' democracy has played in reinforcing the structure of contradictory social relations of power in China's enterprises. Nonetheless, I emphasize where possibilities for engaging the discourse as a counterhegemonic language and practice that Chinese workers could and still do exist. This argument should not be interpreted as a means to 'save' the subjectivity of the Chinese SOE worker or to read into their expressions a counterhegemonic 'destiny.' At best, the cases of workers involved in protests who engaged components of China's discourse of workers' democracy are indicative of possible directions that future SOE workers protests (maybe in larger sized enterprises that the Party decides to more aggressively privatize) might pursue in the future.

CHAPTERS OUTLINE

I begin this book with a chapter on the origins of the discourse of workers' democracy in China in the Maoist period of Chinese state socialism, which lasted from 1949 until Mao's death in 1976. I locate origins of this discourse in the mid- to late1940s, when the CCP developed a rural-based mass mobilization orientation as the core revolutionary strategy. When it came to industry, however, the Party struggled with how to apply such an approach in new industrial enterprises—especially because their main source of financing and advice came from the Soviet Union. The Soviets expected that Chinese industry and socialism would be constructed along similarly hierarchical lines that stressed 'one-man management' and a premium on production at the expense of transforming workplace relationships. Chapter 2 traces the different understandings of workplace democracy that were developed during the Maoist period. These interpretations on what forms of workers' democracy should be utilized to defeat bureaucracy's role in impeding the motivation of workers were contentious and part of broader factional disagreements on how to develop the socialist economy and how to empower workers as the 'masters' of SOEs.

In Chapter 3, I lay out what I regard as key shifts in the political economy of China's transition from state socialism that began in the early years following Mao's death and continue to this day. I provide this as the backdrop for the chapters that follow, which focus on the ways the discourse of workers' democracy in China underwent modifications after Mao. Critically, the political economy of transition from state socialism in China has required that China's SOEs submit themselves to the logic of capitalist markets. In practice, this was not so easy because such a transformation necessitated that workers in Chinese SOEs regard their role in production as something that markets alone should judge. This transition is one that Chinese SOE workers in the 1980s were not expected to make—even as the role of for-profit markets became greater in the rural economy and coastal cities where private export-oriented production drove record amounts of growth and with it new forms of corruption, inequality, and class conflicts that would erupt during the massive demonstrations against corruption in the late 1980s. In the 1990s, however, even when SOE workers in small- and medium-sized enterprises were expected to accept layoffs and the permanent closure of their source of livelihoods, SOE workers did not sit still and accept their role in production as mere commodities—especially when they had no commodities to sell of worth in capitalist labor markets as they actually existed in China. That 'stubbornness' has placed limits on the extent to which the SOE sector of China's political economy could complete a transition from state socialism to capitalism by the end of the 1990s.

Chapter 4 looks at how the political economy of transition from Maoist state socialism shaped the Party leadership's interest and determination in the 1980s to redeploy a discourse of democracy to justify an increasing role for competitive markets in China's rural and industrial sectors. The Party's revised discourse of workers' democracy encouraged elections of workers' representatives as a means to develop support for the Party's market economic restructuring. Although in the 1980s SOE workers showed support for their WRCs, the reactivation of this and other institutions of workers' democracy in China's SOEs did little to make these workers or managers act in a more capitalist fashion. Because the bulk of market penetration of the national economy occurred in the rural economy, China's urban industrial SOEs and the state sector in general remained protected by their parent ministries from exposure to capitalist competition. Thus, the discourse of workers' democracy in the 1980s SOE was not linked to a transformation of production relations in the SOE. At best, it remained an institution through which workers curried favor along traditional models of paternalistic labor relations that characterized the SOE in Chinese state socialism prior to Mao's death in 1976. When the crackdown of student protests occurred in June 1989, some predicted that the Party would end its embrace of the discourse of workers' democracy in China.

In Chapter 5, I show that the opposite occurred. In the 1990s, the Party aggressively reconfigured and promoted a discourse of workers' democracy as it attempted to restructure production relations in small- and medium-sized SOEs via privatization schemes. I argue that increased workers' democracy was promised to SOE workers in exchange for accepting the release of state ministries from fiscal and social responsibilities for their enterprises' and their own human fates. I contend that data collected from official media intended for SOE workers and cadres in China's official trade union (ACFTU) show how this 'official' discourse was developed as a means to rationalize the dismantling of small- and medium-sized SOEs and to force them to compete with Chinese and foreign-owned capitalist companies. This discourse often used rhetoric borrowed from discourses of democracy that originated in the Maoist period, but now with a decidedly neoliberal end. Data that I collected from field interviews with SOE workers at 'model' democratically managed SOEs in Henan Province show that workers were skeptical of the official discourse and engaged an alternative discourse of workers' democracy. I argue that, although by no means radicalized, these SOE workers expressed a discourse that contained the basis for potential resistance to the official discourse of workers' democracy.

In Chapter 6, I draw on interviews with SOE workers who led antiprivatization protests in Henan Province and how they, in the process, drew on a discourse of workers' democracy that ideologically justified their protests and plans to actually practice workers' democracy at the point of production to restore SOE workers' jobs and social security. Typically more radical discourses of workers' democracy were developed when SOE workers saw their enterprises about to be declared 'bankrupt.' I argue that, although the literature focuses on how Chinese SOE workers' protests are shaped and limited by a lack of 'citizenship rights,' the field interviews and observations I draw from in this chapter suggest another and bigger barrier—namely, the level of workers' organization. That is to say, faced with a transitional economy that could not deliver a capitalist welfare state, the biggest obstacle that SOE workers in Zhengzhou faced was their own inability to democratically organize as the means to develop their mass base of support for their demands for democratic control of production at their SOEs.

In the concluding Chapter 7, I begin with the argument that the transition to capitalism in China's SOEs is hardly completed and the struggles that determine whether the SOE will be systematically compelled to submit to the force of capitalist markets remain an open question. I argue, contra much of the literature on the state of today's working-class movement in China, that where struggles are likely to occur in the SOE sector, they probably will occur in the largest SOEs. The Chinese Party state continues to protect these SOEs from full exposure to markets, although how long that will remain the case is unknown. These large-value pumping SOEs certainly are not as secure as they were a decade ago because China has signed onto membership in the WTO. I suggest that lessons learned from SOE workers' discourses of democracy developed in the 1990s and early 2000s still remain relevant to workers in China's largest SOEs, who will quite possibly experience the full power of market forces in the next decade.

2 The Origins of China's Discourse of Workers' Democracy

We have already seen that the Chinese worker is represented on the controlling bodies of the factory and is heavily involved in the criticism mechanisms which have been molded in China over the last quarter of a century. Formally such devices in themselves do not represent any startling differences between China and other industrial countries. The Chinese worker's votes, however, can probably have a veto power. More probably nominees who would not command popular support will not be put forth. Criticism mechanisms, unless integrated into the daily processes of the organization, are capable of becoming institutionalized rituals, though the Chinese criticism sessions seem to be quite alive and also seem to serve important functions. But clearly, periodic voting and criticism would represent minimal kinds of worker self-management.

—Hoffman (1977, 305)

INTRODUCTION

In the 1990s, SOE workers in China encountered a phenomenon that they had not anticipated ever having to deal with in previous generations: namely, privatization and the loss of jobs and basic social welfare benefits. One of the promises that the CCP made to workers in such enterprises, in exchange for such sacrifices, was greater workplace democracy. This was not the first time such a pledge had been delivered to Chinese workers. From the earliest years of Chinese state socialism, the CCP engaged a set of concepts and policy initiatives that I categorize as workers' democracy. A set of ideas that directly or implicitly connote workers' democracy provided a potential terrain for battles over workplace relationships from the earliest moments of the Maoist version of state socialism in the late 1940s through to the present period of market-oriented restructuring. The purpose of this chapter is to lay out where concepts or sets of practices that reflect one or another degree of workers' democracy were both promoted and understood during three periods of Maoist state socialism from 1949 to roughly the mid-1970s. Such a discourse provided workers in the Maoist period with an ideological means to both assess and resist coercive relations of production in Chinese industry, albeit with limited levels of effectiveness. I argue in later chapters that where one sees discourses of workers' democracy present in Chinese SOE workers' protests against privatization in the 1990s and the first years of the new millennium, they borrow from ones developed in the Maoist period of state socialism.

One of the earliest concepts of workers' democracy developed in Chinese state socialism was 'democratic management' (*minzhu guanli*). Robert Cliver (2002), in a detailed paper on the evolution of '*minzhu guanli*' in Chinese state socialism, notes that, " . . . *minzhu guanli* has repeatedly been resurrected as an essential element in everything from the Great Leap Forward to the ongoing reform of state-owned enterprises . . ." (4). In the first section of this chapter, I lay out what conditions made it possible for democratic management to be implemented from 1949 to 1952. Workers' democracy also conceptually encompasses a whole set of ideas and policies in Chinese enterprises that were engaged during a period that ironically saw the *dismantling* of 'democratic management' as Party policy during the Cultural Revolution period. These policies, which are discussed in a later section, reinforced distinctly noncapitalist understandings of the SOE's role in Chinese society.

I lay out how different understandings of what was meant by workplace democracy emerged within the CCP. These different understandings shaped the types of discourses of workers' democracy that emerged during three key phases of the Maoist period: the FMC-SWSC Period (1949–1952), the WRC Period (1957–1961), and the Cultural Revolution Period (1966–1976). Each period's respective discourse was informed by the Party's reaction to workers' collective forms of activity, set up minimally realized *potentials* for workers to experience certain amounts of workplace democracy, and in turn gave rise to workers' collective forms of action when dissatisfied with the fruits of the CCP's workplace democracy policies. This chapter provides the background for making sense of how China's workers' democracy-related programs have influenced Chinese workers in the SOE sector since the transition from Maoist state socialism, which I treat in Chapters 4, 5, and 6.

THE BATTLE AGAINST BUREAUCRACY

Concepts associated with workers' democracy were not new to the forms of state socialism that developed in the Soviet Union or Eastern Europe. However, it was not one that was embraced with much energy in such cases (Sirianni 1982). Yet for two brief periods in Maoist China, the Party took a leading role in promoting a policy of 'democratic management.' During other periods, the Party conducted campaigns that endorsed ostensibly radical forms of worker led takeovers of factories. These variegated and often contradictory polices arguably contained the *potential* to remedy Stalinist forms of hierarchy and bureaucracy if practiced with the same level of energy as they were rhetorically advanced.

Burawoy and Lukacs (1992) argue that the problem of legitimating labor regimes in state socialism is substantively different from that in capitalism. Built into the fabric of state socialist productive relations are *social obligations* on the part of the state to both improve the economic and cultural level of workers as a class and to empower them to control critical processes of political decision making. Although these concepts exist in more abstract ways in capitalism, they are not tied in any sense to political legitimacy—even in the most developed models of social democracy:

> When the problem is to mystify the appropriation of surplus, as under capitalism, ideologies play a secondary role in reproducing society. They are diverse and not essential. However, where surplus appropriation is transparent and has therefore to be justified as being in the collective interest, then ideology comes to play a prominent role everyday life. Thus, state-socialism calls on both its dominant and subordinate classes to proclaim the virtues of socialism—its efficiency, its justice, it equality—in ritual activities from communist shifts, production conferences, brigade competitions, and campaigns to forced' marches and public speeches. (20–21)

Although, in certain respects, the Chinese discourse of workers' democracy often constituted little more than what Burawoy and Lukacs (1992) called in the Hungarian case "painting socialism," it also reflected a wider consensus in Chinese state socialism that there existed a need to challenge the Soviet model of enterprise relations that would render 'painting' socialism unnecessary. Ideas and policies that clustered around workers' democracy in China developed as contested and contestable models, which contributed to the character of Chinese state socialism. This discourse of workers' democracy in China was, as Burawoy and Lukacs would put it, also used by all Party factions to paint over and pretty up the flaws of state socialism in China and to advance their own sectarian interests.

In *Dream of a Red Factory*, Kaple (1994) argues that CCP efforts to construct a 'mass' popularly controlled (what I would call workers' democracy) alternative to Stalinist industrial models were not only mostly fruitless, but also a cover for the CCP's unreflective employment of the Soviet management model in the SOEs:

> The "Democratization of Management" movement, which was ostensibly created to teach workers some self-management techniques, also was aimed at attracting support for CCP policies in the factories. . . . (T)he basic . . . principle . . . was the High Stalinist principle of strong Party control in factory management. The Chinese communists' drive

for Party primacy in management greatly influenced the shape of the CCP proposals for this period. (58)

However, Kaple underplays the reality that workers' democracy initiatives likewise developed in response to the real and strong conviction within China's working class that socialism *should* provide the goods that it promised from the Yenan period onward.[1] At certain moments in the Chinese state socialist experience, the discourse of workers' democracy was not only regarded as worthwhile, but also even worth collectively challenging the Party to *make real* (Sheehan 1998).

Another reason this discourse would filter both downwardly and upwardly from 1949 was the particular context of Chinese state socialist development. In the case of postrevolutionary China, attempts to institutionalize workers' democracy as a component of Chinese state socialism made considerably more headway in the thought processes of China's direct producers, enterprise and governmental cadres, and intellectuals than in the Soviet case. The aggressive embrace of bureaucracy and hierarchy in the industrial workplace, and society generally, which was the cornerstone of Soviet development, attracted considerable criticism within the CCP throughout the Maoist pre- and post-1949 periods (Blecher 1986; Riskin 1987; Selden 1971).

The contentious nature of the Maoists' relationship with the Soviet Union first revealed itself most strikingly during the Long March. In 1934, Mao and Party cadres who survived the Kuomintang of China's (KMT's) near obliteration of the urban-based CCP retreated to the rural countryside and eventually devised a new rural-based guerilla strategy as the foundation of nationalist revolution (the Yenan Model). This new strategy directly contradicted Stalin's advice to develop an urban proletarian-based Communist Party (Harris 1978). During the Yenan period, the CCP needed to create alternatives to absolute vertical decision-making models due to their impracticality in rural peasant-based guerilla warfare. Hence, the CCP was predisposed to experimenting with mechanisms that delivered authority to middle and lower levels in enterprise and Party organizations. In his *Democracy and Organization in the Chinese Industrial Enterprise: 1948–1953*, Brugger (1976) argues that what emerged as a result was an anti-bureaucratic thrust in both rural and industrial policy that reinforced predispositions toward decentralization:

> [From 1943 on] . . . there evolved an organizational policy . . . of . . . centralized authority and decentralized administration. . . . [It] was designed to *inter alia* to prevent growth of hierarchical barriers at middle levels. Secondly, policy formulation at the center was not simply concerned with financial matters but endeavored to devise concrete tasks to meet the requirements of war. A situation [existed] where middle levels of organization had been simplified or eliminated, where hierarchical

barriers had been broken down but where the center prescribed and checked up on the implementation of specific work tasks. (54)

This particular rural revolutionary context, in which all parties concerned presented their positions on workers' democracy-associated campaigns, created a space within the CCP that encouraged experimentation and assorted challenges to vertical one-man management, which Stalinism had developed into a universal art form in the Soviet Union.

PEOPLE'S DEMOCRACY

The CCP was much more 'mass' oriented than the Leninist or Stalinist parties of other state socialisms in 1949 and, as a result, was more open to forms of direct checks and supervision on authority (Sirianni 1982). This does not mean that the CCP consistently provided a model for democratic class-based empowerment of the masses (Wu 2005). From the earliest years of the People's Republic of China (PRC), the Party cracked down on and purged leftist elements that promoted 'syndicalist' challenges to one-party dominance (Harris 1978). Nevertheless, the Party's call for 'People's Democracy' in the early 1950s contributed to a greater space for workers' democracy- related concepts and policies to develop under Chinese state socialism. On the one hand, People's Democracy referred to an umbrella coalition-oriented conception of socialism. Groups that could make what were perceived by the Party as positive contributions to national development (including the National Bourgeoisie and lower and middle-class landlords) were alloted participatory roles in the society and even the Party (Lin 2006). However, this concept was not merely a device to make coalitions possible with the CCP in the early postrevolutionary years. It also contributed to a cultural environment that called for test runs in 'mass' democracy at a number of levels, including the workplace:

> Another dimension of people's democracy was seen in the experiments with community and workplace self-management, which . . . had an origin in the locally diverse revolutionary process of state building. . . . Novel experiments with self-management were phenomenal in large state firms, in which participatory and flexible approaches were introduced as an alternative to Soviet "one-man command" and Taylorism. (Lin 2006, 152–154)

CHINESE WORKERS' REBELLIOUSNESS

However, it would be inaccurate to ascribe workers' democracy-oriented initiatives in the Chinese workplace that took place in the early or later

1950s or the 1960s to the ideological mindset of CCP cadres alone. They were as much a reaction to the rebellious consciousness of collective action evidenced in the Chinese working class just prior to and in the early years following 1949. Indeed, here is an important departure from the Stalinist model worth noting. In the Soviet case, the response to workers' forms of self-organization was to destroy almost entirely the organs of workers' democracy in the Soviet Union after the eradication of the Left Opposition (Sirianni 1982). In the Chinese case, however, in response to workers' collective activity, a concept was developed and promoted by the CCP in the early 1950s: democratic management (*minzhu guanli*).

In the years leading up to the CCP's 1949 victory and after, workers frequently engaged in collective actions in enterprises that were liberated from KMT control. The years 1948–1950 saw some of the highest levels of labor-based collective rebellion at the point of production in Chinese history (Perry 1994). Party leaders in the CCP were aware of and concerned about the level of urban worker activism. Workers often disregarded the centrally made enterprise policies that encouraged moderation in order to maintain an alliance with 'national capitalists.' 'Excessive' appropriation of capitalists' assets was the preference of local workers and cadres.

In many instances, where workers took control of enterprises, they set wage policies that CCP leaders regarded as blindly egalitarian to the point of discouraging skilled workers from productivity. Conflicting perspectives on industrial policy between workers and national cadres led to divergent interpretations of democratization in the realm of the Chinese socialist workplace to come, divisions that remain to this day. Cliver (2002) writes that in April 1947, only 2 years before the culmination of the Chinese revolution, factories in liberated Harbin began a campaign of reining in what the CCP labeled as 'left adventurists' who threatened "the broader goal of restoring and developing the national economy" (7). The Party media organ Xinhua published an editorial that called for "workers to learn how to manage production, suggesting that state-run factories should establish factory management committees with representatives elected by the employees to discuss how to lower costs, improve production, and resolve all manner of problems from supplies to production to sales" (Cliver 2002, 8). In April, 1947, the 6th All China Labor Congress (what was then the precursor to the All China Federation of Trade Unions) passed a series of resolutions officially stipulating *minzhu guanli* (democratic management) as a policy designed to confront bureaucratization *and* workers' activism that violated the spirit of CCP national development policies.

THE MINZHU GUANLI STAGE: 1949–1952

What was meant by *minzhu guanli* led to considerable confusion and, although partially realized in practice in certain instances, disappointment on the part of almost all parties that had a stake in the matter. The response of the CCP to worker-led factory takeovers was generally negative. Cliver (2002) notes that Party leaders were especially concerned with takeovers that resulted in the appropriation of factory property by individual workers as a remedy for their economic hard straits. How, after all, could workers as a class benefit from factories being stripped of their assets by isolated groups of workers? What the Party leaders failed to appreciate was the potential that workers had to collectively control their factory property for more than short-term economistic goals, although numerous examples of that potential existed at the time. Cliver further contends that there existed numerous precedents for such collective takeovers that workers could use to protect their *collective* interests, as opposed to purely individualistic needs:

> The Xinguang Underwear Factory was frequently cited to employees in other firms as a model of worker responsibility. The factory was in dire straits due to outstanding debts and a shortage of materials. The owner had already fled, and the workers were divided over how best to proceed. Some wanted to dismantle and sell the factory's equipment in order to buy food. Others hoped to restore production and manage the enterprise themselves. With support from the Party, some of the workers organized a "temporary committee to maintain production." By August, 1949, some 400 workers struggled to increase production in order to provide assistance, and ultimately employment, to those who had been laid off previously. (10)

CCP leaders did not advocate democratic management as a means to systematize direct worker control over factory production decision. Party leaders did, however, promote democratic management, and, by virtue of its promotion in response to workers' collective activity, debates on how far it should go took place at all levels.

What was meant by *minzhu guanli* in the first few years of the PRC comprised diverse types of workplace organization and practices, which are characteristic of a broader discourse of workers' democracy in China:

> *Minzhu guanli* thus included certain elements which can be understood as "worker control." Maximally, worker control can be understood as syndicalism—direct control over production or collective ownership of factories by workers. In its more quotidian form, worker control may constitute everyday resistance to managerial control made possible by workers' roles in the production process. In opposition to Taylorist "scientific" management, worker control may mean an effort to retain or gain greater input into the conditions and operations of production. Worker control may also include demands for respect, equality, and freedom from abusive treatment. In a broader

context, worker control connotes the ability to form autonomous organizations, to negotiate collective contracts, and to influence the social conditions and public policies which workers face in their homes and neighborhoods. (Cliver 2002, 3).

However, vertical forms of management models of enterprise–ministerial relations imported by the CCP from Stalin's Russia and the calls, stemming from earlier *minzhu guanli* resolutions (not to mention the principles of People's Democracy), for Chinese industrial enterprises to set up factory-level management committees plainly conflicted with each other in a vexing fashion. Following the revolutionary overthrow of the KMT, the CCP relied greatly on Soviet advice on economic reconstruction. However, this advice was not easily carried out in the Chinese context, especially when general imperatives were executed in rural regions far from the urban centers of the political administration or in China's specific industrial settings. Chinese workers and managers quickly realized, for example, that the factory management committees stood in stark contrast to the Soviet system of industrial relations, which had "condemned the 'parliamentary system' of management that had existed in (the Soviet Union) in the early days of the Bolshevik Revolution" (Brugger 1976, 77).

Bottlenecks associated with state-socialist monopolies of Party-state ownership and control of SOE-produced surpluses haunted Chinese state socialism. For 30 years, there were repeated efforts, from the point of production to central party plenaries, to reform and improve the capacity of workers to have a say in the affairs of enterprise production and surplus distribution. Calls for democratic management in China were framed as complementing Party industrial development policies by advocating greater worker involvement in the affairs of production and enabling workers' motivation. Key cadres such as Gao Gang, responsible for massive industrial projects in Northeast China, believed that worker and management participation in production decisions would contribute to the general rise in skills levels of China's working and managerial strata, another key prerequisite for Chinese economic growth (Kaple 1994). Democratic management was advocated as a mechanism to improve the efficiency of CCP urban industrial policy. The emphasis on democratic management's potential to improve productivity enabled almost any Party faction to embrace it:

> Despite differing interpretations, the CCP's top leaders were unified in their belief in the capacity of *minzhu guanli* to revolutionize industry and improve production. It was hoped that *minzhuhua* (democratization) would "liberate" not only the working class, but also the productive forces, leading to the rapid improvement of production by raising workers' consciousness and enthusiasm. A Northeast Daily editorial

published on February 28, 1949, emphasized the connection between liberation and production by combining *minzhuhua* with *qiyehua*, "enterprization," or the establishment of rational factory systems based on Soviet methods. Deploring the lack of responsibility and accounting in state factories, the editorial stressed the need to combine "scientific" management with "democratization," stating that "it is only when the masses' consciousness is raised that workers themselves will willingly respect the system. (Cliver 2002, 12)

Factory directors, therefore, could promulgate forms of *minzhu guanli* that effectively increased their power. Workers' committees could be employed to "educate" workers about production priorities, work rules, and mobilization of production. Workers' representatives assigned by factory directors were the most effective means to accomplish this end. This would leave unresolved the basic problem of these representatives' inability or unwillingness to challenge factory directors' production decisions.

The *Minzhu guanli* policy called for two institutions within factories to provide Chinese workers with the opportunity to supervise and make changes in directors' production-related decisions: the factory management committees (FMCs, *gongchang guanli weiyuanhui*) and the Workers and Staff Representative Conference (WSRC, *zhigong daibiao huiyi*). Elections of the WRSCs were to be organized at production team levels by the (Party-controlled) union (Brugger 1976; Cliver 2002; Sheehan 1998). Representatives could be recalled, were to meet once or twice a year, and were expected to relay workers' suggestions and criticisms. In addition to these duties, WSRCs were granted the right to review reports by the factory director and oversee the FMCs' management of the factory.

However, as Cliver (2002) points out, complicating the potential of the WSRCs was the establishment of the superior bodies known as the FMCs:

> The factory director chaired the FMC, and the committee's decisions would only be implemented if promulgated as an administrative order by the factory director. The director was also granted veto power over any decision of the FMC which he felt would harm the interests of the enterprise, or which violated the directives of higher administrative organs. In an emergency situation, the director could act unilaterally to resolve pressing problems, but he was required to inform the FMC of his decision and obtain approval after the fact. If members of the FMC disagreed with the director's decision, they could appeal for intervention, while carrying out the director's decision in the meantime. (14)

Furthermore, the WSRCs could only be successful as an organizing force for workers if the unions had power, since they were the mediating force that often determined whether a WSRC could act as an actual 'representative' of workers. However, there were serious institutional obstacles to unions' capacity to play that role. The official Party-controlled unions were not that strong within SOEs. Calls for better disciplined and skilled union officials, who not only understood but responded effectively to workers' needs, failed to produce desired outcomes. Even where they did exist, union officials were relegated to bureaucratic tasks such as "organizing production competitions, participating in management, attending to workers' welfare needs, carrying out education work, and maintaining labor discipline" (Cliver 2002, 17–18). As necessary as these tasks were, they took away from union leaders' abilities to spend more time actually *organizing* SOE workers. This bureaucratic orientation, combined with Party domination of their activities, made it unlikely that union leaders could be counted on to contribute positively to the development of independent and powerful institutions of workers' democracy in the SOEs.

On the one hand, these initiatives had created the opportunities in many instances, although hardly enough or even the majority where democratic management was implemented, for Chinese workers to participate in and challenge decisions made by factory directors and management. Where the conditions were optimal, workers could take advantage of the policy to advance their interests and make changes in production policies. Cliver's study of *minzhu guanli* in the early 1950s would seem to support such a conclusion:

> In certain factories, workers were able to achieve improvements in working conditions through the exercise of *minzhu guanli*. However, success depended on leaders' attitudes and the resources available to the enterprise. The iron workshop of the Fengtai Locomotive Depot had no ceiling windows, and the smoke affected the blacksmiths. When workers raised the issue through the FMC, the administration installed two windows, solving the problem. At the Northeast Smelting Plant, however, the union possessed limited resources, and did not, at first, have the support of the party and administration in improving safety and welfare. There were a number of accidents, as well as much waste and inefficiency. Once *minzhu guanli* was implemented, however, the administration took measures to improve safety, and by 1950, more than 100,000 pieces of safety equipment, such as work clothes, facemasks, rubber gloves and rubber shoes, were distributed to workers. (37)

Even Kaple (1994) suggests that *minzhu guanli* policies were translated effectively in practice in some instances, if sporadically and inconsistently:

> Just as with the factory management committee, the rules for creating and utilizing the (WSRCs) were adapted to each factory's needs. For instance, when Beijing People's Printing Plant began to implement the Democratic Management Program in 1950, the plant manager decided

that all workers and employees at the plant had to study for twenty five days to make sure they all understood the concept of "democracy" in management. . . . At (this) . . . factory, the (WSRC) was used as a forum for meeting with the older workers, whom the (WSRC) members now counseled and criticized. The factory director said that before "liberation" the same workers had been afraid to talk but now they had learned that they themselves were "the masters" (*zhuren*), they were speaking up. One old worker commented: "It is as if we all are family members; if there is something to say, we say it." (68)

However, the structural conditions of democratic management's execution were, as already noted, hardly ideal. Regardless of whether the policy was carried out or effective had much to do with location and skills levels of the workforce. Skilled male workers participated in management during this period more than their female counterparts, who disproportionately occupied less skilled positions and were taken less seriously by factory administrators and cadres. This meant that in sectors that employed higher skilled crafts workers, *minzhu guanli* was more relevant and served as a means for the Party to attract and develop the skills of workers in these sectors—a national development priority in the first decade of China's socialist reconstruction.

THE WRC AND TWO PARTICIPATIONS PERIOD: 1957–1961

The lack of enthusiasm for the policy on the part of many cadres and administrators was certainly an important factor in the decline of *minzhu guanli*, as was the lack of resources for meeting workers' needs as expressed through WSRCs and FMCs. Relying on 'the masses' to manage enterprises and improve production, although attractive in theory, was complicated, inefficient, and frustrating in practice. This was the opinion of proponents of Soviet management techniques, who felt that the implementation of centralized planning and a vertically integrated command structure in industry would be impossible without granting factory directors the authority to carry out plans and directives without FMC/WRSC permission.

Although the first early revolutionary *minzhu guanli* initiative was short lived (it was rescinded by 1953), the discourse of workers' democracy did not disappear with it. Its impact continued to be felt. This is likely due to three important facts: (1) *minzhu guanli* further stimulated the discourse of workers' democracy in China because workers in SOEs did have opportunities to challenge factory leaders, thus raising the expectations of workers for the goals of socialism; (2) in the mid-1950s, despite the clampdown on *minzhu guanli*, SOE workers literally erupted in open rebellion in the forms of slowdowns, strikes, and other types of collective protests against conditions of production that kept the issue of labor relations and workers' democracy at the fore; and (3) Maoists incorporated other components of the discourse of workers' democracy into their anti-Soviet and mass mobilization campaigns from the late 1950s onward as a means to counter what they viewed as the pitfalls of 'formalistic' policies such as *minzhu guanli* to achieve workers' democracy.

Commenting on the first set of (post-1949) wide-scale workers' rebellions in 1956–1957, Sheehan (1998) writes:

> Workers' response to the thwarting of their aspirations to run their own enterprises in this early period does not seem to have extended to organizing themselves in opposition to management or the party, but judging from press accounts and official reports, it did include often harsh criticism of leading cadres which could not be safely ignored. Workers' alienation from enterprise leadership is frequently mentioned. . . . (T)his first confrontation between workers and the party left a legacy of dissatisfaction among workers and unresolved problems regarding the implementation of democratic management which would also form the basis of the second major confrontation in 1956–7. (45)

Although there were, from a practical strategic perspective, understandable reasons that the Party would ditch *minzhu guanli* as a means to improve industrial productivity and national development, at the state enterprise level, Chinese state enterprise workers were hardly taking to this 'solution.' Sheehan (1998) describes a "backlash against authoritarian or undemocratic management in general, and against the system of one-man management in particular" (49), which took on a life of its own in the media for workers and union cadres.

Undemocratic means of factory management were met with rebellion in the Chinese SOEs. One key catalyst for such upheaval was the type of industrial ownership transformation that occurred in China throughout the 1950s, especially from the middle of that decade. From the mid-1950s onward, the Party consolidated its control over industry through the nationalization of privately owned capitalist enterprises. This set up a level of high expectations among the workers in these enterprises as they went from being employed by capitalists to being putatively the 'masters of their enterprises,' in which 'democratic' forms of management were practiced. Because of their experience with autonomous unions before their enterprises became nationalized, they also had a sense of bargaining rights and independence:

> So we find that in state enterprises, early fears about the tendency for the factory director to override institutions of workers' participation in management had been realized, as Soviet-influenced styles of highly centralized management spread through Chinese industry and cadres appointed by the state came to behave as if their every action had the

personal sanction of Chairman Mao himself. This, then, is the style of management and enterprise atmosphere which the private enterprises inherited when they were taken into joint state-private ownership early in the 1956, as the "transition to socialism" in the Chinese economy was completed. But it was in sharp contrast to the expectations of many workers in private enterprises who seem genuinely to have looked forward to attaining the status of a state employee, and who were gravely disappointed by the reality of their working lives as 1956 progressed. (Sheehan 1998, 51)

The Party's response to the rebellions that occurred from 1956 to 1957 was, in part, recognition that its resort to one-man management only increased the alienation in the workplace experienced during the FMC/WSRC period:

By 1956, many industrial workers were increasingly angry at what they saw as a betrayal of their vision of socialism. In August of that year, following the wholesale nationalization of industry and commerce in the "socialist high tide," an article in *Chinese Worker* quoted a worker as saying, "This quite simply is feudal order; the 'managers' in these enterprises have become the feudal kings of petty kingdoms. How can this phenomenon be allowed to continue in socialist enterprises?" Frustration with the unions and the failure of democratic management, as well as resentment at the privileges and arbitrary power of managers and party cadres, led to wholesale criticism by dissatisfied workers of the party state and the socialist system in the spring of 1957. (Cliver 2002, 44)

Reforms designed to bolster the significance of democratic management were introduced, most notably the invention of a new enterprise-level institution that would remedy the fault lines inherent in the FMC/WSRCs: the WRC (*zhigong daibiau dahui*). The WSRCs of the early 1950s could not be regarded as independent organs of workers' representation in the state enterprises because of their membership in the FMC, a unit that factory directors essentially controlled. The WRC was designed to overcome this flaw by allowing only workers to be elected as representatives and increasing greatly the number of representatives who served on the WRC. Furthermore, although they could serve for a lifetime, representatives also could be recalled by workers (Andreas, Core, and Zhan 2007). The WRC was no longer accountable to the FMC any longer, but it was still organized through the union, and this remained a fundamental impediment to workers' *real* representation. Furthermore, the WRC's focus was supervision of Party officials, and these included, of course, enterprise managers and directors. However, this was not easily accomplished as long as the union chiefs, through which WRCs conveyed workers' sentiments to Party officials, were appointed by the Party. As a result, although the WRC created institutional opportunities for workers to supervise factory administrators in certain instances, it retained similar structural binds that constricted the WSRCs of the past.

Impediments to workers' democracy inherent in the WRC policies were unable to resolve the kinds of anger that gave rise to workers' rebellions from 1956 to 1957. The 1958–1961 Great Leap Forward (GLF) did little to mollify this, although it included sets of policies to specifically address the distance between workers and cadres that contributed so greatly to the failure of the WRCs (Sheehan 1998, 85–86). The GLF industrial policy called for 'two participations' (of workers in management and managers in labor) and 'one reform' (of antiquated rules and regulations). These policies were presented in the media for workers and union cadres as further developing democracy in the workplace by expanding workers' direct participation in management (Sheehan 1998, 87). Between sending cadres 'down' to the work floor and allowing workers to engage directly in tasks traditionally delegated to management, it was hoped that a new type of relationship in the SOEs would contribute to the effectiveness of already existing institutions of workers' democracy such as the WRC. Reforms in industry went as far as the elimination of piecework and unprecedented innovations in worker participation in management roles, with concomitant investments in skills training for production workers.

In fact, this policy represented an effort to go beyond the WRC as the centerpiece of workers' democracy policy (Andors 1977). Bureaucracy and the division of labor were seen as fundamental impediments to the implementation of policies designed to democratize work relationships in the Chinese SOE during the GLF. However, cadres resisted policies that effectively reduced the status they enjoyed *by virtue of* the division of labor in the state socialist factory system. What is perhaps most noteworthy is that, as Cliver (2002) argues was the case for the FMC in the first three years of the PRC, where workers democracy reforms occurred from 1956 to 1961, the greatest benefits again appear to have gone to workers in larger heavy industrial SOEs (Sheehan 1998, 91).

For about three years after the GLF, the CCP was in a state of flux, desperate to devise policies to deal with the unexpectedly disastrous outcomes which that policy had produced. The GLF reforms in Chinese industry saw a revised discourse of workers' democracy and associated set of policies that encouraged decentralization, challenges to hierarchical divisions of labor, and redistribution of skill levels in SOEs. The enthusiasm that was often a part of this effort simultaneously stimulated workers' participation in enterprises that enjoyed new autonomy from central ministries. However, workers also were driven to a point of exhaustion because their participation in management often was work performed *after* a day of production. Safety regulations intended to protect workers were lifted to 'free' workers to participate in management 'without restriction' (Sheehan 1998, 94–95). Finally, this policy also infamously led to massive distortions of production reports sent back to the central ministries, which greatly damaged the CCP's capacity to address famine-related crises in outlying regions.

Such catastrophes led again to a reversion to one-man management and a general questioning of the GLF faith in workers' participation in management. Nonetheless, Maoists would soon proceed to a campaign that came closest to embracing mass management of factories as a means to democratize workplace relationships where the FMC/WSRC, WRC, and the 'three participations' policies fell short of the goal. This was the case, even with Mao's ringing endorsement of the Anshan Constitution in 1960.[2] The reasons for this extended beyond mere intra-Party factional strife:

> Although the results of the (Great Leap Forward) were often inimical in the extreme to workers' interests, this was mainly due to the continual upward revision of production targets already at unrealistically high levels and the consequent pressure to increase production at all costs. . . . The stated aims in (Great Leap Forward) policies, however, did not necessarily run contrary to workers' interests and aspirations: workers did want to participate more in management; they did want cadres to lose their arrogant disdain for workers and reform their workstyle by coming out of their offices and participating in productive labor; and they did want their suggestions for innovation and reform taken seriously and, if feasible, implemented promptly, rather than being shunted off into some labyrinthine process of upward referral and endless discussion. So support for the (Great Leap Forward) policies at both the highest and lowest levels did exist, and to a certain extent continued into the 1961–6 period (Sheehan 1998, 92–93).

In the years between the GLF and the Cultural Revolution, a variety of policies emphasized workers' congresses as an institutional mechanism to minimize the more hierarchical social relations of work that one-man management necessitated. Yet again, Chinese state socialism was in a period in which workers' democracy oriented 'reforms' that accompanied one-man management only spurred growing resentment among Chinas state enterprise workers.

THE CULTURAL REVOLUTION PERIOD

The consequences of the Cultural Revolution are hardly a matter of uniform agreement. For most scholars within China and abroad, it was the most repressive and totalitarian period of Chinese history. However, even the harshest critics of the Cultural Revolution will not deny that *efforts* to transform social relations in virtually every realm of life occurred during this period. Although Maoists in the earliest stages of the Cultural Revolution eschewed organized forms of revolt in the factories, workers' democracy-oriented concepts arose within the context of the Cultural Revolution. They were promulgated in a way that linked notions of workers' democracy with workers' direct control of production through the overthrow of leaders within and outside the factory (Perry and Li 1997).

During the Cultural Revolution's most militant worker-based activism, no longer was democratization of the SOE merely a matter of electing leaders through WRCs or a union, or even participation in management; now the rhetoric that spread throughout Chinese society appeared to legitimize the exercise of mass (i.e., worker) *administration* the Chinese workplace. Yiching Wu (2007), in an eloquent revisionist commentary on the significance of class in the Cultural Revolution, argues that workers' demands and ultimate objectives during the Cultural Revolution were both economic and political. Where demands appeared 'economistic,' Wu argues, "it was always possible to trace yearnings for genuine popular democracy, and for working-class power both in factories and in various spheres of the state" (22).

Emblematic of the Cultural Revolution discourse of workers' democracy, writing in the mid-1970s, Gong Qing,[3] a University professor of political economy, declared:

> From the early days of the post-liberation period to the beginning of the First Five-Year Plan, most factories, through democratic reform, eliminated capitalist administrative structures and rules such as the system of having foremen and supervisors, the system of searching the workers entering or leaving a factory, and so forth. . . . (T)heir extermination greatly enhanced the workers' revolutionary spirit of being masters of their own affairs. . . . (cited in Andors 1977, 365–366).

The words 'democratic reform' referred to here do not simply connote laws that politicians enacted. The language that Gong Qing employs (even if propagandistic) references the activities of workers in China's enterprises to make them more directly objects of their own control or 'mastery':

> How can the administrative structure of an enterprise provide free access to and maintain close ties with the masses? One of the most important factors for this is reliance on the participation of the toiling masses in management. In the "Anshan Steel Constitution" (Chairman Mao) has listed the worker masses' participation in management as a basic principle for running socialist enterprises well. . . . (M)any industrial enterprises have created various approaches relying on the worker masses for management and have scored great achievements. . . . As practice has shown, workers have directly participated in the administration of factories (cited in Andors 1977,, 368).

The discourse embedded in this passage is strikingly similar to that disseminated by earlier advocates of the FMCs, WSRCs, and WRCs, which institutions the Cultural Revolution actually diminished, if not outright eliminated through 'mass struggle.' "Mass participation" in management was a premium in discourses of workers' democracy deployed by factions that were most 'red' prior to the Cultural Revolution, especially in the GLF period. In the Cultural Revolution, however, one finds calls for direct 'mass' administration and even, where 'feasible,' takeover of enterprises by workers. For almost a decade in Party propaganda, the idea circulated among cadres that workers could (under the right conditions) take over factories to promote the interests of the masses and that this had something to do with 'democratic' reform in the factory (and society generally).

New policies of enterprise work relations developed in the Cultural Revolution period, which emphasized a mass-based approach that rejected what was perceived as the formalistic nature of workplace democratization that took place during the FMC/WSRC, WRC, and 'three participations' reforms. Bettelheim's (1974) favorable assessment of the Cultural Revolution's impact on factory relations makes frequent references to the ability of workers to, through their own initiative, use Mao's teachings to rebel against managers:

> Li Chou-hsia, a woman worker and member of the Peking General Knitwear Factory's . . . explained the masses not only rejected the revisionist line, but were also . . . demanded participation in management, in keeping with the Anshan Constitution. The first experiment in workers' participation in management was proposed by the revolutionary committee before the formation of the new party committee. . . . [It] focused on the abolition of the 'unreasonable rules' imposed by the old management—regulations concerning work organizations, discipline, etc. which reflected a lack of confidence in workers' initiatives. . . . (21–22)

Bettelheim's (1974) observations are meant as an affirmation of the way the Cultural Revolution ostensibly delivered real direct democracy, in contrast to the formalistic elections of managers that *minzhu guanli* provided:

> The election of workers' management teams is organized by the members of a work team or shop and is entirely under their supervision; management is concerned only with the principle of workers' management teams. Team members are elected at various levels corresponding to the levels at which the teams themselves are organized—factory, shops, work teams. (22–23)

However, and critically, Bettleheim declares in the next breath that "candidates must be actively engaged in the study and application of Marxism-Leninism and Mao (ZeDong) Thought, have some experience, and be representative of the masses" (Bettelheim 1974, 23). Only a paragraph later, he continues, "both the workers' management teams and the revolutionary committee are under the ideological and political direction of the party committee" (Bettelheim 1974, 23). Bettelheim's reports reflected a discourse of direct worker participation in the affairs of enterprise management, which could be accomplished by the removal of company leaders that stood in the way of this goal.[4] Prominent in this discourse was the call for the elimination of the division of labor within the SOE as a means to redistribute power within the factory. Only now it could conceptually be accomplished via the removal of leaders in the factory altogether. In a manner markedly different from the Soviet model, and even the most prominent Eastern European alternative found in Tito's Yugoslavian self-managed enterprises, the Cultural Revolution called on workers to take factories into their own hands when all other means failed to bring about real reform of SOE power relations. Workers in China responded in 1967 with rebellious activity in their enterprises on a scale that was even greater than the outbreaks of worker-based collective activity that workers participated in from 1956 to 1957 (Sheehan 1998, 104).

Perry and Li's (1997) work on Shanghai labor militancy during the Cultural Revolution suggests that this 'revolution' became a mechanism that, at times, enabled Chinese workers to justify spontaneous attempts to bring the Anshan Constitution to the enterprise and extend the level of the working class' power under state socialism. Economistic demands were prevalent in many instances where "temporary" and lower skilled workers took advantage of calls to rebel against profit-driven managers to win wage increases. Still, Perry points out that workers also were just as driven in instances like the Shanghai Commune by politically inspired desires to challenge the organization of factory relationships, if not the power of the CCP in workers' lives. In fact, it is possible to describe the Shanghai Commune effort as the closest that Chinese workers ever came to experiencing a form of factory relations that had the potential to supersede both the contradictions of state socialism and capitalism:

> If Beijing spawned the most famous social force of the CR in the form of student Red Guards, then Shanghai must be credited with producing a more enduring and politically more influential mass organization: The Workers' General Headquarters. Having dubbed his grand experiment a *"proletarian* cultural revolution," Chairman Mao was elated when a rebel movement broke out among the workers of China's industrial capital. Worker rebels were soon hailed as the main fighting force of the CR; before long, they surpassed the Red Guards in both numbers and political significance. (29)

In the final analysis, however, the concept of workers' democracy that developed in the Cultural Revolution era remained almost as limited in terms of goals achieved as earlier efforts at *minzhu guanli*. This was the case despite the putative intent to address and overcome the flaws of *minzhu guanli* formulated in the previous decade. The resolution of central contradictions within state socialism was not the end result of the Cultural Revolution. Indeed, by the end of the Cultural Revolution, the power of the Party leadership had been restored and strengthened to counter mass-based and/or Red Guard-organized rebellions in the enterprises. There were a number of important factors that worked against the possibility that the discourse of workers' democracy during the Cultural Revolution could be anything but limited in its results. Most critically, factionalism made it difficult to move beyond the dominance of cadres in the affairs of production, thereby rendering many of the "rebellions" little more than switches from one cadre grouping to another:

> Since each of these factional groups claimed to be the "true revolutionaries" and denounced their opponents as "reactionaries and revisionists," there was no organizational basis for carrying out reforms. . . . Since the mass organizations could not be relied upon to reform themselves, the only resort was to fall back on the Army and eventually rebuild the Party. Thus, the possibility, that Mao appeared to have raised, of abandoning the Leninist vanguard Party and its state structure in favor of "extensive democracy" (as might have been realized through an experiment like the Shanghai Commune) was firmly rejected, and the process of rebuilding state, Party, and factory organization began. (Watson 1978, 178)

As a result, although the Cultural Revolution period saw a discourse of workers' democracy, workers' democracy remained, as it did in the 1950s, unachieved. That it was not realized, however, would feed new kinds of rebellion and workers activity on the occasion of Mao's death in 1976. The discourse did not die with the end of Maoism in the late 1970s. Indeed, it would once again be revised and shape the way enterprise relations would be problematized and restructured in the post-Maoist period of Chinese state socialism. An admixture of 1950s' style *minzhu guanli* and Cultural Revolutionary calls for mass-based workers' participation/direct control would shape a revived discourse of workers' democracy in the 1980s as China's political leaders sought to legitimize exposing China's economy to greater amounts of market-based competition.

3　China's Post-Mao Political Economy in Transition

CHAPTER INTRODUCTION

From the late 1970s, the political economy of transition from state socialism shaped transformations in the discourse of workers' democracy in China. In this chapter, I offer an overview of China's transitional political economy during the post-Maoist period (from roughly 1978 to the present). I argue that capitalist markets had not systemically dominated the SOE sector by the end of the 1990s. Even at this late stage of restructuring, the largest value-pumping SOEs in China continued to be shaped by conflicting values of collectivism and for-profit markets. The outcomes of such ideological conflicts in the Chinese SOEs, even in the present moment, remain critical for the direction of Chinese transition from state socialism.

Until the mid-1990s, theorizing the political economy of China's transition from state socialism required one to take a stand on whether China was 'market socialist,' 'capitalist,' or some 'hybrid' form of capitalism and socialism. These debates have thankfully become less prominent as new forms of inequality between rich and poor rendered the 'socialist' component of 'socialism with Chinese characteristics' less and less palpable, much less even noticeable (Greenfield 1997). However, both those who believe that China has become 'half pregnant' with both capitalism and socialism or who take for granted China becoming capitalist tend to ignore the problem of what kinds of struggles must occur in what was the traditional heart of Chinese state socialism before such a transition could ever be said to have given birth to capitalism. This chapter cannot answer the question, 'Is China capitalist?' However, in this chapter, I suggest that the struggles that have occurred as China transitions from state socialism remain incomplete from the vantage of what is necessary for the logic of capitalist markets to be *systematically* dominant in China's national political economy. In the chapters that follow this one, I focus on how, from the early 1980s to the end of the 1990s, various social actors with an interest in the future of the Chinese SOE deployed a revised discourse of workers' democracy. This renewed discourse was institutionally made possible and constrained by the political economy of China's transition from state socialism since the death of Mao Zedong in 1976.

THE LIMITS OF THE 1980'S ECONOMIC RESTRUCTURING

China's transition from state socialism proceeded in a fashion that diverges noticeably from the Russian shock therapy model and with transparently more dynamic results (Clarke 2002; Nakagane 2000). For most of the first decade of China's transition from state socialism, exposure to market competition and capitalist investment was limited to peripheral areas of the national economy, focused on the rural sector where producers experienced the earliest release from the state's direct involvement in and control of production and surplus distribution (Nee 1996; Selden 1993, 1994).[1]

China began (considerably more slowly) to implement market-oriented policy shifts in the SOE sector by the mid- to late 1980s. Many commentators took note of what seemed to be dramatically altered relations of urban industrial surplus production (Howard 1991; Howard and Howard 1995; Sabin 1994; Solinger 1995). The large and historically dominant SOEs appeared to pale in dynamism compared with the rapid growth of small urban collectively owned enterprises (COEs), which were freed of many of the restrictions on hiring and firing that were enforced by ministerial control of production-investment decisions. COEs grew in number and output swiftly, in part, because a good number of them were actually private companies whose 'collective' status secured a license to operate in private markets (Sabin 1994). Concurrent development of foreign export zones only created greater room for industrial production for profit. The absorption of large numbers of rural migrant laborers into sectors that primarily produced for export and demonstrated the most glaring features of exploitative relations associated with Dickens' novels added to the impression that Chinese capitalism was in full force (Chan 2001; Howard 1991). Just as conspicuous were dramatic changes in the thrust of the social security system. Growing numbers of urban workers no longer enjoyed access to the traditional iron rice-bowl social welfare benefits that came with a job in the state sector (Chan and Chow 1992; Philion 1998; Wong 1996).

All of these phenomena were regarded increasingly as contributing to the demise of the SOE sector. However, exposure to market competition was not the primary mechanism deployed to stimulate SOE production throughout the 1980s. Although motivations for increasing SOE investment in production and profits were introduced, SOEs continued to follow the traditional extensive pattern of operation:

> Instead of seeking to maximize profits, managers sought to maximize enterprise wealth by maximizing inputs including raw materials and

means of production, labor, wages, and state-supplied capital—with little concern for efficiency (productivity) or demand (the market). Instead of plowing surpluses back into production, to increase their competitive edge, they systematically sought to divert profits toward consumption (especially to build housing, etc.) even when this threatened the financial health of the enterprise and/or caused it to fall into debt. (Smith 1993, 65–66)

The labor process in the SOE, contrary to expectations and despite new market-oriented policies, underwent little in the way of systematic revamping. Piece wages were introduced; however, the apportioning of earnings continued to be dictated by traditional Chinese socialist SOE mores, as Walder (1991) reported in a review of changing labor relations in China's SOEs:

> By what criteria are salary rises and large money bonuses to be distributed? Initially, Chinese managers attempted to use the methods of the Mao era: laborious collective work group evaluations whose results could be manipulated by factory leaders. . . . Managers (thereupon) adopted different strategies after this experience and for the rest of the decade sought to keep differences in bonuses to a minimum and keep them and pay ráises liked only loosely to individual and group performance. Instead, they sought to win the cooperation of labor by bringing about steady increases in compensation and benefits. Workers came to expect such increases. (476)

SOE directors and managers did benefit from regulations that were redrawn to give them greater authority over the labor collective (Warner 1987). Party cadres within[2] and outside enterprises benefited by skimming considerably from a dual price track for industrial inputs, and workers saw augmented wages and social welfare benefits in line with productivity gains. Instead of experiencing rationalization in the Chinese SOE sector, rentier behavior further took hold in China at all levels in industry and with it the expanded reproduction of urban SOE investment.

The limits of this accumulation strategy came to the surface in the late 1980s, despite demonstrably rapid rates of growth in the national economy during the first decade of economic restructuring, which had been spurred on by a combination of inflows of private capital in the rural and light industrial sectors plus government subsidies to state producers.[3] The contractual responsibility system, which gave farmers greater autonomy over what to produce and sell in private profit-driven markets, did indeed stimulate production in China's rural areas. However, by the mid-1980s, when the central government began to decrease its purchases (and subsidies[4]) of agricultural products, agricultural production dramatically declined as farmers transferred investment energies into nonagricultural activities. By

1988, nonagricultural production accounted for some 53 percent of rural output total value, up from 31 percent in 1980 (Hartford 1990). Increasing shares of that percentage were geared toward export manufacturing orders. Labor surpluses grew exponentially when large population movements of former peasants migrated to cities in search of wages in coastal export-oriented companies (Singh 1995).

Foreign currency revenues were employed to maintain the loyalty of the Party's traditional base of support (urban SOE and government workers, intellectuals, and Party cadres) in the form of subsidies that undercut the conditions necessary for the circulation of capitalist accumulation (Cheng 1995). New tensions associated with this pattern of development emerged and were characterized by increasing rural inequality that fueled (1) the growth of a 'floating population' of rural to urban migrant laborers who were denied access to social security benefits reserved for holders of urban residence permits (Li, Tan 1994), and (2) a boiling sense of dissatisfaction among urban intellectual/skilled strata with the role of Party corruption in the procurement of new wealth since 1978 and (critically) their *lack* of opportunities to share in that experience. Inflationary trends (in 1988 reaching 27 percent) only exacerbated these strains; central government revenues stagnated and deficits tied to foreign borrowing accelerated as money (credit) in circulation expanded more quickly than output (Hartford 1990). This paradigm led to a crisis situation by the late 1980s. Economic restructuring strained the Party's capacity to retain the loyalty of its traditional base of support, as evidenced most explicitly in the form of the 1989 spring protests, which had been percolating from as early as 1986 in urban areas, especially on elite university campuses.

WORKING-CLASS RESPONSE TO 1980S' ECONOMIC RESTRUCTURING

A good number of scholars (Black and Munro 1993; Walder 1991; Walder and Gong 1993) argued that the Party's June 1989 crackdown was inspired by the 'threat' posed to the Party by workers' involvement in the Tiananmen demonstrations. However, Lau's (1996) detailed study of the protest literature and timeline of demands made by participating independent workers movements concludes that independent workers' level of activity was overestimated. The level of workers' activity was limited to support for the students' right to protest and anticorruption slogans. The direction of economic policy in China in the post-Tiananmen 1990s supports Lau's thesis that the Party was much more concerned about the discontent of urban intellectuals than of workers. The Party leadership was, however, concerned about workers' eventual support for the protests should the liberal democracy movement not be stopped in its tracks. If protests and the contradictions between the state and the intellectuals and urban petit-bourgeoisie that gave rise to them were not checked, greater threats to the Party's monopoly of political power could potentially grow out of hand. By rolling back (and, most importantly, making requisite concessions to) the intellectual and petit-bourgeois strata that led China's liberal democracy movement, the Party essentially found a successful formula to nip the crisis in the bud.

The Party's resolution to the 1989 crisis was not the imposition of capitalist rule on the organization of production relations in the SOEs. Instead, although migrant workers coming to the cities from rural areas suffered the brunt of repression during the June 4th crackdown, urban state workers experienced, for a period of several years in the early 1990s, a renewed policy of state protections for SOEs ensued. Indeed, by the end of the 1980s, the attempt to create labor markets in the heart of China's economy had fallen so far short of its goals that researchers such as Michael Korzec (1992) were declaring the 'failure of Chinese reform' and predicting that the CCP would never impose a labor contract system on Chinese labor:

> Although, at the end of August 1989, more than 10 percent of the labor force of state enterprises in China were registered as "labor-contract-system workers," half a million more than the number at the end of 1988, the time for drastic experiments with the labor market was over . . . the labor contract system has disintegrated. . . . It is improbable that contract workers will eventually replace permanent workers as the backbone of the Chinese economy. (50–51)

POST-TIANANMEN RENEWED ATTEMPTS TO RESTRUCTURE CHINA'S ECONOMY

However, the June 1989 repression of the intellectual led liberal democracy movement did not lead to a widely anticipated withdrawal of the CCP's commitment to economic restructuring. This was the case despite austerity policies, the pronouncement of renewed restrictions on private enterprise activity, and recommitment, in principle, to Chinese SOE sector production in the early aftermath of the Tiananmen crackdown. Although the Party remained committed to investment in the SOE sector in the early 1990s, this period also saw a massive influx of private sector investment from Hong Kong, Taiwan, Korea, and Japan, encouraged in the wake of American capital flight in response to the June 1989 crackdown (Hsiao and So 1996). By 1992, when, on his pivotal *Southern Tour*, Deng Xiaoping made declarations in support of the role of private enterprises in 'socialism with Chinese characteristics,' a much more public resurgence of market-entrepreneurial activities and correlated incidences of labor exploitation of labor took hold in China's urban areas, especially in, but not isolated to, the more developed coastal cities (Lu 1992). The devaluation of China's currency in 1995 only further intensified the attraction of foreign capital to investment in China's economy. Notably dramatic increases in the levels of American, European, and Japanese investments were felt, with ever greater amounts moving into longer term capital-intensive projects, contributing to surging double-digit levels of economic growth from 1994 through late 1997. Expectations that the June repression of the liberal democracy movement would bring an end to market-oriented experiments in China gave way to a renewed sense of *certainty* that China was, alas and ironically, becoming capitalist.

Indeed, if the 1980s looked like Chinese capitalism's decade of incremental development, the 1990s took on *the appearance* of capitalism's full fruition (Biddulph and Cooney 1993). Reports of exploitative labor relations and widespread profiteering in industry were no longer limited to privately owned companies that were springing up everywhere to feed the insatiable foreign exporters' appetites. Research emerged asserting that many state sector companies were now experiencing similar conditions, especially in the small- and medium-sized companies (Lee 1999; Leung 1994; Zhao and Nichols 1996). Regional disparities, both inter and intraprovincial, grew rapidly despite double-digit growth (Bramall and Jones 1993). The 'floating population' of rural-urban surplus migrant laborers provided a seemingly endless supply of cheap labor for a stratum of *nouveau riche* owners of restaurants, construction companies, hotels, and other private-sector work that urban workers refused to take (Yan 2002). At the 14th and 15th Congresses, the Party resolved to and did enact a policy of 'letting go' of state subsidies to smaller sized SOEs while increasing their exposure to domestic and foreign competition.

By 1997, it looked as if China was finally about to shake off the yoke of the social obligations long associated with the SOE. Almost all SOE workers had become contract workers, and huge numbers of those in failing units were classified as 'laid off' or 'on vacation' (Lau 1997; Sabin 1994). The position of SOE workers was plainly weakened by the raised level of (foreign and domestic) private investment in China's economy. That only added to the certainty of both liberalizers and restructuring's critics that a commodified proletariat and capitalist counterpart, both substantially freed from state interference, were alas the new subject contenders for political-economic control of China on the eve of the new millennium (Lu 1992; Nee 1996). This idea coincided with the prevalent belief that China was experiencing a corporatist type of capitalist development, over which the state exercised a large role, but that enabled capitalist markets to expand their reach with every passing day (Unger and Chan 1996). A slightly modified variant of this position saw China as a 'mixed' economy, one that combined the best of capitalist markets and state-socialist nationalist guidance and economic redistribution.

However, even by the end of the 1990s, it still was not clear that capitalist relations of production would 'inevitably' dominate the Chinese political economy. Monkey wrenches were thrown into the expectation of a 'gradual' Chinese transition to capitalism with the onset of the Asian Financial Crisis (AFC), upsetting expectations that the combined market-state guidance model of late industrializing growth would necessarily produce a smooth transition to capitalist development in China. By mid-1998, the AFC was making itself felt in China (Lau 1999a, 2001a, 2001b; Lo 2001). East Asian investors reduced or withdrew investments due to credit collapses and bankruptcies back home. Chinese producers in export sectors that competed with newly devalued South East Asian currencies saw sudden decreases in foreign purchase orders. On top of these dilemmas, the economy also faced the same ominous aggregate drop in prices in an already overheated national economy that was giving East Asian economies major headaches prior to the AFC (Cooper-Ramo 1998; Yuan, Yang, and Xun 1998). Just when SOEs were slated to compete for domestic and foreign private investors, foreign investors suddenly were holding back. Investment from Asian countries fell by 21 percent in 1999, whereas overall foreign direct investment (FDI) dropped 11 percent. Exports to Asia fell by 9.9 percent in 1998, with those damaged by the AFC facing the most serious declines (Lau 2001a). To make matters even more worrisome, consumers, lacking faith in the Chinese economy, were holding onto bank deposits even as interest rates were pushed to near zero, not circulating money for either investment or commodity consumption.

Meanwhile, the capacity of provincial and national officials to command funds for failing SOEs that would placate laid-off and retired workers diminished considerably. As a result, during efforts at restructuring SOEs, factory/ministry cadres characteristically maneuvered to drive down the value of SOE assets to attract 'investors' who virtually dictated the terms of SOE stockholding conversion. In the process, the conflict with SOE workers only intensified as they observed inside deals for SOE assets designed to transfer public wealth to a new class of wealthy cadres and private investors, few of whom had any interest in investing in SOE production (or frequently enough in any private production for that matter) because of declining growth rates and overproduction that characterize Chinese markets. This trend became increasingly endemic in the late 1990s as China edged toward enforcement of provisions in the WTO agreement that called for loosening tariffs in most agricultural and key industrial enterprises within less than a decade and further elimination of subsidies to uncompetitive SOEs. In response to those who believed that, regardless of economic growth rates, China's economy would enjoy smooth success, a *Business Week* commentator pointedly declared:

(Confidence) . . . is born of a conviction that the massive unemployment, poverty, and corruption, being produced by China's market reforms will not swell into a social revolution. . . . (A) Hong Kong based managing director for Goldman Sachs & Co. says even in a best-case scenario, reforming the state sector will cause "tremendous stress, lots of difficulties, pain, and potential for social unrest." If the (Chinese development) stats skeptics are right, the strains on the system may prove greater than anyone is now predicting. (Balfour 2002)

EVER UNCERTAIN TRANSITION IN CHINA

China, when not viewed from the world of immediate and undeniably strong appearances, has in fact never been on any *set* road to capitalist relations of production. Even on the eve of China's entry into the WTO, much about its transition remained in need of greater empirical inquiry (Lardy 1998, 2002; Rawski 2000, 2002). China has experienced a much deeper integration into world markets than did its Russian counterpart, *despite* a continuing one (CCP)-Party monopoly (So and Chang 1998). Nonetheless, even with the higher levels of investment in China by foreign and domestic capitalists, the process necessary for capital to act as capital in the heart of the Chinese political economy has not taken place due to the level of exigent class conflict called forth by capitalist transition. The reasons are of critical importance because they are pertinent to positions that China's working-class movement takes in the period of transition from state socialism.

It is true that by the end of the 1990s China's SOE sector underwent considerable restructuring (Parker and Pan 1996). However, it would be hyperbole to assert that the greatest value-pumping (large) SOEs were subjected to the laws of market competition such that capitalist markets determined how they were operated and financed (Qian 1996; Qian and Xu 1998). Liu and Link (1998) noted the continuing prominence of the SOE sector in China's political economy into the late 1990s:

> Notwithstanding the widespread discussion of the effects of the "private market" on China, China's state enterprises, although they were never very efficient, still dominate the urban economy. . . . With few exceptions, only state enterprises receive loans for China's banks (which are themselves exclusively state owned) and only state enterprises can have access to foreign currency. Still the state sector's share of the economy has steadily declined. Twenty years ago it was the only sector, and today it produces about 30% of the gross domestic product. But the 70% of the "non-state" GDP includes all of agriculture and rural industry, which together are 60% of GDP. Contrary to the impression given in the Western press, only about 10% of GDP comes from urban private enterprise. The state sector of the economy also dominates the concerns of the Chinese leadership-concerns that are, as always, essentially political. (Liu and Link 1998)

There is no question that private enterprises expanded rapidly in China, particularly since Deng's 1992 'southern tour.' However, throughout the 1990s, their contribution to GDP, compared with SOE counterparts, remained small. Furthermore, in contrast to the literature on the failing performance of SOEs, Lo (1999, 2002) countered that the difference in performance by scale within that sector was overlooked at the cost of a more accurate picture of what fueled the engine of Chinese economic growth during the 1990s. For starters, the SOE sector continued to dominate the largest value producing large- and medium-sized enterprises (LMEs). LMEs also constitute the most protected, soft budget-oriented, and least market-exposed part of that sector of production. The majority of declines in growth occurred in the SOE sector in the smaller companies and the COEs, which overwhelmingly tended to be the most exposed to international markets and least tied to state ministries as far as production prerogatives are concerned (Lo 1999). In this sense, quite differently from the Russian model, China actually managed to improve productivity in the greatest value-producing enterprises of the still dominant and least market-dominated state sector.[5] That is to say, even with entry into the WTO, the SOE has remained both a vital and substantial contributor to state revenue in China. Meanwhile, Lo points out that there is also good reason to be wary of grandiose assessments of how much capital was generalized in China's economy at the start of the 21st century:

> For the first time since the start of the reform era, the trend of the secular decline of the enterprise pre-tax profit rate has been reversed (in the SOE sector): it increased from an all-time low level of 5.5% in 1998 to 6.4% in 1999, and further to 8.4% in 2000. . . . It is spectacularly obvious that industrial investment has been experiencing a slump since the mid-1990's: its share of the total capital construction investment in the economy has decreased from the average level of 47% in the 1981–85 period, 53% during 1986–90, and 47% in the 1991–95 period, to 38% between 1996 and 1999. But it is precisely in 1998 and 1999, when the Keynesian-type fiscal packages were forcefully put into effect, that the slump in industrial investment was most severe. . . . What this phenomenon indicates is the reluctance of economic agents, particularly financial interests, to involve themselves with industrial production. . . . (This) is consistent with the argument that private capital that has accumulated in China over the reform era is mainly speculative financial capital, and that it is in significant measure responsible for the profitability decline of Chinese industry— through a process of "rents" squeezing profits. (Lo 2001, 262–263)

Cooper Ramo (1998) noted that even Shanghai's economy, awash in money from worldwide and Chinese investors, was distorted by speculative short-term finance capital markets that militate against the systematic implementation of capitalist production relations. Liberalized rules for foreign investment in 1992 brought in a massive flow of currency that was directed toward Shanghai's real estate sector. However, that sector no sooner took off like wild fire in 1994 than the housing market began a sudden collapse. As a result, FDI in Shanghai slipped in 1997 to $6 billion from a 1994 high of $10 billion, due in large part to a burst in the real estate bubble encouraged during the previous three years.

Excitement generated in the late 1990s by China's entry into the WTO notwithstanding, concerns continued to be expressed about the kinds of sociopolitical stresses that would result from tariff removals in state-dominated sectors that the WTO membership demanded of China (Han 2000). Additionally, representatives of institutions tied to U.S. capital and international financial institutions (IFIs)expressed anxiousness about Chinese leaders' willingness to fulfill WTO obligations, that is, the systematic imposition of the capitalist norms of competition on Chinese manufacturers. An analyst in *The Financial Times* summed up this view with the following admonition:

> One lesson of the collapse of socialism in Eastern Europe is that profitability, not quantity of investment, is the key to sustained economic growth. Here, arguably, lies China's fundamental problem. There is no doubt that massive investment is being made—more than Dollars 300bn in foreign direct investment in 20 years, and vastly bigger amounts by the state. All this shows up as growth because the sums are spent, the workers are hired and the cement is poured. But what about actual return in a decade or two? This is much less clear. . . . Many . . . think, mistakenly, that China is capitalist. In fact, China's system is exactly what its leaders call it: socialism with Chinese characteristics. In practice, that means a large state sector, party committees even in private enterprises, corporate boards that are unable to fire managers, no market for corporate control and massive changes in economic policy (such as consolidation of the motor industry) dictated without consultation. (Waldron 2002)

CHINESE TRANSITION AND THE PROBLEM OF ATTRACTING INVESTMENT

Attracting capitalist investment into the heart of the economy such that capital dominates a society in transition from state socialism is not merely contingent on *desire* alone to secure that investment. It is just as much determined by the actual market conditions in which capital invests. Capital, after all, does not invest simply because investment is desired. If it did, the problem of capitalist reproduction long ago would have been solved forever. When markets, viewed from the vantage of capital, are deemed insufficiently ready for investment due to perceived burdens of costs (i.e., social security, payments to 'corrupt' rentiers, high tariffs, etc.) or lack of buyers, capital can simply withhold investment. Capitalist markets do not just exist by virtue of their being declared 'opened.' They must be opened in a fashion that capital sees worthy of its investment—that is, its return is high enough. Naturally, capital will try to find a way to enter markets such that entry is lowest in cost and highest in profitability, and capacity to dominate is premium.

China's rulers clearly hoped to pursue a newly industrializing country (NIC)-style development plan of utilizing currency generated by foreign exports to sustain restructuring and revitalization of protected state sectors.[6] However, as shown by the frequently tense WTO negotiations and American irritation with the amount of regulation of key markets in China since entry into the WTO, international investors and credit institutions have had quite a different perspective on how China should develop markets. Lo (2001) argues that, for Chinese leaders who intend to continue with a national development plan based on large SOE development with simultaneous consumer growth across strata, capitalist development in China is anything but certain:

> From the 1992–94 financial liberalization and the 1995–97 enterprise downsizing—both have fundamentally undermined the existing (anti-market) regime of accumulation—it could be posited that . . . Chinese state authorities have been captured by these newly emerged speculative financial interests in the economy. The anti-market nature of the politics adopted in the 1998–2000 period, however, suggests that this capture is in no sense total. What remains, therefore, is the continuation of enormous uncertainty over the future prospects of the political economy. (262)

Foreign capital and international financial bodies (especially, but not only, the WTO) also increased the pressure on China to conform to its expectations, placing China's rulers in a rather precarious position. Cadres do enrich themselves in the process of making greater compromises with international investors. However, that fact alone does not mean that cadres will fall in line with capital on the social and political prices to be paid for attracting further investment in the heart of the Chinese economy. The stress caused by this ostensible 'stubbornness' during negotiations on WTO and similar international trade agreements designed to secure greater capitalist investment in the Chinese economy is perpetually bubbling to the surface. In a February 1999 article, *Business Week* reported that foreign investors were increasingly concerned with the often arbitrary policies of Beijing:

> [1999] marks the 10thanniversary of . . . at Tiananmen Square, as well as the 50th anniversary of the founding of the People's Republic. Celebrants

can easily turn into demonstrators if they're angry enough and poor enough. With these threats looming, Zhu has quietly set aside much of his politically destabilizing reform plan. He is also engineering a crackdown on the provinces, shutting down heavily indebted, corrupt investment trusts and sealing the exits for any Chinese company that wants to ship money out of the country. There's some merit to this crackdown: China needs a better regulated and less corrupt economy. But the moves show Zhu is as much a Party cadre intent on control as he is a reformer. And while Zhu in the past used the levers of state power to curb inflation and promote growth, this time his policies seem likely to lead to even more stagnation. Ministries are changing the rules to favor local players—and sideswiping foreign investors in the process. Foreign ventures are losing distribution deals and forking over more of their profits to tax collectors. "Multinationals have been in the economy for six or seven years, and they're not getting the returns [they want]," says Padraig Lehane of Dun & Bradstreet in Shanghai.

Before capital invests in labor as a commodity, labor must be transformed into a commodity, that is, tradable in labor markets. For that transformation to take place, labor must trade at the *price* set in existing capitalist labor markets. This is not a process that occurs as a result of new opportunities that markets present to labor. It arises as a result of a process of struggle, whereby previously noncommodified labor has no other means to access means of subsistence than to compete for wages in labor markets (Wood 1994). Marx and Engels (1935/1847) summed up the power relation as an explicitly unequal one:

> The worker leaves the capitalist, to whom he has sold himself, as often as he chooses, and the capitalist discharges him as often as he sees fit, as soon as he no longer gets any use, or not the required use, out of him. But the worker, whose only source of income is the sale of his labor-power, cannot leave the *whole class of buyers, i.e., the capitalist class,* unless he gives up his own existence. He does not belong to this or that capitalist, but to the *capitalist class*; and it is for him to find his man, *i.e.,* to find a buyer in this capitalist class. (20)

Capitalists don't merely invest in labor markets because there are workers willing to work; reference post-Soviet Russia or millions of unemployed workers in China today. Capitalist investors are in search of workers who will work at or below the going *market rate* for the labor they perform in specific sectors of production. The value capital accords labor in a transitional economy is determined in comparison with rates in existing capitalist markets elsewhere. Conflicts arise, then, between workers in post-state-socialist societies with their own sense of value informed by collectivist and/or nationalist ideologies and those who collaborate to compel them to accept the going valuation of labor power in international capitalist markets (Burawoy 2001; Clarke 1993a, 1993b).

Just as important, capital seeks to dominate new markets of investment and eradicate whatever obstacles that prevent that from transpiring. Thus, capital is seeking more than cheap labor costs for exports back to the home country or other advanced capitalist regions of the world market. Indeed, it is entirely reasonable to estimate that the greatest source of conflict as China 'restructures' will concern how much of China's *domestic* market becomes open to foreign investors. A factory director in a Changsha large SOE water pump producer that had undergone major progress toward privatization stated the WTO provisions were not of real concern to his factory.[7] He explained that his company was able to underprice foreign competitors' imports even after tariffs were lowered. What *did* concern him, however, was what would happen if and when American or Japanese producers should invest in factories in China to produce similar goods for Chinese consumption. CEOs of major foreign companies have told interviewers that they expect the biggest conflicts to arise over the matter of how much of China's domestic markets will be opened up to foreign investors in the near and long-term future.[8] The largest capital-intensive investing companies are quite frank about their willingness to take losses in the short term on their investments on the assumption that future tariff revisions and eliminations of SOE competitors' subsidies will open up massive Chinese domestic market opportunities. In the case of China's transition, there remains a battle over the terms of capitalist investment. Resolution has hardly been reached, nor is it in any sense guaranteed to bring about the systemic submission of producers and appropriators to the laws of capitalist competition.

The obstacle to capitalist transition remains, as it has from the beginning, China's working class, most critically in the largest value creating sector of production (i.e., the SOE). How that struggle continues to play itself out is what will determine and, invariably, what it will mean for China to become capitalist.

THE WORLD MARKET AS A SOURCE OF UNCERTAINTY IN CHINA'S TRANSITION

Quite simply, China's transition to capitalism is tenuous due to the social relations of production domestically, which are also aggravated by the problem of overproduction and intercapitalist competition internationally. Cumings (1998) comments on the impact of the AFC on the East Asian NIC 'developmentalist' model that Chinese leaders attempt to mimic:

> South Korea and Japan have been sheltered economies, indulged in their neo-mercantilism and posted as engines of economic growth,

because of the great value they had in the global struggle with communism. Now that that struggle is over, however, the issue of their
"fit" with a new era of free markets and neo-liberalism comes to the
fore. . . . The deep meaning of the Asian crisis, therefore, lies in the
American attempt to bring down the curtain on "late" development
of the Japanese-Korean type, and the likelihood that they will be successful—because the strong, nationalistic neo-mercantilism of Japan
and South Korea was propagated in the soft soil of semi-sovereignty,
and because . . . the Americans have, paradoxically, had willing ac-
complices in Northeast Asian peoples who have sought to reform or
nullify this same model themselves. (45)

Because of the international environment of capitalist restructuring,
despite comparably high levels of FDI in China, 1990s China bore a closer
resemblance to Russia than many observers seem to recognize. In the
1990s, Russia faced a virtual global boycott in its industrial base because
its central enterprises and financing institutions continued to carry out
nonmarket-oriented patterns of investment and credit. After foreign capital
finished its feeding frenzy on raw materials procurement schemes, it largely
left Russian managers and workers in the core manufacturing enterprises
without investments of capital (Clarke 1992; Clarke and Biziukov 1992;
Clarke and Kabalina 2000).

The question remained, by the end of the 1990s, both if and how China
would make a transition to capitalism in its SOE sector. This was no small
matter given the disconnect between the social relations of production in the
commanding heights of China's economy and the expectations from international and domestic capital in terms of further restructuring (i.e., confronta-
tions with SOE workers) in its economic center. The regime of accumulation
pursued by China since Tiananmen was caught in a contradictory moment
of both requiring greater investment of capital into its economic heart and
maintaining the loyalty of workers in that vital sector of production. It was,
after all, the former that threatened the position of the latter.

The problem China faced at the start of the 21st century in complet-
ing a transition to capitalism was intimately tied to the limits of the social
relation called capital. Overproduction has led dominant capitals internationally to redraw the terms of investment such that capitalists are able to
withdraw greater portions of surplus from productive activities as the price
for its investment (Harvey 2005, 2006).[9] This has only served to exacerbate
the level of social conflict required for an attempted transition from state
socialism to capitalism in China.

Brenner (1998) has argued that the present economic trend of 'global
turbulence' is an outcome of the attempts on the part of postwar advanced
capitals, since the early 1960s, to reverse declining aggregate rates of profits, which stemmed from intensified international capitalist competition. In
the same vein, beginning with the dismantling of Bretton Woods, a whole

series of international treaties, accords, agreements, and the like have been signed that progressively remove barriers to capital flows in and out of regions. This has rapidly subjected formerly protected political economies to two potential threats to national economic integrity—namely, imports from advanced (i.e., the most competitive) capitals[10] and credit/currency speculators (Bello 2002; Brenner 2002; Cumings 1998).

The AFC was tied in closely to this process. As Bernard (1999) has pointed out, the rush to liberalize foreign lending in East Asian countries came in response to pressures put on state leaders from domestic manufacturing capitalists, who were reacting to increasing competition from other producers in South East Asia and China. These state leaders likewise acquiesced to pressures from the United States to open up formerly protected domestic markets. This only served to increase the pressure from domestic capitalists who utilized the option of capital flight and simultaneously increased their calls for privatization, reliance on foreign laborers, rewriting of finance, tax, and labor legal codes to combat competitive challenges from producers in South East Asia and advanced capitalist countries, especially the United States.

The AFC, initially set off by IFI's lack of confidence in the viability of short-term investments in Thailand, was closely linked to the intensive competitive pressures placed on the export 'engine' of Thailand's economy in the aftermath of China's devaluation of the Yuan. This set off a domino effect in star NIC countries such as Korea, where foreign investors likewise experienced a 'sudden' collective angst over the integrity of loans to Korean companies that happened to be overinvested in Thailand's now defunct real estate and stock markets (Bello 2000). The result for workers was devastating because the International Monetary Fund (IMF) then demanded unprecedented (for East Asian NICs, that is) harsh bailouts that threatened to undermine the institutions that once enabled East Asian NICs to control the direction of capital flows into national development projects *and* actively participate in world commodity markets (Cumings 1998).[11]

Wade and Veneroso (1998) note that East Asian NIC development was premised on the capacity of the state to accumulate and distribute sufficient funds to (protected) firms that had the potential to compete in world markets. This resulted in a debt-equity structure that radically differed from those traditionally found in Western countries, whereby the debt load frequently was higher than the value of equity capital.[12] In the case of Korea, for example, it was just this structure (as opposed to the capacity of Chaebols to compete in the international arena) that would make Korean companies in the post-bailout era especially vulnerable to foreign reassessments of their *value*:

> The [IMF's] much higher real interest rates will tip many high debt/equity firms into bankruptcy—and the resulting financial instability and unrest may cause net capital *outflows* instead of the inflow that the

Fund expects. Meeting western standards for the adequacy of banks' capital requires a rapid fall in banks' debt/equity ratios, and a sharp cut in their lending, causing more company bankruptcies. Opening up the financial sector to foreign banks will result in a large scale take-over, because after the liquidations foreign banks and companies will be the only ones with the capital for recapitalizing the domestic ones. But foreign banks may not lend to high debt/equity local companies and may not participate in the kind of alliances between government, banks, and companies that (that) financial structure requires. If Citibank buys up Korean banks and applies normal prudential limits . . . it will not lend to a company like Daewoo with a debt/equity ratio of 5:1. The amount of restructuring of Daewoo before its debt ratio comes close to 1:1 is hard to imagine. (Wade and Veneroso 1998, 14–15)

The subsequent neoliberal recipe of restructuring Chaebols and government financing called for dramatic increases in unemployment, attacks on trade unions (for not meeting their patriotic duty to accede to calls for 'flexibility'), and a general program of austerity that redirected wealth upward as the paradigm for future development (Hart-Landsberg and Burkett 2001).[13] Excited forecasts were offered by many economists that East Asian NIC economies would quickly recover after this round of reintegration and 'structural adjustment.' However, reports as recent as spring 2003 indicate that local companies and banks face greater exposure to foreign buyouts.[14] Furthermore, East Asian NICs are now even more susceptible to shifts in the U.S. economy because the prime mechanism for dealing with the fallout from the AFC has been the combination of increased exports to the United States and constricted domestic demand. When the volatility of the current global market and its incapacity to generate sustainable growth is taken into account, the problems facing workers in East Asia are transparently on a scale that neither romanticizing past 'developmentalist' state models nor further 'integration' into global capitalist circuits of production and exchange are likely to resolve. Brenner (2002) prophetically noted that, despite the early signs of East Asian recovery:

The international recovery that has gathered force since 1999 has provided little clear evidence that the world's leading manufacturing economies can finally expand together, at least without the benefit of a US current account deficit that is setting new records every year—i.e., without the continuation of a US consumption boom. . . . [F]or the world market to expand sufficiently to absorb US export growth at its current rapid rate, it would seem that US imports and the US current accounts deficit must increase disproportionately. The implication is that for the American and world economy to continue to grow vigorously, the reigning pattern of expansion must continue to prevail—though this would obviously do nothing to reduce the current account deficit, indeed would be likely to make it worse. (40)

What differentiates China from East Asian NICs, such as Korea, Taiwan, or Japan, whom CCP leaders hope to emulate, is that in East Asian NICs the terms of capitalist development is a settled issue. Capital has long flowed in and out of these countries as capital in accordance with contemporaneous global market conditions. For China, there is little likelihood that it could attract capitalist investment into the heart of China's economy and, at the same time, continue with its national development strategies, which are politically dictated. There is not a lack of desire to restructure production relations such that capital acts as capital in the Chinese economy systematically. However, the matter is clearly one of more than adding a little market here and taking out a little socialism there. Chinese restructuring has not brought forth the kind of investment and consumption patterns from domestic and foreign investors and consumers that would sustain a 'developmentalist state' patterned on the East Asian NIC experience. The Chinese ruling party continues to cling to and base its legitimacy on a twofold developmental policy of (1) securing (and increasing) its accumulative capacity through traditional access to state resources (*guanxi*, corruption, speculative ventures, etc.), and (2) pursuing nationalist political and economic development strategies that limit (albeit increasingly less so) the level of capitalist control over state institutions that control the direction of capital flows.

THE TRANSITION TO CAPITALISM, THE LIMITS OF CAPITAL, AND THE UNCERTAIN CHINESE TRANSITION

Since the beginning of post-Mao economic restructuring, there has clearly emerged an ever-widening gap of power between those who produce value and those who accumulate wealth in China. As markets have become employed more and more widely in China, cadres have sought to accomplish two objectives. They have sought to take advantage of their access to the state bureaucratic apparatus to benefit from the state policy of letting go of companies deemed to be no longer of value to the state. The objective of this policy has been to stimulate investment in that sector by private capital in addition to restructuring companies as productive independent shareholding corporations. Central to this policy would be loosening the politically based ties between the state and SOEs. These companies, thanks to their new market-driven basis and independent shareholder ownership, would contribute to the revitalization of failing enterprises while enabling the state to focus its energies on the engine of the Party's national development plans—the largest SOEs.

However, the 1990s policy of restructuring (e.g., shareholder corporation conversion, merges, and/or outright sell-offs) in the small- and medium-sized SOEs did not sufficiently redirect capital derived from 'privatization' into productive market-based investment, nor did they successfully compel workers to give up their claims to social protection from the state and (critically) SOEs in the aftermath of the AFC. It is true that China was protected from the worst encroachments on national markets that foreign capital made in post-AFC Southeast Asian and Asian economies. This is especially the case due to the nonconvertible status of the Chinese Yuan, which served as a buffer zone in the face of hits on currency by foreign currency speculators. Nonetheless, as noted earlier, the devaluing of Southeast Asian currencies and the concurrent rapid and numerous bankruptcies of East Asian companies that invested in China impacted China's economy by the late 1990s. At the same time, China's booming growth rates slowed down significantly, although China continued to outpace its neighbors who were in a state of unprecedented financial crisis. A reminder of the late 1980s returned with numerous sectors of production encountering overproduction, deflation, and low levels of consumer demand. Indeed, consumers consistently responded to frequent lowering of bank interest rates by throwing even greater amounts of Yuan into the bank, expressing votes of no confidence in the Chinese economy and prospects for reform. Increases in unemployment due to mid-1990s policies of 'letting go' of small- and medium-sized SOEs only intensified a situation already laden with potential for social unrest.

On the one hand, China's response to the AFC and declining domestic investment and consumer confidence was to throw some 1.2 trillion Yuan into public works projects while pushing through a series of initiatives to restructure SOEs. Critically, efforts were made to make state workers accept layoffs as inevitable and to seek new 'opportunities' in labor markets. This was widely interpreted as a 'get tough' on state workers period in order to resolve SOE (and associated central government) debt burdens. By April 1998, Zhu Rongji was already backing away from this punitive approach in the face of rapidly spreading SOE worker protests in urban areas suffering from surging unemployment rates and inadequate provincial government payments of retired workers' pensions and health care insurance. An order sent down from Zhu to all provincial governments called on them to ensure that every laid-off SOE worker was enrolled in reemployment programs, allotted subsistence payments, and so forth.

Meanwhile, the competitive position of China's exporters faced renewed threats as neighboring NICs gradually started to rebound due to their credit and enterprise relations restructuring efforts to resolve economic havoc tied to the AFC. In 1999, leading Chinese economists were complaining that China's economy would continue to lag as neighboring exporters were able to produce higher value-added exports and outperform Chinese in overseas markets (see "China to Lag" 1999). Projections for SOE profitability were geared downward in order to meet definitions of program 'success' (see "Rust Sets in on Reform" 1999). Company managers in hard-hit districts complained of facing contradictory demands to both streamline production and simultaneously maintain government set levels of employment. In the interim, government financing maintained balance sheets of ailing enterprises (see "State-Owned Enterprise Reform" 1999) through special loans, tax breaks, and so forth.

As it became clear that eventually the state was letting go of as much responsibility for SOEs as was possible, provincial cadres and SOE directors/managers sought 'private buyers' of enterprises (see "SOE Sell-off Prospects" 1999) This only further inflamed SOE worker anger as corruption became not only more common, but more transparent (He 2000; Jiang 2002). Critically, much of the transfer of assets that occurred in the process of cadre/manager-orchestrated company 'conversions' resulted in little or no new productive investment. Indeed, the most likely scenario that was sought frequently was land speculation after all factory assets had been sold off or run down to near zero value. This was especially more likely to be the 'option' resorted to in instances where no outside buyer could be found or, even worse in the eyes of both workers and liberal reform-oriented cadres, when there was more wealth to be made through speculation than investment in production by a capitalist. The growing consensus in China was to push forward entry into the WTO to resolve such a dilemma or be faced with greater economic stagnation.

Although, as Lau has documented, by the end of the 1990s Chinese capital made quite significant advances in its capacity to buy out state assets, Chinese investors remained quite hesitant to invest in state industries. This is not terribly surprising because private companies in China are not generally equipped with the economies of scale or the access to state credit needed to invest in post-purchase production. This was especially the case because state workers, even in sectors that have been 'let go,' still consider said enterprises to be their possession and to be responsible for their subsistence (Philion 2008). This predicament was magnified by the lack of sufficient consumer activity due to excessive rates of SOE failure-related unemployment. Instead, private business owners, especially in regions experiencing financial difficulties, were more likely to join up with state cadres to buy off companies, only to engage in speculative schemes that are shared with state and factory cadres. It is hardly the case that 'reforms' in small- and medium-sized SOEs that were 'let go' either created or solidified the role of capital as the dominant signifier of value in China's SOE sector. Accumulation in this sector became more 'gangster' like, but hardly 'capitalist.' Nor did foreign capital step in to buy out small- or medium-sized SOEs because it was interested in capturing more lucrative markets typically dominated by larger scale SOEs in China.[15]

Large scale SOE corporatization and restructuring was widely ballyhooed inside and outside China in preparation for China's entry into the WTO. However, considerable skepticism remained about prospects for capitalist techniques of production becoming systematically implemented and able to attract sufficient capital into sectors of production dominated by large SOEs. The 'problem of labor' or 'labor strife' in the state sector continued to be a focal impediment to SOE market integration.

The labor strife in China that intensified in the late 1990s should be considered in this light. State sector workers, across the board, suffered considerable losses in status and social protections, with the exception of more skilled younger workers and workers located in (to date) the most protected large companies. However, despite stories of labor militancy in response to SOE dismantling, SOE workers in China hardly succeeded in organizing as a coordinated collective force by the end of the 1990s. This was not simply a matter of heavy repression as a price for protests. In fact, the Chinese state strategically treated cases of SOE worker upheaval on a case-by-case basis, here making small payments to buy time, there sending in police to isolate key workers' leaders. Critically, in almost every instance of SOE protests, government ministries responsible for enterprise funding comprised the primary target of workers' criticism and negotiation. Protests became increasingly ritualized in terms of government handling and met with less and less sympathy, not to mention compensation payments (Lee 2002). They became a kind of safety valve switched on to mollify workers' anger and, just as important, as a way to forestall the force of capitalist markets. Workers in SOEs that failed due to bankruptcy or government policies did not, by and large, go hungry due to their lack of participation in labor markets dominated by capitalists. They continued to eke out a level of subsistence through a variety of classically nonmarket techniques, including relying on government subsidized 'reemployment' markets in which they peddled goods, depending on children's income from employment outside the state sector, severance payments, meager pensions, and so forth. When these failed, China's SOE workers resorted to demonstrations to receive what they continued to insist the state owed them for their past roles in once productive SOEs.

THE UNCERTAIN TRANSITION SINCE THE 1990S

Since the end of the 1990s, Chinese economic restructuring stressed market-based rationalization in the largest value-pumping SOEs. In the larger protected SOEs slated for restructuring, initial hopes that they could implement ample streamlining measures to increase competitiveness with foreign companies have not met with actual achievement. SOE restructuring has certainly aimed to make larger sized SOE managers act more like capitalists, yet they still are guided by priorities other than profit maximization—especially in periods of uncertainty (Choe and Yin 2000). For example, a study by Hassard et al. (2002) on efforts to corporatize[16] 10 major steel companies in China finds that major SOEs have encountered significant difficulty meeting their original goals of laying off half of their workforces.

Workers are relocated to sideline subcompanies instead of removed from the company roster. Anxiety about workers protests against restructuring that China saw with frequency in small- and medium-sized SOEs during the 1990s, combined with lingering notions of managerial responsibility to workers, has held back layoff goals in SOEs in Hassard's study. Furthermore, aside from housing, the enterprises have been unable to shift responsibility for school and health care to local governments, thus retaining many of the social welfare costs with which private companies need not concern themselves. The study contends that, although state interference has been reduced since 1999, when corporatization efforts began in these enterprises, extensive state interference in production decisions remain. Top management appointments still need government approval. And permission is also needed for SOEs who want to convert their debts to banks and suppliers into shares in the company, and for stock market listings to raise desperately needed capital. . . . One of the aims of this phase of SOE reform was the achievement of a level playing field for all companies, ending the "sweetheart deals" that gave certain large corporations a competitive edge in the 1980s and early 1990s. But this has not been achieved: some of the SOEs that the team visited are so certain that they would be turned down for stock market listings and debt-to-equity swaps that they have not even asked for state permission. (Hassard et al. 2002, 119)

Reform initiatives have most benefited local governments that transfer jurisdiction of failing SOEs to newly corporatized large SOEs. Instead of increased movement on the restructuring front, the result is that failed companies, which would otherwise have been bankrupt long ago, remain operative as shells of their past selves and workers remain unemployed and dissatisfied with their new 'owner.' Companies under local government control often do better than those under national industrial bureaus. Because local government has a vested interest in their success, they are less likely to be forced to take over other loss-making firms and make cost-of-living payments to their workers, as well as being better placed to win local contracts. (Hassard et al. 2002, 121)

The interest of local government cadres in retaining access to economic surpluses generated by politically based access to enterprise surpluses continues to dominate the logic of production relations in large SOEs. SOE managers hardly act as 'state capitalists,' let alone capitalists; their power continues to depend on the priority of sociopolitical priorities over competitive performance in capitalist markets (Choe and Yin 2000). As a result, key facets of assets restructuring such as layoffs, ending the social welfare role of companies, and management independence remain stunted versions of original projections. It is for this reason that, even with the WTO entry matter settled, whether capital will flow in and dominate the heart of China's economy as capital remains yet an empirical question.

This situation is appreciably different from the capitalist context that characterized East Asian NIC development in the postwar era. In the case of the NICs, capital circulated in the economies and stimulated the development of state-based industrial development by virtue of the agreement reached between dominant (domestic and foreign) capital on the role of state institutions in setting boundaries (through the maintenance of powerful state-controlled banks, control over surplus investment flows, high tariffs in critical growth sectors, etc.) for capitalist investment (Chibber 1999; Hart-Landsberg and Burkett 2001; Lim 1998). These 'irrational' state-aligned institutions supplied needed credit for research and development to competitive enterprises seeking footholds in emergent cutting-edge global markets.

China's ruling class faces class relations of production and conditions of international overproduction that make it considerably more difficult to effectuate the coercive force of capitalist markets in the same manner. Several scenarios are possible, none of which takes for granted the inevitability of capitalist transition in China. Despite the inroads that profit-based markets have made on Chinese society in all realms of life, the present and dominant class relations that characterize production in the heart of China's political economy continue to militate against the likelihood that China's economy will be subordinated systematically to capital acting as *the* primary determinant of value creation. This is not to say that China will not make a transition to capitalist relations of production in the SOE sector. However, that feat remains far from accomplished. If such a transition is realized, there is no reason to presume it will necessarily empower the Chinese working-class movement. This is the case because, if for no other reason, it seems unlikely that capitalist investment in China's economy will resolve the crisis of unemployment and hardship that China's workers face. This predicament alone indicates that, aside from the benefits of increased individual and collective organizing rights, Chinese workers as a whole would likely be in a seriously weakened bargaining position when confronting capital over the price of its labor power in labor markets when China's economy is finally systematically dominated by the competitive logic of capital.

4 The Discourse of Workers' Democracy and Economic Restructuring in Post-Mao China
The 1980s

In 1980, when the Polish Trade Union *Solidarity* emerged, it stood opposed to its own vanguard (the Party). I believe that what remains most critical is the working class masses, for a long period, lacked creative power in their assigned role as masters of their enterprises. At the time Central Party Secretary Office called on Feng Tongqing and me to revisit the earliest instances of the Workers' Representative Committees. This showed how much the lessons from the Polish crisis had been absorbed and understood as related to the problem of motivating workers. . . . However, new reform policies in the PRC have been implemented that contradict these lessons. I've been telling people that we have to give greater attention to these problems. If the masses of workers can regard their enterprise performance as one that directly affects their lives such that they feel concretely their class status and effectiveness, our Party will have a very reliable class based foundation. Only in this way can we keep the slogan "Completely rely on the working class" from becoming an empty slogan.

—Economist Jiang Yiwei (cited in Zhang 2001, 47)

CHAPTER INTRODUCTION

A discourse of workers' democracy reemerged in 1980s China, which coincided with economic restructuring geared toward greater employment of for-profit markets to stimulate national development. However, consistent with my argument in Chapter 3, by the end of the 1980s, this transition had not transformed the distinctly noncapitalist way of surplus production and distribution in the urban SOEs, which constituted the heart of China's economy;nor, for that matter, did the discourse of workers' democracy that emerged in the 1980s, as it was engaged by Party officials, enterprise administrators and managers, and workers. Instead, the decade ended with a growing crisis in the SOEs due to their refusal or inability to 'become' capitalist and general political repression during and after the Tiananmen protests of 1989.

The discourse of workers' democracy in the 1980s was redeployed by CCP leadership as a means to challenge and overturn Maoist SOE workplace relationships. Nevertheless, workers' democracy concepts and practices throughout the 1980s did not fundamentally throw into jeopardy the core noncapitalist forms of ownership and the social obligations inherent in the SOE model. That is to say, distinct from the 1990s, the 1980s discourse of workers' democracy in China did not accompany an attempt by China's leadership to systematically submit SOEs to the coercive force of capitalist competition.

MAO'S DEATH, WORKERS ACTIVITY, AND RETHINKING NATIONAL DEVELOPMENT

A spate of workers' activism followed Mao's death in the 1970s, which accompanied and influenced a national rethinking around issues of national development and how social relations of production (rural and industrial) should be reformulated. Workers' own participation came in response to dissatisfaction with unresolved issues of both wages and democratic participation in the SOE during the Cultural Revolution years. Deng Xiaoping's call for reform of austerity policies that the Cultural Revolution promoted in the SOE reflected the declining social base of the Gang of Four. Jackie Sheehan suggests that workers faced a choice of no power and no money with the Gang of Four and no power and money with Deng (Sheehan 1998, 158–161). In exchange for better salaries for workers in the SOE, managerial powers lost in the political battles stirred by the Cultural Revolution would be restored—at least theoretically. However, before such a policy would be implemented, Chinese SOE workers would collectively make known their ideas on their place in China's transition from Mao.

China's population reacted viscerally to the deaths of both Zhou Enlai and Mao Zedong, with mass actions at the grassroots level with a leading role played by workers. The failure of the Mao's Cultural Revolution to address SOE workers' material dissatisfaction played a large role in fueling the April 5th and Democracy Wall movements. Both movements took aim at the difference in how workers and Party cadres experienced Chinese state socialism.

The earliest sign of pent-up grievances showed itself in the form of the Tiananmen Incident on April 5, 1976. Over half a million Chinese showed up at Tiananmen Square to view wreaths left as memorials for Zhou Enlai, the highly revered Chinese premier who had died in January that year. The Party leadership, then still controlled by Mao's anticipated successors in the Gang of Four, (quite accurately) read into this huge outpouring of sympathy a mass expression of dissent from their policies and responded by removing the wreaths from the square. This only sparked further frustration and anger from below, which translated into further mobilization of collective acts of defiance against the Gang of Four and, more generally, the gap between Party cadres and the masses over the previous 25 years of Maoist state socialism.

This series of protests led to the fall of the Gang of Four by the fall of 1976 and Deng Xiaoping's capture of Party leadership. Deng, however, would himself encounter collective forms of dissent as he laid out his plans for China's transition from Maoism:

> The end of austerity policies and successive catch-up pay increases from 1977–1979 proved extremely popular, but other aspects of Deng's reforms, with their emphasis on ending the 'iron rice-bowl' and management's right to manage, soon came to threaten workers' security, and the policy of sharper wage differentials, too, was resisted and subverted by workers who proved very set in their old, egalitarian ways despite their rejection of low-pay austerity policy of the first half of the 1970s. 1976, then, was not quite such an unalloyed triumph for Deng Xiaoping as it might have appeared, while the Maoist line in industry, based on the Anshan Constitution, was rejected because it had failed to materialize in important respects rather than because its concerns with workers' participation in management and political equality with cadres were not important to rank and file. (Sheehan 1998, 155)

Indeed, China's SOE workers would participate in collective forms of rebellion in response to Deng's new policy directions in industry by utilizing concepts and beliefs solidified in the discourses of workers' democracy that developed in the topsy-turvy of ideological battles over state-socialist national development strategies during the Maoist periods. Chinese workers, quite appropriately, played a prominent role in the Democracy Wall movement, which originated in December 1978 in the form of posters that criticized Deng's policies, along a wall located several blocks from Tiananmen Square. Ironically, the wall posters emerged in response to the declaration of the Party that the Tiananmen Incident was a positive revolutionary act against the Gang of Four by the masses.

In any event, it presented an opportunity to express grievances that accumulated as Deng sought to 'reform' what remained of Mao's state socialism in the mid- to late 1970s. Workers' concerns under Deng were also both matters of wages and democratic participation in the SOE workplace. The problem of inequality in housing allocations that were regarded as tied to cadre corruption combined with workers' anxiety about growing differentials in salaries within enterprises and industrial sectors. Workers' perception that their salaries had not kept pace with prices only added to their relative sense of deprivation. These tensions were only aggravated by SOE workers' belief that Deng had hardly addressed himself to the discourse of workers' democracy from the Maoist period.

That discourse shaped Chinese workers' calls for real democratic participation in China's SOEs in the post-Maoist period:

> More obviously political issues, such as how workers could exercise control over their working lives and how their views and interests should be represented in the enterprise and in society, were also reflected in the 'people's publications.' Behind a large number of criticisms raised in the unofficial publications and posters of Democracy Wall was one overriding question, namely whether, or to what extent, workers' theoretical status as masters of the enterprise and the leading class had been realized. It is this debate, which is behind all arguments about the role of management, the enterprise party committee and the union, the powers and the scope of the workers' congress, the possibility of self-management, democratic election of cadres, and the problems of public ownership (Sheehan 1998, 161–162).

In the Democracy Wall posters and in the unofficial journals it spurred for the short period the movement was tolerated by Deng, demands were put forth for greater democratization of enterprise management in China and the right to directly run enterprises. This rhetoric clearly borrowed from past Cultural Revolution language and the ill-fated attempts to construct models that approximated Paris Commune like formulas of direct factory production control by workers. This was surely not a route that Chinese authorities would accept as either feasible or desirable given their ideological disdain for the Maoist discourse of workers' democracy. Moreover, embedded in the calls for greater workers' democracy by the Democracy Wall activists, many of whom were workers, was the belief that a new kind of workers' democracy was needed to remove the power of Central Party ministries' bureaucrats in shaping how the enterprise conducted its affairs. However, the Party would, in response to the discourse of workers' democracy evident in mass-based movement activity in the mid- to late 1970s, encourage a return to *minzhu guanli* to assuage Chinese workers' alienation from the CCP's developmental move toward for-profit markets in the 1980s. To the extent that this ideological thrust was successful in the 1980s, no small part of that can be explained by the CCP's *not* imposing the logic of capitalist competition on the heart of Chinese economic development—namely, the SOE.

NATIONAL DEVELOPMENT AND CHINA'S INCREMENTAL TURN TO FOR-PROFIT MARKETS

Where shifts in the discourse of workers' democracy occurred in the Maoist period, they did so under the pretext of strengthening the (Party-controlled) state-owned component of the Chinese economy as the means to achieve socialism. However, the post-Mao CCP leadership moved national development strategy in another direction—toward much greater involvement of for-profit, market-based exchanges and production in the national economy. This new policy shift was most aggressively adopted in the agricultural sector.

At the same time, because the location of urban-based SOEs in relation to Party-state revenue was so strategically pivotal to Party-state legitimacy, SOE market-based restructuring proceeded at a much slower pace. From the early 1980s, CCP leaders were concerned that hastily made moves toward incorporating the logic of capitalist markets into the SOEs would tear away at the socially based guarantees of welfare that Chinese SOE workers enjoyed. Such initiatives conceivably would eventually threaten the legitimacy of the Party's claim to be the genuine representative of SOE workers (Wilson 1987). The example of Poland's Solidarity movement stood out as a real concern to the CCP leadership and was frequently cited in the literature as motivating elements in the Party to advocate carefully implementing democracy in the workplace as part of economic restructuring (Zhang 2001, 47).

The restructuring that took place in the 1980s SOE sector rarely caused Chinese workers to lose their jobs, wages, or, most important of all, the social security perks that accompanied the status of SOE production workers. In fact, during the most of the 1980s, urban SOE workers, especially those in the medium and larger industrial enterprises, enjoyed substantial salary increases in addition to investments in factory infrastructure (Walder 1989). When the Party sponsored discussions about workers' democracy in post-Mao China, they emerged in a context of nervousness about the potential for worker unrest with the turn to for-profit markets and potential threats to the forms of social welfare security that SOE workers enjoyed. Party leadership realized that mechanisms were needed to convince Chinese SOE workers that the potential sacrifice of their social welfare rights at the point of production would be countered by the gains they would enjoy from increased opportunities to represent their self-interests in restructured SOEs (Chen 1995, 1999; Wilson 1987; Zhang 2001).

THE RETURN TO *MINZHU GUANLI*

The core institutions found in *minzhu guanli* were the key components of the reconfigured discourse of workers' democracy in the 1980s. *Minzhu guanli* was the centerpiece and most valued concept and practice through which workers' democracy would be both rethought and presented as a component of China's new developmental direction away from Maoism. China's first post-1949 *minzhu guanli* initiative was short lived (it was rescinded by 1953). However, as I argued in Chapter 2, the Chinese discourse of workers' democracy did not disappear with it. *Minzhu guanli* further stimulated the discourse of workers' democracy in China because it provided workers in various locations with an institutional language in the SOEs that allowed for the possibility to challenge factory leaders' decisions, thus raising the expectations of workers for the goals of socialism. Despite the clampdown on *minzhu guanli* in favor of the one-man management model imported from Stalin's Soviet Union, in 1956, Chinese SOE workers erupted in open rebellion in the forms of slowdowns, strikes, and other types of collective protests against conditions of production that kept the issue of labor relations and workers' democracy at the fore. Maoists, in turn, incorporated other components of the discourse of workers' democracy into their anti-Soviet and mass mobilization campaigns from the late 1950s onward as a means to counter what they viewed as the pitfalls of 'formalistic' policies such as *minzhu guanli* to achieve workers' democracy.

THE WRC RESURRECTED

In the run-up to the Cultural Revolution, *minzhu guanli* and its attendant institutions (i.e., the WRC and the AFCTU) came under heavy criticism from Maoist cadres in the CCP for not accomplishing the aims that the policy presumably was designed to accomplish. In their view, there was little point in reforms like *minzhu guanli* if, in the end, the overall social condition of the Chinese working class was not keeping pace with the bureaucratically driven cadre strata. The Cultural Revolution was putatively intended as a set of mechanisms that could be engaged to deliver mass-participatory democracy across Chinese society, which would include eradicating built-in bureaucratic barriers to democratizing Chinese state-owned enterprises. This was, in large part, what explained extreme policies such as the shutting down of the Party-sponsored ACFTU and the WRCs during the Cultural Revolution. With capitalists, trade union bureaucrats, and Party secretaries removed from power, real *mass* administration through direct takeover of factory production was ostensibly possible. However, appearances and reality were not neatly matched, and this version of mass-based democratic control and administration of SOE production was reined in first by Mao and then by the post-Mao CCP leadership.

Almost from the start of the post-Mao transition in the mid-1970s, the CCP leadership endorsed a policy of reviving two institutions that the Cultural Revolution had eliminated: the WRC and the ACFTU. These two institutions would complement and monitor the enterprise director in accordance with the factory director responsibility system, which delegated greater decision-making powers to enterprise directors as part of a program of greater SOE autonomy from state interference. As Deng Xiaoping put it in as early as September 1978, "Workshop directors, section chiefs, and group heads in every enterprise must in the future be elected by the workers in the unit. Major issues in an enterprise should be discussed by workers' congresses or general membership meetings" (cited in Chen 1999, 55).

It might appear that Deng was continuing a Maoist tradition of calling for greater 'mass' involvement of workers in the management of the enterprise. However, this call was a clear departure from the Maoist past and not merely because of the revival of the Party-sponsored ACFTU and WRCs. The emphasis that Maoists in the preceding decades placed on confronting authority through mass mobilization, in order to 'equalize' state socialist relations of production, was clearly rejected by the new leadership.

As I argued in Chapter 2, during the Maoist period, workers did have (limited) occasion to make use of the varying elements of that discourse to fight for expanded benefits and powers within the confines of state socialism. In the post-Mao 1980s, the revival of *minzhu guanli* became the CCP leadership's theoretical rationale for restructuring the SOE. Enterprise directors secured unprecedented decision-making powers while SOE workers retained the socialist promise of worker empowerment:

> In the ideological realm, the CCP . . . derives its legitimacy from its claim to act as the vanguard of the proletariat. . . . [N]ot even Mao ever sought to sever the Party's theoretical links to the proletariat as the leading class of the revolution. The 1982 constitution [continuing that tradition] designates the People's Republic of China as a "socialist state under the people's democratic dictatorship led by the working class and based on the alliance of workers and peasants." The institution democratic management serves to augment the Party's claim that the proletariat, in the final analysis, exercises a contributory role in formulating the affairs of state. Worker participation in the enterprise provides necessary symbolic evidence of the status of the working class as the masters (*zhurenwong*) of Chinese society. (Wilson 1987, 301)

The Party leadership revised its discourse of workers' democracy in a fashion that suited the social relations of post-Mao economic restructuring even before major restructuring occurred in China's SOE sector. It was not until the mid-1980s that the Party actually began to seriously broach the topic of enterprise restructuring. Even then the moves toward outright privatization would only be directed at a certain sector of the SOEs and would not become official policy for another decade.

Wilson (1987) argues that ideas about enterprise democracy were also reformulated by the Party leadership to justify a growing trend of putting (profitable) productivity over all other (social) considerations:

> Enterprise democracy [in China] is closely related to the perception of socialist democracy as a response to the needs of modernization . . . [and] of enterprise democracy as a factor of productive efficiency. In this view, the forms of worker participation is presented as an objective demand of

modernization. . . . From the Chinese perspective moreover, enterprise democracy is directly linked to productive efficiency.

Minzhu guanli, as concerned enterprise restructuring, made for the ultimate bridge to (predominantly Western and Eastern European-informed) theories of *market socialism* that Chinese intellectuals were adapting to their interpretation of 'Socialism with Chinese Characteristics.' Since Deng Xiaoping took hold of CCP leadership, Chinese intellectuals and cadres carefully studied translated documents from Eastern Europe, with special attention to how democratic management stimulated economic efficiency, in addition to its role in socialist construction. (303–304)

This theoretical admixture provided Party leadership with a means to rationalize the mélange of state socialist and potentially capitalist components that featured in economic restructuring during the 1980s. *Minzhu guanli* in the 1980s constituted a set of ideas that the Party leadership hoped to use to win over the support of urban workers to the kinds of restructuring in SOEs and in Chinese society generally. However, *minzhu guanli* did not remain at the theoretical or ideational level alone. It comprised, carried out in a manner far more comprehensively than in the 1950s *minzhu guanli* campaigns, an institutional arrangement within enterprises that called for the active involvement of enterprise cadres and production workers alike. In the process, there were collective winners and losers.

DEMOCRATIC ELECTIONS IN THE SOE AS THE MEANS TO DIMINISH ENTERPRISE-BASED OPPOSITION TO POST-MAO ECONOMIC RESTRUCTURING

In the early experimental phase of post-Mao *minzhu guanli* (October 1978–1982), the CCP leadership encouraged elections of SOE directors and managers by workers and staff. Institutionally, the Party-controlled *ACFTU* was in a position to gain greatly from restructuring because its role had been considerably downgraded during the Cultural Revolution. Indeed, the union media organs were where the greatest effort to promote the new *minzhu guanli* policies could be found. The ACFTU was one of the biggest institutional actors to gain directly from *minzhu guanli*'s revived role in 1980s China. The role of the ACFTU in educating workers about restructuring policies and the new types of labor discipline they required was considered critical. Of course, the ACFTU already was a unit that had a history of working at the behest of the central Party leadership until it was disbanded for much of the Cultural Revolution.

However, the resurrection of the ACFTU was hardly sufficient to accomplish the goal of limiting Party intervention in the affairs of SOE production. Indeed, the most enthusiastic advocates for greater commitment to *minzhu guanli* argued that it was needed to ensure that the revitalized ACFTU not replicate its traditional subservience to the Party and that it actually served the interests of workers. The question, of course, was how to make *minzhu guanli* accomplish such a feat because SOEs were still controlled by the Party state, as were the unions.

Minzhu guanli hardly removed roadblocks to the autonomy of the ACFTU in the SOEs. However, this did not necessarily cause much concern because Chinese SOE workers did take advantage of what this new form of *minzhu guanli* offered them in its early experimental stage—namely, the chance to directly elect new managers and to throw out ones that they believed were not up to the task of management (Chen 1999). It is quite clear from the literature that workers participated in *minzhu guanli* far more than in the 1950s. For example, Chen states that, in Beijing by 1982, workers had cast votes to elect directors in 560 enterprises, with 240 new ones elected to replace incumbents. In the same city, enterprises run by the local government saw "only 130 of 1,200 directors or section heads retained" (Chen 1999, 30–31). The pattern of Chinese workers' enthusiastic reception to elections of administrative personnel and directors is pretty widely documented by those who have written about the topic extensively (Brugger 1985; Cliver 2002; Sheehan 1998; Taylor, Chang, and Li 2003; Unger and Chan 2004; Wilson 1987; Zhang 2001). That directors were turned out in such large numbers was consistent with the tradition of the Chinese SOE labor force, which took advantage of nearly every opening made available or that it created during the Maoist period to challenge enterprise directors and cadres. In this instance workers had good reason to be enthusiastic about elections.

However, from 1982 onward, this policy would change to one that encouraged workers and staff to vote for their WRC. The democratically elected WRC would monitor enterprise decisions made by the director and managers. Although the idea of *minzhu guanli* was received positively by SOE workers, most observers note that, like earlier such workers' democracy-oriented policies in Mao-era China, the results were far from ideal. Reports on the disappointment with proportions of SOE enterprises that experienced elections of WRCs were many. More to the point, many a WRC barely functioned as an actual body that supervised enterprise managers and directors. Sheehan (1998, 183) notes that even as the WRC replaced the Enterprise Party Committee, its capacity to supervise managers and directors, even where directly elected by workers, remained minimal. Reporting on the state of the WRC in the 1980s, Taylor, Chiang, and Li (2003) found outcomes of democratic management initiatives to be less than optimal:

> In the "economic responsibility system" and "contract management responsibility System" in the first stage of reform, (WRCs) were already ineffectual restraints on managerial power. Nevertheless, managers were

required by State Council regulations to work with the (WRCs), which amounted to little more than a duty to complete the paperwork to show superior regulatory agencies, rather than a responsibility to be accountable to (WRCs). In this first stage of urban economic reform, it was officially reported that effective (WRCs) had been established in most public owned enterprises. However, workers' evaluation was consistently low. In a nationwide survey, of 10,000 workers and staff, few people gave a positive assessment of (WRCs), while 45.19 percent viewed them merely as managerial requirements to satisfy senior agencies. (141)

The new authority that managers enjoyed in SOEs in many instances simply rendered the WRC formalistic entities. Arguably, *minzhu guanli* was a mechanism (like *minzhu guanli* in the 1950s) that Chinese SOE workers and cadres were both able to take advantage of, and how they did so shaped the way the discourse of democracy would be yet revised and battled over in the 1990s. As Chen (1999) puts it, a "three-cornered [power struggle ensued] among the workers' congresses, the enterprise Party committee, and the enterprise director" (30). How this struggle transpired is worth attention because it speaks to how and why social actors with divergent interests supported or opposed this initiative in China during the 1980s market-oriented transition. Holding elections of enterprise directors was the first form of *minzhu guanli* to be put into motion at the start of China's economic restructuring. Generally, the incumbent directors were supported by most enterprise Party committees, which had previously assigned them. This explains a practical side of the new post-Mao central leadership's push for *minzhu guanli* as a key to economic restructuring, which resonated with SOE workers' interests:

> Given the newly established authority of the director, his or her capability and qualifications to a great extent determined the enterprise's quality of management and hence its efficiency. . . . [T]he workers elected their director not just for the sake of democracy or self respect but also for their material interests. Elections tended to expand the resources available for welfare and also resulted in a more responsible welfare policy. (Chen 1999, 34)

The Enterprise Party Committee tended to be dominated by cadres who had secured their appointments during the Cultural Revolution. Those cadres were most likely to oppose the type of market-oriented restructuring plans the Dengist leadership had in mind for SOEs. SOE enterprise directors and cadres on the Enterprise Party Committee were, after all, primarily responsible to ministerial superiors, which exacerbated alienation among SOE workers (Chen 1999). Furthermore, Chen (1999) points out that materially SOE workers, especially in the early 1980s, had a strong interest in elections because:

the [restructuring policies] increased [the] power . . . enterprise director[s] wielded over enterprise affairs [which was directly linked] to income and bonus. . . . [Under] [t]he factory director enterprise responsibility [system] . . . executive power began to expand while the Party committee was discouraged from interfering in enterprise administration. (33)

Although the enterprise director elections experiment was regarded by Party leaders as positive, it did not encourage direct elections of enterprise directors by workers in the SOEs. Party leadership did, however, call for elections of enterprise administrators to be conducted by the WRCs. In this sense, then, the Enterprise Party Committee was to be further removed from direct involvement and control of the elections, with the result that SOE workers could thereby possess greater capacity to monitor and affect enterprise decision making.

Enterprise Party Committee cadres, especially those aligned with Mao's Cultural Revolution, complained most vociferously about the new policies as 'window dressing' and 'competitions of eloquence' (Chen 1999, 34). They resisted *minzhu guanli*, to the extent possible, by using their power to scratch non-Party-approved candidates. Party leaders countered such efforts by assigning the task of approving candidates to the FMCs, which worked at the behest of the director.

The type of election held in factories also corresponded to the type of state-owned enterprise. In the aftermath of the initial elections, the SOEs with closer ties to the central ministries and more vital to the national economy were pushed in the direction of developing worker participation through involvement in the WRCs instead of direct elections of leaders (Chen 1999, 36). However, it was constitutionally stipulated that COEs (Collectively Owned Enterprises) should have direct elections of their enterprise administrators. Such an arrangement made perfect sense in terms of the greatly loosened ties between industrial ministries and the COEs. In the case of the COEs, the CCP wished to see such enterprises subjected to more direct forms of competition in for-profit markets. This required the Party to let go of what social obligations it had to workers in the COEs as part of their new autonomy. However, such fuller autonomy and the release of the Party from its commitment to SOEs, in the form of 'iron rice bowls,' were matters that neither SOE workers nor ministries were willing to confront until the mid-1980s and then only sporadically so (Korzec and Howe 1992; Smith 1993; Walder 1986). Thus, save in the early experimental phase, the central Party leadership rarely promoted direct elections in the SOEs during the 1980s.

Instead, in the heart of the 1980s Chinese industrial economy, prioritizing the role of the WRC in SOE democratization was a preferred mechanism to reinforce an image of the CCP's post-Mao commitment to workers' democracy. This maneuver, initiated by the Party leadership, only exacerbated conflict. The WRCs were assigned roles that were largely supervisory and consultative to act as a bridge between enterprise administrators and production workers, which set up a clear conflict in the SOE between the WRC and the Party committee:

> Although the main argument against policy leadership by the Party Committee centered on competence, it was also explained that, since the enterprise is now to be considered a legal person, it would be wrong to treat a Party committee in that way; Party committees may not be sued, for that would damage the prestige of the Party. To be sure the image of the Party in industry was already pretty low. . . . Typically Party membership in a state enterprise ranged from 15 to 40 per cent; factory administration, however, concerned the *immediate* interests of the workers on the spot and all workers should have the right to vote for policy makers, and ultimately senior administrators too. (Brugger 1985, 76–77)

Throughout the 1980s, the WRCs were increasingly presented to SOE workers as the organization through which workers could express their interests and gain access to SOE leaders. Regardless of whether the WRC was truly empowered to do much for workers, the Enterprise Party Committee stood to lose its status as the WRC grew. In media organs such as the *Workers' Daily* and ACFTU union cadre bulletins, SOE workers' displeasure with WRC performance was blamed on Party cadres. In response to such palpable dissatisfaction, in October 1984, the Party committee was further separated from management, whereas the WRC was granted greater say in decision making. This coincided with other SOE policy changes in 1984 that accorded greater power to enterprise directors and experiments in using labor contracts to move away from the iron rice bowl system of lifetime employment.[1] This only further opened up rifts between enterprise based Party cadres and Party leaders. One might have expected that *minzhu guanli* could have become a weapon that workers would, thereby, be inclined to use against the Party leadership and its reform policies. To the contrary, the target of workers' ire was squarely enterprise-level cadres. Furthermore, local (i.e., provincial and city government level) cadres teamed up with Party leaders to support the use of policies such as *minzhu guanli*. Both had a vested interest in confronting obstacles to SOEs' exposure to greater degrees of market competition:

> The mutual political distrust and conflicting interests on reform between Party elites became a major motive in . . . reform. . . . Party cadres at different levels and in different areas suffered to different degrees. Local and regional cadres were higher up in the Party's hierarchy of power and could even play a role in the choice of central leaders, whereas cadres at the basic level were too distant from the center to have any bearing on policy—or decision making. They were unlikely

to establish personal relations with leaders and so the leaders had few scruples in enforcing reforms at their expense. . . . [I]n urban enterprises reform sharpened the conflicts between workers and cadres, and the leaders found in workers a reliable force to circumvent cadres' attempt to block reform. (Chen 1999, 44)

THE WRC AND MEDIATED CONFLICTS WITHIN THE 1980S SOE

Most of the literature on the 1980s WRC and its impact on China's SOE workers relies on official reports in the form of quantitative statistics or media reports and AFCTU bulletins. Such reports are surely useful, but they tend to paint the story of the WRC and other attendant phenomena found in the discourse of workers' democracy in black and white. Qualitative investigations of actual existing enterprises' experiences with the WRC fill in such gaps. If, at the macrolevel, renewed and altered workers' democracy-oriented policies served to legitimate Party policy on economic restructuring in the 1980s, what role did this discourse's key institution— the WRC—play within the enterprise in that decade?

There are only a few in-depth studies of the WRC as an institution in the Chinese SOE (Feng 2005; Unger and Chan 2004; Zhang 2001; Zhu and Chan 2005). A field study conducted by Peking University sociologist Zhang Qin (2001), drawing on factory records from 1985 to 1994 and on-site interviews, reveals that the WRC, as it was designed in the 1980s, reinforced the relations of state-socialist production that reform appeared to undermine. The reason was quite straightforward: The primary acting body of *minzhu guanli* in the enterprise, the WRC, was organized by the ACFTU.

The enterprise trade union and the WRC were technically independent of each other in the SOE. Indeed, from the vantage of production line workers, the most attractive feature of the WRC is that receives its authority from elections by workers. However, as Zhang argues, the WRC reinforced the tradition within the Chinese SOE to avoid the establishment of opposing and distinct group (or class)-based interests. Instead, the WRC was an institution that workers engaged to curry favor with the factory director in order to secure social welfare needs and protections. Zhang (2001, 7–20) contends that, contra the predominant view of Chinese SOE workers as 'dependent' (Frazier 2002; Lee 1999; Walder 1986) and unable to independently express their collective self-interests, the WRC was an institution that, even as it was not autonomous from the control of enterprise officials who were appointed by the Party, nonetheless provided a channel for workers to express their collective interests, regardless of whether it was realized as distinct from enterprise administrators and the Party. What was significant about the reconstituted WRC in the 1980s is not that it 'failed' or 'disappointed' workers as much as it militated against SOE workers or administrators creating *capitalist* kinds of workplace relationships as the SOE was 'reformed' in the 1980s.

This is an ironic outcome in the sense that the WRC was ostensibly desired by workers and Party leaders alike because it was supposed to help clarify the autonomous interests of managers and workers in enterprise production. However, both SOE workers and Party leaders alike had good reason to resist the full realization of this goal. The former clung to their expectations that the SOE is a unit that is obliged to play a social welfare role and provide job security. The latter had no strong interest in allowing workers to have an autonomous power base from which to challenge the direction of enterprise restructuring or the Party's monopolized authority over that process.

At the enterprise level, this trend has been reinforced by how alliances and power structures were reorganized in the restructured SOE during the 1980s. WRC elections are organized by the factory trade union. This is crucial not so much because of the union's ties to the Party and its legally stipulated obligation to carry out Party policy within the enterprise. Just as important is the fact that the factory union chief must maintain the favor of the factory director in order to maintain that position, especially to gain access to factory provided funds in order to distribute services unions are expected to deliver to SOE workers. The union chief has a vested interest in making sure that union cadres are elected to the WRC, which makes the WRC more able to maintain an amicable relationship with the factory director. That outcome strengthens the rapport between the union chief and the factory director; 'troublemakers' on the WRC create a potential for tension between the union chief and factory director:

> The relationship between the union and the enterprise, due to the former's role of administering services, is one characterized by great caution, with the union taking care to accommodate factory leaders by sticking to a strictly self-enforced role of providing "suggestions." The union has no capacity to independently administer services. If it tried to do so, it would receive no support. Union cadres are assigned by the factory leaders. They are not elected. The bulk of their funds are from administrative funds [i.e. enterprise allotted service budgets], not union members' dues. As a result, it plays a meditative role to ensure that it receives a greater amount of administrative funds for its budget. (Zhang 2001, 94)

Additionally, a significant proportion of WRC candidates are cadres and/or skilled technological workers who have little in common with production workers as concerns income and workshop related issues (Zhang 2001, 62–63). This does not mean that the renewed WRC then has no function in the factory or that workers, despite their often negative view of the WRC, have not participated in the WRC to pursue material gains. The key for

SOE production workers becomes finding ways to win election of their shop floor managers to the WRC and thereby to represent one's workshop unit's social welfare interests through that representative in their contact with the union chief and factory director.

Given such structural parameters, Zhang (2001, 88) contends that the 'substantive' democratic potential of the WRC is institutionally constrained to the point of almost no return. She draws this conclusion from a study of how the WRC functioned in a large-sized machine producing SOE. This factory's WRC convened elections of representatives every four years since the enterprise was established in 1961. Furthermore, the WRC met every year several times to discuss the enterprise director's plans, financial situation, and workers' social welfare benefits. Notably, the majority of the representatives elected to the WRC were administrative staff or union cadres.

On the face of it, this would seem to only reinforce the view of WRCs as formalistic entities without any real beneficiary role as concerns workers' interests. However, as a means to protect social welfare provisions when they are threatened by enterprise administrators' reform proposals, in the 1980s and into the 1990s, the WRC in this machine factory was able to be engaged by contending parties to maintain a power balance within the enterprise that prevented administrators from severing their social welfare obligations to workers (Zhang 2001, 89–92). Election to the machine factory WRC was not something that workers saw as terribly urgent. Such a possibility represented at most an opportunity to take time off from work with little other benefits from direct involvement. What did matter was electing union cadres to the WRC to secure greater access to administrators and to negotiate social benefits.

On the one hand, then, the WRC as it was constructed in the 1980s was a mere formality as Maoists had insisted until Mao's death in 1976. Nevertheless, it provided an institutional mechanism that workers engaged as a tool to protect or defend basic social welfare rights. In the best-case scenario, the WRC was an institution through which administrative initiatives to cut services to SOE workers could be forestalled to another day (Unger and Chan 2004; Zhang 2001).

THE WRC AT DECADE'S END

On the face of it, the Chinese workers' democracy initiatives that emerged in the 1980s satisfied the desires of SOE workers for job and social welfare security in the face of the party's push to increase the power of SOE factory directors and managers. At the same time, as evidenced in the nationwide discontent with cadre corruption that led to the Tiananmen protest by 1989, an institutional reform like *minzhu guanli* was hardly sufficient to smoothly reproduce the class relations of post-Mao transition. Wilson

(1987), only two years before Tiananmen, sums up neatly the contradictions that were surfacing in China as a result of economic restructuring:

> Since coming to power in 1978 . . . Deng . . . has instituted . . . measures, including wage rises and the reinstatement of piecework and bonuses, designed to counter the falling wages inherited from the Maoist era and to improve workers' standard of living. At the same time the economic reform movement poses a threat to certain institutionalized expectations held by Chinese workers about the nature of the relationship between workers and the state. The intention of the state to do away with the state guarantee of employment for urban dwellers, to abolish the system of permanent job security, to widen wage differentials, and to eradicate the complex system of urban price subsidies infringes upon the "social compact" forged between the state and its workers since 1949. . . . The considerable challenge . . . is to convince the majority of workers that the sacrifices demanded by the reforms will be exceeded by increased material benefits . . . in the long run. (317–319)

Chen (1995) argues that capitalist-oriented restructuring only exacerbated the tensions that reforms like *minzhu guanli* were designed to mollify:

> Moreover, the workers' congresses as an organ of power tended to decay as China's industrial enterprises accelerated their pace toward capitalist style management since the late 1980s. In many places, the director was authorized to hold supreme power to handle relationships between the state and enterprises and to deal with the increasingly complex economic environment. It is ironic indeed that, as manifested in the management structure of China's foreign funded enterprises in recent years, the development of capitalism not only undermines the foundation of Party dictatorship but also make workplace democracy suffer. (399)

At the same time, the discourse of workers' democracy in China did not disappear with the tumultuous Tiananmen crackdown as might have been expected. In fact, if anything, it picked up steam and was renewed yet again in the 1990s, only in ways that, I argue in the next chapter, contra Chen and Wilson, although often ironic, are entirely in keeping with the social relations of coercion that characterize China's transition from state socialism.

5   The 1990s

Chinese Privatization and Reframed Discourses of Workers' Democracy

INTRODUCTION

The discourse of workers' democracy in 1990s China was redeployed in response to shifts in the CCP's economic development strategies, which attempted to move small- and medium-sized SOEs in the direction of privatization. The changes were most dramatic in China's small- and mid-sized SOEs in the 1990s, and it was in that sector that the official discourse of workers' democracy was most vociferously promoted.

The official discourse of workers' democracy during the 1990s, in turn, was aggressively harnessed to this effort to compel, in absolute numbers, a sizable segment of China's SOEs to submit to the logic of capitalist markets. However, transition from state socialism to the coercive relations of capitalist markets is more than simply a process imposed from above without any contestation from workers. Workers in post-state-socialist societies have often turned transitions from state socialism to capitalism into complex and ideologically contested processes (Burawoy 1996; Clarke 1993a, 1993b). I found such ideological contestation in the words of China's SOE workers I interviewed in 1999 and 2000, even those who appeared most 'resigned to' the logic of capitalist markets. SOE workers in China possessed their own ideas about the workplace democracy policies and toward what ends they should be employed. Their reactions to the official discourse of workers' democracy in China could be easily confused for 'confirmation' of official 'ideology' (Blecher 2002). Nonetheless, in the context of workers' struggles that accompanied privatization in China's late 1990s and early 2000s, they did not embrace Party leadership's plans for market restructuring at the start of the new millennium.

Instead, workers' ideologies and struggles in the 1990s reflected the zig-zagging political economy of restructuring in the SOE sector in China's post-Mao period discussed in Chapter 3. Even in a period of more aggressive restructuring in the SOE sector, the discourses of workers' democracy hardly 'ideologically' closed the deal for smooth or certain capitalist transition in China and point to the limits of that transition. Neither the actions of factory SOE administrators or workers in the cases discussed in this chapter conformed to a capitalist logic. They also planted the seeds for challenges to future policy initiatives designed to submit China's political economy systemically to the coercive force of capitalist competition.

WORKERS' DEMOCRACY IN 1990S CHINA

In this chapter, there are three principal sources of data that I rely on to examine how the official ideology of workers' democracy was put to use during the 1990s. This chapter focuses on how workers' democracy was framed in official Party-sponsored literature and the reactions to this literature among workers in Henan Province. The analysis draws on (1) news stories from *Workers Daily* in the last quarter of 1998 and the first quarter of 1999; (2) articles or columns in ACFTU bulletins on the significance SOE workers' democracy and reform; and (3) field interviews with SOE workers in the cities of Luoyang, Anyang, and Xinxiang at 'model democratically managed' enterprises on the topics of SOE restructuring and workers' democracy in China, which I carried out in late 2000.[1] I begin with literature that was designed for national audiences of workers and trade union cadres. I then drop down a level to literature and data I gathered that specifically addressed workers' democracy policies in Henan Province, including field-based interviews with SOE workers from 'model democratically managed' SOEs in three major cities in Henan Province. Henan Province was chosen as a site because it was frequently cited in the Party-controlled news media organs I read or watched on a daily basis as a location of aggressive workers' democracy reforms. Furthermore, in the late 1990s, labor activists in Beijing informed me that Henan was an important location as word spread of dramatic and militant collective protests by Henan's SOE workers against fraudulent privatizations. Specifically, these activists had developed contacts with a number of persons in Henan's capital city of Zhengzhou, who were once members of the 'rebel faction' in the Cultural Revolution. They were actively developing links with and supporting SOE workers' protests in Zhengzhou. Henan, therefore, seemed like an ideal location to assess both the actual state of workers' democracy in SOEs that were touted as 'models' of one or another type of workers' democracy-oriented policies *and* how protesting SOE workers were influenced by concepts that dominated China's discourse of workers' democracy.

I show how national-level Party-based discourse rationalized and promoted the pattern of privatization in the small- and medium-sized sectors of China's SOEs, linking the types of economic restructuring that occurred in the 1990s to a radical language of worker participation in management *and* enterprise autonomy from the state. Calls for democratic elections of factory directors in the small- and medium-sized SOEs became prominent in much of the discourse of workers' democracy in the 1990s, even though the Party had largely discouraged such a policy when *minzhu guanli* was revived in the 1980s.

I then compare the ideological content embedded in the 1990s official discourse of workers' democracy to data collected from interviews with SOE workers' and managers on the topic of workers' democracy policies in Henan Province. These interviews enabled me not just to compare and contrast workers' views on workers' democracy-oriented policies with official media assessments and document the unhappiness of China's SOE workers with the type of restructuring that they have faced since the 1990s, but also to show that, even in late 1990s model 'democratically managed' SOE enterprises, one could find Chinese workers who interpreted the discourse of workers' democracy in ways that reaffirmed a core (and socialist) belief in something that the Party was trying to end as it advanced the policy of SOE privatization: guaranteed social benefits and job security.

THE TURN FROM THE SOE

Although initially anticipated by some to be put on the backburner in the aftermath of the crackdown on the 1989 liberal democracy movement, SOE restructuring received increased support from the central leadership of the CCP in the 1990s. This was not as surprising a turn of events as it appeared to some at the time (Korzec and Howe 1992). Given calls for financial austerity, combined with support for the SOE in the early post-Tiananmen years, it followed that new sources of funds to the state would have to be found to offset growing deficits brought on by lagging SOE productivity and debts. Furthermore, greater involvement of foreign and domestic capitalist investment in the Chinese economy would also be key for the Party to retain the complacency (if not loyalty) of the intellectual and petit-bourgeois strata emerging and competing with Party cadres for surpluses in expanding markets. The impact of the Tiananmen liberal democracy movement was a compromise that created opportunities to accumulate wealth for groups that did not traditionally enjoy Party connections. Among those groups, the small private merchants and factory owners in urban regions and university students and graduates were the primary beneficiaries of post-Tiananmen policies that increased the role of private investment in the Chinese economy. Through most of the 1990s, and even into the 2000s, these two strata were largely coopted and pacified as social forces of political protest (Li, M. 1994).

However, for SOE sector workers, especially those in companies faced with increasing debt burdens and marketplace competition, 1990s SOE restructuring policies aggravated nervousness about future social and job security. Indeed, as the 1990s progressed, SOE access to state fiscal support became tied more firmly to productivity, potential for profitability, and, critically, the perceived capacity to repay loans to bank lenders. This threw the fate of greater numbers of SOE workers and administrators into jeopardy, a departure from the 1980s policy of leaving urban SOEs alone and a direct challenge to the Party's traditional commitment to SOE workers as the masters of Chinese socialism (*zhurenwong*).

TWIN PHENOMENA: EXPANDED DISCOURSES OF WORKERS' DEMOCRACY AND PRIVATIZATION IN CHINESE SOES DURING THE 1990S

Despite the 1989 Tiananmen Square repression, many of the key components of the workers' democracy discourse and policies that emerged in the 1980s carried over into the 1990s. For example, the WRC continued to be heralded in Party-controlled media organs as a key institution in SOE reform success. An assortment of new concepts also emerged, encompassing 'transparency of enterprise affairs (*Changwu gongkai*), and, the "Employees Director and Supervisor" system (*Zhigong dongshi he jianshi zhidu*), which placed workers on the board of directors in SOEs that were converted (usually through mergers with more competitive SOEs or privately owned enterprises) to limited shareholding companies (*Yoxian gufenzhi*). Further, the official discourse of the 1990s suggested it was necessary to go beyond more indirect and passive forms of workers' democracy found in the typical SOE during the 1980s. Workers' elections of new factory directors in SOEs became a frequently and exalted component of the discourse of workers' democracy in the official literature. Reminiscent of the production control tendencies from the Cultural Revolution era, media reports praised the decisive role of managers and even directors working side by side with workers on the factory floor. Side-by-side exhortations for more market-based forms of competition were seemingly Maoist celebration of direct workers' control of production (*Shengchan zijiu*), found in enthusiastic reports of workers' spontaneous takeovers of factories, cooperative administration of shop floor activities, and workers' direct election and recall of new managers.

In the 1980s, the CCP had encouraged China's SOEs to implement worker participation in elections of WRCs to monitor and provide comments on SOE directors' production plans. This version of workers' democracy was designed as part of a policy direction to gradually subject the SOE to private competition. However, it was not intended or carried out as a means to transform the SOE into privately owned entities. Throughout the 1980s, the only units that the Party suggested *should* move in the direction of privatization and a more thoroughgoing break with fiscal reliance on state ministries were the smaller scale COEs, which did not contribute a significant share of value to China's overall industrial economy in any event. More important, in the COE sector, the sense of 'collective' (i.e., collective security and guaranteed social welfare benefits that were enjoyed by SOE workers) was quite underdeveloped (Philion 1998). It was in this sector that the CCP had promoted direct elections of directors and managers by workers in the 1980s. These elections served as a means to complete a process that divorced the Party from any fiscal responsibility for subsequent failures of privatized COEs to generate profits in competitive private markets. Would workers' democracy function smoothly as an official ideology of privatization for small- and medium-sized SOEs, which were more firmly integrated into traditional state-socialist networks of financing and social welfare obligations?

By mid-1997, Premier Zhu Rongji announced a policy of "grasping the large and letting go of the small"[2] In a move that mimicked the East Asian NIC formula for state-guided developmental success, a select number (roughly 1,000) of large and protected SOEs that the Party relied on for China's national development plans were targeted for renewed state protection and huge capital investments. For these select SOEs, this promised increased fiscal commitment from the state and protection from (foreign and domestic) private market-based competition. However, the measure targeted small- and medium-sized SOEs for privatization, which far outnumbered large-sized SOEs in absolute numbers of workers and staff employed. It did so by strongly 'encouraging' small- and medium-sized SOEs to experiment in varying degrees of shareholding schemes with the stated goal of increasing SOE autonomy from dependence on the state for fiscal revenues. To the extent that small- and medium-sized administrators did not assimilate the message, looking to non-state forms of revenue supply in these SOEs became less and less an option as state-operated banks and ministries refused to guarantee financing in the event of debts due to failures of production to generate profit.

However, this policy only further exacerbated the problems of unemployment in the SOE sector and rising levels of discontent in the SOE sector overall, which would be revealed in a rapid rise in numbers of strikes, factory occupations, street demonstrations, petition campaigns, and the like that workers would lead in a quest to spare themselves the price of being 'let go' by the state. Nevertheless, the print and televised news organs in China presented a fairly optimistic picture of markets renewing the possibilities of workers' democracy. If anything, the discourse of workers' democracy took on a whole new fervor in the late 1990s, even as the price of letting go of countless millions of small- and medium-sized enterprises and experiments in privatization in that sector became harshly transparent when the East Asian financial crisis hit unprotected small- and medium-sized SOEs in China.

CHINESE OFFICIAL NEWS MEDIA AS PROMOTERS OF WORKERS' DEMOCRACY IN CHINA'S SOES

The idea that privatization-oriented economic restructuring could benefit SOE workers and democratize their enterprises was prevalent in newspapers that Chinese read daily in the 1990s (and to this day, for that matter). For a country in which almost universally issues that involved either workers' self-organization or democracy were taboo, newspaper articles in 1990s China that discussed both in the same breath might have appeared somewhat unexpected. Yet they were not difficult to find on almost a daily basis during a research stay in China for two years from 1998 to 1999. For example, a headline for the December 14, 1998, *Workers' Daily* reads, "All the Workers Participate in Enterprise Transparency, Democratic Supervision, and Collective Decision Making." The article reported dramatic transformations in the way all decisions in the Shijianzhuang Tractor Factory took place since implementing democratic reforms:

> Whether it's the enterprise director's salary, apportionment of workers' housing, or managers' expense accounts, in SOEs these have been considered top secret matters. But at the Shijiazhuang Tiantong Tractor Factory "Enterprise Transparency Wall," these are all items posted and updated for workers and staff to see on a regular basis. As a result, Tiantong's workers can understand enterprise issues and the wall serves as a means for workers to participate in enterprise decision making. . . . In 1994, the factory's total accumulated debt amounted to 80 million Yuan. In the face of such a grave situation, the new director, after extensive consultations, came to the belief that the two main reasons for an SOE's failure or success were mistaken production strategies and corrupt managerial staff (*ganbu*). The best and most effective alternative would be to promote a system of enterprise transparency and democratic supervision (*minzhu jiandu*).

This article reported that this factory was dramatically turned around as workers gave input on enterprise production decisions, but also provided democratic evaluations of managerial performance (*minzhu pingyi*). In many ways, the narrative reads like (and incorporated language from) news reports that one would find from the height of the Cultural Revolution or GLF, excitedly renarrating stories of workers' responsibility for supervising managers and managing factories. Only now enterprises were apparently making such democratic reforms while successfully competing in markets with private capitalist-owned companies or being directly invested in by capitalists.

Furthermore, the CCP seemed quite willing to allow its media organs to suggest that the capacities of the WRC should expand as the economy became more subjected to competition from domestic and foreign capitalist-owned companies. The WRC now was presented as an institution that should not only make comments to factory directors, but also have a more active role in production-related decisions. The November 30, 1998, *Workers Daily Weekend Magazine* featured almost a whole front page of headlines that feverishly praised the impact of transparency and democratic management in the SOEs and called for the strengthening of core institutions of workers' democracy: "Beijing Promotes Enterprise Transparency Everywhere," "Enterprise Restructuring Must Respect the Democratic Choices of Workers," "The WRC: One Ballot," and "Let the Workers Know about All Major Problems in the Enterprise," "Rationalizing Production Must Not Be Used to Dissolve Union Organization." These policies presumably made production in the SOEs more able to remove old hierarchies that prevented workers from exercising a democratic voice in production. A headline from the January 21, 1998, *Workers' Daily* declared, "Winning the workers' hearts is the biggest benefit: Yongji Electronics factory succeeds at promoting 'non-hierarchical management':

> Only by nurturing enterprise democracy and, thereby, respecting workers will we get in exchange workers' enthusiasm and best efforts for our enterprise. This is the best way to achieve SOEs' source of momentum. The only way to sustain a solid SOE is to thoroughly rely on the workers; not by the old way of relying in word but not in actions.

The workers at Yongji Electronics, the article reports as part of this new nonhierarchical and transparent policy, made all hiring at every level to be subjected to open competition, including management. Bureaucratic offices that once 'assigned' new positions and promotions in the enterprise were eliminated. Other matters, such as bonuses and housing distribution, were also given to workers to decide.

Whereas the Party seemed to tread carefully in terms of what powers were granted the WRC during the 1980s, in the 1990s, Party-controlled newspapers that targeted rank-and-file SOE workers and union cadres now openly exhorted a more powerful WRC in Chinese SOE:

> At present, as China's SOEs undergo restructuring, there are instances of enterprise directors not consulting with workers, not holding a meeting with the WRC, not respecting the democratic choices of workers. This one-way decision making process when it comes to enterprise restructuring is worth our serious attention. For example, as a pharmaceutical factory in Changchun city began restructuring, enterprise administrators set a date for selling off the enterprise.[3] When the workers caught wind of this news, they rejected the rationale for the planned sell-off and countered that their products still had a future. They suggested that it was better to turn the enterprise into a stock-holding company instead and in numerous instances beseeched their enterprise director to convene a mass based meeting of the WRC, to let the WRC decided the format restructuring would follow. Thereafter, enterprise administrators essentially ignored this democratic demand. Upon the selling off of the pharmaceutical manufacturer, the workers were forced to sell off and sever their labor relationship with the enterprise

and forced into labor markets to fend for themselves. Workers' interests and rights were profoundly damaged by this experience. (*Workers Daily*, December 12, 1998)

News articles reported approvingly how SOE workers, through their active role in their WRCs, asserted their democratic right to reject plans by factory directors to convert factories to privately shareholder-owned companies. An article headlined, "Workers Look to Get Back Their Democratic Rights," sympathetically recounted a case of SOE workers' anger about a plan by their enterprise director to relocate factory infrastructure and sell the enterprise to private buyers:

> This aroused a strong and angry reaction from the workers who felt that the price being offered for the factory and its land (5.4 million Yuan) fell short of the relocation costs alone of 5.7 million Yuan, not to mention the enterprise's actual worth (8 million Yuan). Certain workers in interviews insisted, "Such a big decision and they didn't even consult with the workers, as though in their eyes we didn't exist." Workers then approached factory administrators and union representatives, demanding the return of the workers to decide on important enterprise matters. (*Workers Daily Weekend Magazine*, February 1, 1999)

This article goes on to report that factory administrators continued to ignore the workers' sentiments and called a meeting of the WRC, which rubber stamped the plans for relocation and selling off of the enterprise. The workers then took their case to the Decheng City ACFTU Branch, which investigated the WRC and declared it not in compliance with regulations that required it to represent the workers' interests in the enterprise. Thereupon, Decheng City ACFTU Branch Headquarters in Shandong Province put forth an order for all major production decisions to be made by the workers.

The official discourse endorsed the idea that SOE workers should vote on retention of managers and directors, and even select new ones. A February 22, 1999, lead article in *Workers' Daily* shouted out the headline, "Jiangxi workers' use democratic elections to exert control over factory directors." The story tells readers that in the Jiansi district of Jiangxi Province, 21 small- and medium-sized enterprises had subjected their factory directors to democratic elections. In many instances, a factory's rebound was attributed to the workers' choice of a more qualified factory director. In another example, a February 2, 1999, front-page article in *Workers' Daily* featured a story entitled "Hechi City promotes democratic direct elections for SOE directors":

> According to sources, the Guanxi Provincial City of Hechi has seen 55 of its 136 SOEs experience direct elections of directors and managers.

Rank and file and administrators now work together and are experiencing noticeably higher levels of economic efficiency. Bankrupt or economically strapped enterprises are especially prominent among the 55 whose WRCs have, beginning in 1997, taken the lead in organizing direct elections of enterprise directors, vice directors, managers, and vice-managers.

A crucial factor in the success or failure of this policy in enterprises was said to lie with the strength of and support from the factory union for such elections. On any given day, SOE workers in China could find stories about elections of new factory directors in the Party newspapers or in radio and televised newscasts.

A recurring thread in these articles was the expanded comprehensiveness of workers' democracy. A headline from the January 4, 1999, edition of the *Workers' Daily Weekend Magazine* read, "Democratic Management should only be strengthened and must not be weakened." The article reported on a declaration from the Guizhou Provincial Vice-Secretarial Conference calling for "enterprise projects to rely on the democratic participation, supervision, and management by workers that should only become stronger, not weaker." Although the WRC and the ACFTU factory-level unions were accorded the key role in carrying out elections that would be officially sanctioned, nonetheless newspapers reported instances of workers' democracy that were born of spontaneous and unsanctioned rebellion on the part of SOE workers. Another article from the December 21, 1998, *Workers' Daily* carried a headline that read, "The Key to Bankrupt Enterprises' Recovery is Workers' Production Control." Workers' Production Control is a rough translation of the Chinese phrase *Shengchan zijiu*, which refers to workers taking over production to carry out the task of saving their factories. This article announces in glowing language the story of workers at an SOE that produced conveyer belts in the Inner Mongolian city of Baotou. These workers fought for their jobs by taking over their factory and democratically electing new leaders. In many such media narratives, the workers typically engage in a mass-based takeover of their factory and elect a new factory director through a democratic election. Such articles indicated how the CCP now verbally propagated a concept of workers' democracy for SOEs in a way that went beyond the more limited versions the Party espoused in the 1980s.[4]

THE DISCOURSE OF WORKERS' DEMOCRACY IN A NEWSPAPER THAT CHALLENGED THE PARTY LINE

Not only official Party-controlled media circulated this discourse of workers' democracy. It was also picked up by a nationally read newspaper that was regarded as more independent of the Party for financial support. The

Southern Weekend (*Nanfang Zhoumo*), a newspaper that was famous for its harder hitting investigative reports on Party corruption, and more 'Western' orientation on issues of political and economic policy, also featured articles that positively featured cases of workers' democracy in 1990s China. For example, a March 27, 1998, article published in *Southern Weekend* entitled "Qiqihar Workers Cast Ballots, Elect New Director, and Face Violent Repressions Three Times" reported what looked to be a remarkable case of workers taking control of production democratically:

> On October 11, 1997, workers at the Qiqihar Tent Factory took matters into their own hands in an effort to save their factory, which was on the brink of bankruptcy. Workers organized their own WRC, recalled their director who had originally been appointed by state bureaucrats, and democratically voted in a new enterprise director. Thereafter, from December 1997 to February 1998, there occurred three successive incidents of bloodshed against the workers' representatives, activists, and candidates for the post of enterprise director.

The story recounts how this small COE thrived throughout the 1980s and was a model factory that employed 300 workers and won many awards for its productivity. Only in 1988 did the tent factory begin to go downhill as the unit saw the Qiqihar light industry ministry bureau appoint six different enterprise directors who sold off enterprise infrastructure, including the kindergarten for workers' children. With the accumulation of some 2 million Yuan in debt, the workforce was laid off (*xiagang*), and the factory's life was suffocated by one after another corrupt enterprise director. In September 1997, workers met with a lawyer who informed them of their rights stipulated by the State Council's draft of COE Management Law and Heilongjiang Provincial Governmental Codes for COE Management. This gave them the impetus to call a WRC mass meeting on September 11 to vote on a resolution to oppose the proposal by the enterprise director to relocate the factory infrastructure and tear down the factory buildings. This, the WRC argued, the laws clearly stated could only be done with the consent of the WRC. The workers' overwhelmingly opposition to the plan was disregarded by the last of the Light Industry Ministry's appointed factory director (Li Jintao) at this meeting. This led the workers to call for her immediate recall, and the WRC voted unanimously to reject the resolution to relocate and raze the factory. Additionally, it passed a resolution demanding that Li Jintao return the lost assets and infrastructure of the factory immediately.

The *Southern Weekend* recounts the refusal of the Light Industry Ministry to stop the subsequent efforts to prevent the razing of the factory, which only further radicalized workers, who then took their case to the municipal branch office of the ACFTU to make known their wish to democratically elect a new enterprise director. Again they met with bureaucratic stumbling blocks and, even worse, the continued razing of their factory in violation of their resolution. On October 17th, the workers marched in the street chanting the slogan, "Recall Director Li and Give Us Back our Factory!"

Despite the organized election of a new factory director by the workers, they met with police and gang violence, the Municipal Light Industry Ministry Branch's rejection of the election, and reinstatement of Li as the factory director. In this particular article, the *Southern Weekend* followed a frame that rather directly suggested that the Party stood in the way of the tent factory workers' goal of democratically electing managers and that workers' self-management was a worthy goal. Here, the source of the problem was not the laws, but the lack of enforcement of laws already on the books. These Party-controlled ministries and bureaucrats were able to outright violate or manipulate laws in their favor at the expense of workers' democracy. Rarely did the more official and directly controlled newspapers express such sentiments. However, whether more loyal to the Party (*Workers Daily*) or quasi-independent media sources with more wWestern liberal orientations (*Southern Weekend*), both promoted a view that workers' democracy was or should be compatible with China's economic development strategy to increase the role of competitive markets as a means to resolve the ongoing crisis of stagnation and bankruptcy in the SOE sector. They made such arguments, ironically, with appeals to workers that Cultural Revolutionaries once used to exhort SOE workers to mass actions in their workplaces only three decades earlier to fight what they regarded as capitalist roaders.

OFFICIAL REPORTS IN PUBLICATIONS FOR PROVINCIAL UNION CADRES ON THE NEED FOR DEMOCRATIC MANAGEMENT IN FAILING SOES

This official discourse did not stop with mass news media. It was evident as well in the manifold literature (in the forms of periodicals, magazines, and bulletins) that targeted ACFTU cadres at local, provincial, and national levels. Selected editions of the 1997 ACFTU journal[5] (*Workers' Movement Forum [Gongyun Luntan]*, hereafter *Workers' Forum*) provide representative material from the Party-controlled union documenting the understanding of the role workers' democracy played in 1990s SOE restructuring. *Workers Forum* is a national periodical published for trade union cadres and provides a compendium of articles that appeared in either provincial editions of *Worker's Forum* or in the trade union newspaper *The Workers' Daily*. *Workers' Forum's* purpose was largely to keep cadres abreast of the latest labor policies and positions. The focus of these editions was when, how, and why various manifestations of workers' democracy succeed or fail in China's moment of transition.

Articles in *Workers' Forum* that treated matters of workers' democracy policies were not only written to report success stories. They also clarified for union cadres the link between workers' democracy policies and the CCP's overall developmental goals, and how the two complemented each other. Union cadres in China play a crucial role by backing the Party's developmental policies and, in addition to taking care of workers' social welfare needs, conveying reasons for that support to rank-and-file workers. Additionally, because the factory union still played a leading role in organizing WRCs, union representatives and chairs shaped the WRCs' attitude toward the Party's economic development. However, reports in *Workers' Forum* typically contained the success story element as part of its overall content. For example, a September 1998 report from the Liaoning branch of the ACFTU on the impact of "Worker-Staff Democratic Choice and Democratic Review of Enterprise Administrators" epitomizes reports on workers' democracy policies in the 1990s:

> These past years have brought difficulties for state and collective enterprises in Liaoning Province. In an effort to overcome them, as a result of either workers' demands or administrative ministries arrangements, these enterprises have instituted democratic elections, democratic suggestions, or democratic hiring competition to democratically select enterprise administrators.

This report then proceeds to catalogue the seemingly extensive evidence that widespread elections were being carried out in SOEs with statistics on percentage of participating companies and the advantages enjoyed as a result:

> 1,820 state and collective enterprises have democratically selected administrators in Liaoning Province. Wherever workers and staff democratically choose enterprise administrators, the absolute majority considerably improved the performance of company leaders. Management has been reformed, economic efficiency has had varying levels of improvement. For example, Shenyang City Transportation Company . . . democratically selected and hired administrators in 1996. Soon thereafter the company went from indebtedness to turning profits. . . . In Shenyang's Heping District there were 46 enterprises that implemented democratic choice, of which more than half turned a profit; the remainder cut their losses. . . . In Anshan, 5 enterprises experiencing losses were designated test sites for democratic, of which, except for one still experiencing losses, 3 companies recovered profitability and one has broken even. In Dandong, by the end of 1996, some 136 state owned and collectively owned enterprises promoted democratic recommendations and democratic elections. 26 companies stabilized development, 55 turned profits, and 35 clearly experienced declining losses.

The report proceeds to applaud different success stories at the individual enterprise level. Sources of success included improved cadres' caliber when elected, a more motivated and stable workforce, better assignments of tasks, greater willingness to take risks, and high annual or biannual approval ratings for managers who were elected democratically. In one example given, after workers at a failing tool factory elected its director, the spirit changed dramatically, so much so that wages that had been paid only three times a year were now paid every month. The company adopted new, more aggressive tactics to take advantage of any markets that provided potential customers in addition to other measures of enterprise restructuring.

In the 1990s, literature distributed to union cadres highlighted the problem of SOE debt in China and the critical role that workers' democracy could play in its removal, along with the return of enterprise profitability. These types of connections were made less frequently during the 1980s and almost never made before the 1980s. One further leitmotif was when enterprises that were both democratic and exposed to greater market competition advances could be made in workers' economic situations. This would be due not only to the increased shop floor motivation that democratization inspires in workers, but also to the opportunities that stem from clever (democratic) management strategies in competitive markets. Enterprises that implement democratic management were likewise proclaimed better able to improve their productivity and were regarded favorably as targets of investment by foreign investors. The link for union cadres was thus established between the influx of foreign investment and the democratization of management.

Various forms of workers' democracy were heralded as preventive mechanisms against the problem of corruption that plagued enterprises due to the opportunities presented to managers and directors for skimming from subcontracting deals. For instance, a March 1996 article, written for ACFTU cadres in Jilin Province, declared:

> Asset subcontracting is also a key concern of workers. Enterprise affairs council laws stipulate clearly that the size of assets subcontracted, value, and limits are all set forth and must be subject to democratic audit. The WRC must approve the agreements before they are official. . . . [U]pon democratic audit, one company was found to have had an arrangement between the company accountant and subcontractor, with the latter providing the former a bonus for the agreement. The subcontractor owed back wages, didn't pay into the workers' health care insurance fund while simultaneously using health insurance to pay for the general manager's dog. As a result, the company nullified the subcontracting arrangement, fired the general manager, and reassigned the accountant to a non-finance position.[6]

The subtext developed in such passages was that workers' democracy will help root out corruption, which transpires when managers and directors

collude to take advantage of their Party-based social status to absorb surpluses that should be invested in production. It followed that workers would
benefit when they have an institution like the WRC and elections of administrators to ensure that restructuring of enterprise relationships occurs in
a fashion that optimizes outcomes in competitive markets for company
employees. Again, the dovetailing of workers' democracy policies with the
Party's national economic development strategy was made clear in such
reports intended for ACFTU cadres around China in the 1990s.

It would be a mistake, however, to regard such reports as ones written entirely to move union cadres to embrace outright and direct paths to
privatization as the means to improve SOE workers' worsening conditions.
Workers' democracy also was presented as a mechanism to counter over-
zealous privatization thrusts among ministerial bureaucrats and enterprise
directors. This thrust is framed as a product of cadre misinterpretation of
the calls on the Party to diminish the ties between the state and small- and
medium-sized SOEs:

> For some companies that are in the midst of SOE reforms, selling off
> companies is taken to be the only method of implementation . . . re-
> jecting other options that would make it possible to save a SOE. Jiang
> Zemin, at the 15th Party Congress, stated, "We need to improve the
> overall state owned economy by shoring up large enterprises and letting
> go of the smaller ones by choosing to restructure, partnerships, merge,
> lease properties, subcontract, conversion to shareholding (*gufenzhi*) or
> sell off companies to private buyers." This is a call for local policy
> of loosening state-enterprise ties to be made according to the on the
> ground situation of small enterprises. However, many cities have slated
> small companies for sale to private buyers as their only option, plainly
> ignoring the central leaders' intent. It is our opinion that revival of small
> and medium sized SOEs is a complex and difficult task, one which im-
> pacts on the problem of disappearing state assets and the ability of the
> Party to grow. Loosening state ties to revive small and medium sized
> the SOEs should be conducted enterprise by enterprise, with enterprise
> self-revival (*zijiu*) as the most preferred endpoint. (*Workers' Forum*,
> National Edition, October 1996)

Union cadres did not only receive signals that SOE restructuring in the
direction of privatization was proceeding smoothly. The official discourse
delivered to union cadres reflected the tension within the Party, in SOEs, and
society generally about the pace of privatization and wisdom of compelling
SOE workers to give up their social relationship with and dependence on
their SOEs. This literature for cadres was quite frank and open about the
limits of "democratically choosing and auditing" small- and medium-sized
SOE administrators. It would therefore be incorrect to read into the content
of these materials for union cadres in this period only upbeat assessments

of workers' democracy policies as growing numbers of small- and medium-sized SOEs embarked on variegated paths toward privatization. An article from the February 1999 *Liaoning Workers' Movement* was quite straightforward about the gap between stated goals and real outcomes when it came to workers' democracy policies as the Party pushed for greater SOE privatization from the mid-1990s onward:

> These past several years have seen considerable development in the democratic selection of enterprise leaders in Liaoning, proving that this policy contributes positively to the revival of small and medium sized SOEs. Still, there remains a great way to go. . . . From areas where the policy has been implemented already we know that theoretical comprehension of the policy is not a major problem. The crucial problem is at the level of enterprise leadership. Under the present system, wherever administrators give the right to select enterprise leaders, the democratic selection of leaders proceeds very smoothly; where the situation is the opposite, democratic selection simply cannot be carried out effectively. When leaders are not willing to let go of power, the problem is usually one of old habits and prejudices, though desire to benefit from corrupt insider deals as enterprise leaders cannot be ruled out as a contributing factor.

This was indeed one, if not the major, point of conflict in the 1990s process of restructuring—the desire on the part of managers to coordinate deals with 'buyers' of enterprises from which they could secure bribes and promises of leadership rank in "restructured" companies. Small- and medium-sized SOE leaders stood to gain especially if they found buyers for their enterprises. As the author of this article notes, this threw the entire possibility of "democratic selection of managers and leaders" into jeopardy because companies that are privatized without consent of the workforce are de facto not subject to any kind of worker control, not to mention state regulation.

The extent of this corruption was evident since the late 1990s in report after report about managers and directors involved in one after another fraudulent scheme to team up with outside buyers of small- and medium-sized SOEs, allowing for no consultation with workers. However, there existed little in the official discourse of workers' democracy that provided an in-depth examination of how workers end up in this position in small- and medium-sized enterprises, which would go beyond the ideological boundaries of the official discourse of workers' democracy. That is to say, how could workers who had been exercising varying forms of 'democratic management' since the onset of the post-Mao economic restructuring have not noticed and done something about schemes by factory administrators and Party cadres to pilfer the source of their livelihoods, namely the SOE?

This points to another key element of the discourse of workers' democracy in Chinese small- and medium-sized SOEs in the 1990s: privatization. The focus on the role of enterprise leaders in the implementation of workers' democracy only further reveals the ideological nature of the discourse. The privatization policies opened workers up to the threat of both corruption and complete loss of any legal claims to social security as state workers. At the same time, the policy of workers' democracy, ostensibly designed to protect workers from bad managers and directors, entirely depended on the willingness of directors and managers to subject their social power to democratic election, selection, or audit. The official discourse of workers' democracy narratives reproduced the status quo, with no theorized mechanism for resistance to the unequal power relations of privatization in small- and medium-sized SOEs outside official Party channels. Such channels were, after all, often a party to and benefitted from the stripping of social security from workers during SOE sell-offs.

THE DISCOURSE OF WORKERS'
DEMOCRACY IN HENAN PROVINCE

In the course of plumbing through articles in the media and ACFTU documents, the experience of Henan Province consistently cropped up as a model province when it came to promoting and executing the national Party policy of expanding the substance of workers' democracy in China's SOEs. The ACFTU published several special edition volumes of *Workers' Movement* from 1995 to 1997, published during the Party's promotion of 'letting go of the small SOEs and reviving large SOEs,' which highlighted what it referred to as the 'leading role' of Henan Province in the quick and wide-scale implementation of the policy of 'democratic selection of enterprise administration' (*minzhu xuanze jinin guanli*). Articles in these editions of *The Forum* also contained numerous references to Henan Province's aggressiveness in carrying out the policy of encouraging city governments to find ways to let go of small- and medium-sized enterprises. This was not the first time that Henan had taken the lead in China. The provincial capital of Henan, Zhengzhou, was the city in which the Chinese workers' movement was 'born' and experienced heavy blows in an infamous 1927 massacre.

Henan was widely cited in these editions of *The Forum* for its early and positive response to the call from national Party leadership to deepen enterprise restructuring in small- and medium-sized SOEs and to link it to the democratization of SOEs. Henan was the location of large numbers of small- and medium-sized enterprises engaging in many of the industrial sectors that were opened to foreign investment and competition following Deng's 1992 endorsement of private capitalist investment during his 'southern provincial tour.' Provincial and city leaders received clear messages from the central leadership that small- and medium-sized enterprises could not rely on the center for guarantees of credit. At the same time, Chen (1999) reports that:

> In 1994 the Henan provincial government decided to establish a "system of open and democratic elections" in all state enterprises that failed to show profits. By late 1995, nearly 200 state enterprises in Henan were managed by democratically elected directors who reportedly brought back the dying enterprises back to life. (39)

Chen surely found these kinds of data from articles, such as one from the November 1995 national edition of *Workers' Movement* entitled "An Investigative Report to the National ACFTU on the Implementation of Transparent Elections of SOE Administrators to Turn Around Bankrupt Enterprises in Henan Province," which praises Henan Province as a leader in workers' democracy:

> "Enterprises Rely on Us (workers) to Develop, We rely on the Enterprise for our Development" is the core belief that guides Henan's policy of open democratically elected and hired SOE administrators, as part of its distinctly determined effort to revive SOEs in debt and facing bankruptcy In June 1996, The Henan Provincial Council convened an "Henan Provincial Economics Workshop Conference," in order to gather research on the problem of bankrupt or indebted SOEs in Henan and to set in motion the appropriate policy resolutions for their crises. One of the most important components of this conference was listening to the experiences of workers, union cadres, and administrators at enterprises that had carried out the strategy of saving their factories by electing new enterprise directors and managers.[7] . . . The result was the passing of Resolution 14, passed by relevant ministerial cadres present at the conference, clearly recommending that all 17 pertinent cities promote the holding of elections for SOE enterprise administrators and managers.

The article cites the achievements of Henan Province in the short time since the resolution passed. Referencing "as yet completed statistic investigations to date," by March 1995, already 152 SOEs in Henan had carried out democratic elections to hire new enterprise directors and managers. The overwhelming majority were small- and medium- sized SOEs, of which 74 percent had undergone dramatic turnarounds from debt-ridden to economically efficient states.[8]

A speech by a Party cadre from Beijing who attended this meeting explains why Henan's promotion of workers' democracy in its SOEs was so much more aggressive than in the 1980s:

> My own sense of things is that our policy is basically following the spirit of socialism with Chinese characteristics as envisioned by Deng

Xiaoping. . . . The different accounts given of Henan's current strategy of promoting democratic elections of SOE directors and managers reminds me that this is not the first time such a policy has been called for by the Party. The first time was from late 1979 through early 1980. One of Beijing's municipal industrial ministries carried out a comprehensive policy of democratically electing SOE directors and managers. The main reason for this was the chaos of enterprise leadership, which stemmed from the ideological turmoil the Gang of Four period left behind. Because many of the enterprise leaders under the ministry's jurisdiction were Gang of Four holdouts, many SOEs were in a tumultuous condition, which invariably affected production. . . . The second time was in 1988, a SOE in Beijing's Congwen district was operating as an enterprise that elected its leaders. The reason for this was that the leaders weren't united in vision. Most of the managers were near retirement age, which made it difficult to choose a new director from among current managers. As a result, the district cadres decided to have an election based on the principle of open competition (anyone from within or outside the enterprise could be a candidate).

This official did not merely confirm what I argued in the last chapter—namely, that this policy was implemented far more widely in the 1990s than in the 1980s. He also clarified a major difference in motivation for democratic elections in SOEs during the 1990s. For starters, the crises faced by SOEs as the Party moved in the direction of increasing the role of private investment in the national economy were not regarded as political in orientation. Instead, they were portrayed as managerial crises caused by failures that were linked more to economic strategies in competitive markets. The problem could not come from either ministerial appointments (because they proceeded along a bureaucratic logic that attached more importance to *guanxi* [social corrections] than competitive market norms) or from elections within the enterprise. In the 1990s, he declared, elections would be competitions that could enable workers and managers to independently choose (elect) persons who were not members of their unit and had no relationship with the responsible ministries.

A report from the Anyang City-Provincial Organizing Committee and Anyang ACFTU Branch reported that early on in the enterprise restructuring process many enterprise administrators in Anyang could not make the necessary adjustments to fierce competition under market conditions[9]:

(As a result) . . . state assets have disappeared, enterprise debts hit new heights, losses more serious than ever, and workers unpaid for long periods. Workers reacted with intense dissatisfaction and collectively demonstrated and petitioned the government for redress, in many instances demanding the recall of their enterprise administrative leaders. These factors attracted a high level of attention from the city council and government. The city general secretary took it upon himself to meet with and listen to WRC representatives' suggestions. Committees studied the relevant laws, and researched how, under conditions of socialist markets, democratic management could be carried out in order to improve the caliber of enterprise leaders, improve leaders' output, and fundamentally stabilizing enterprise productivity and the workforce. (31)

The report then goes on to state that the city government departments and committees were united in their understanding of the role that the democratic selection of enterprise administrators would play in restructuring and revitalizing failing companies. A lack of understanding of democratic management in SOEs was to blame for the problems of debt in Anyang. The principles underlying the initiative are noteworthy—namely, 'transparency,' 'autonomy,' 'competition,' and 'selecting excellence.' These reflect the incorporation of Western capitalist market ideals, notably prominent in the 1990's excitement about globalization and lean production, into the Chinese concept of workers' democracy. Heads of selected industrial departments were chosen democratically, it is reported, whereupon efficiency and output improved dramatically, and profitability and wages both were possible again. The extent of democratization, in terms of both numbers of enterprises and activity, appears to surpass any other era since 1949:

> Of the 10 companies chosen as original test sites, the largest of them was Henan Province Pharmaceutical Company, with 3800 workers. It was also one of Anyang's indebted enterprises with a transparent and latent debt of over 200 million, the largest of them was Henan Province Pharmaceutical Company, with 3800 workers. It was also one of Anyang's indebted enterprises with a transparent and latent debt of over ¥ 200 million and on the verge of bankruptcy. (33)

The story presented in reports about Henan were familiar: New company leaders and new (foreign) markets are found, workers' suggestions are taken seriously, productivity and efficiency increases, and the relationship between enterprise administrators and workers improves dramatically. In the three-year series that comprises these editions of *The Forum*, the results of numerous meetings on the accomplishments of democratic selection of managers are reported on by different branch investigative committees of the Henan ACFTU. One can see almost a copycat pattern in the manner of reportage, with little difference between respective cases outside of company name and products. This is not unique to China. Under the state-socialist rubric, reports on policy implementation are designed with the need to affirm policy decisions delivered from on high (Burawoy and Lukacs 1992).

However, there is a more nuanced picture that emerges outside the official 1990's discourse of workplace democracy, which reflected the strains being placed on the Chinese political economy in transition and the rising discontent on the part of SOE workers who faced the most deleterious consequences imposed by transition. Interviews with SOE workers in Henan revealed another side of the discourse of workers' democracy in China existed in the 1990s, which was engaged as a means to defend something that China's economic development strategy was denying SOE workers, especially those in the small- and medium-sized enterprises: their right to a job.

FIELD INTERVIEWS AT MODELS OF DEMOCRATIC MANAGEMENT IN HENAN PROVINCE

The SOEs that comprised the cases in this section were selected in the fall of 2000. The enterprises were chosen because they were small- and medium-sized enterprises that were proclaimed as examples of enterprises that successfully restructured (*gaizu*) as a result of implementing democratic management. The enterprises were located in three cities (Anyang, Xinxiang, and Luoyang) in Henan Province.

Interviews with company leaders were initially conducted in advance of later interviews with workers at the enterprises. The enterprises I chose to focus on in this section reveal the character of the discourse of workers' democracy in Chinese transition during the 1990s, particularly where enterprise restructuring was occurring at the greatest pace—namely, in small- and medium-sized enterprises that are either collectively or state owned. They were also companies that, at the time of the interviews, had experienced relatively low levels of direct collective forms of conflict between workers and administrators. These interviews were set up to analyze, in ways the official Party-based literature did not make possible, what actual level of 'enterprise democratization' occurred at these selected model companies.[10] In one case, it was not possible to interview workers. However, two in-depth interviews with the enterprise union chief pretty much revealed the distance between the official version and on-the-ground reality.

The purpose of these interviews was not exposé in nature (i.e., to prove the policy does not meet the description in the official literature). I took it for granted that this policy was largely not able to meet its lofty goals. Nor was the aim to draw a general theory from these cases about the national implementation of this policy. I was more interested in how SOE workers in model cases of SOE 'democratic management' in China interpreted the discourse of democracy, if they engaged it at all, and how it shaped their responses to the social relations of 1990's SOE restructuring.

Interviews were conducted or attempted at six models of democratic management over a period of six weeks in September and October 2000. I also entrusted further interviews to a colleague from Henan who provided me with an extra set of interviews. Although I am fluent in Chinese and was able to conduct many of the interviews myself, it was decided that, due to time limitations, arrangements would be made for my contacts in Zhengzhou to do interviews at factories where I had begun the interview process. This worked out well in some cases and in others did not meet original expectations.[11] On the basis of the quality of the interviews,[12] four of the cases are discussed and analyzed in the following sections: the Luoyang Number One Dyed Fabric Factory, the Anyang Chemical Fiber Textile Factory, the Xinxiang Yellow Tiger Wire Tubing Factory, and the Xinxiang Wireless Electronics Factory.

THE CASE OF THE NO. 1 DYED FABRIC FACTORY, LUOYANG, HENAN PROVINCE

Of the four SOEs discussed in this section, Luoyang No. 1 Dyed Fabric Factory (hereafter "the #1") is the case in the official media that was brought up most often, not only as a model, but as the *most ideal* model of all the democratically managed factories in Henan. As I noted in Chapter 1, it was one that supporters and oppentents of China's reliance on the growing role of private capitalist investment for economic growth used to bolster their calls for increasing or diminishing state support for China's SOEs. To hear all ideological sides of the spectrum, this SOE, from all appearances was, in fact, a model of enterprise autonomy and worker-controlled democratic management well into the mid-1990s.

In 1991, due to declines in productivity and being overburdened with debt, after searching unsuccessfully for an SOE willing to merge with the #1, the enterprise was slated by the city government to be sold to a Township and Village Enterprise (TVE), which happened to be a slaughterhouse. Under the terms of the deal, the #1 would be turned over to the TVE. Thereupon, the TVE would lay off all workers more than 35 years old, take no responsibility for the pensions or subsistence of laid-off workers, and eliminate the trade union along with the relationship between government and the factory unit altogether. The sale would effectively end the status of SOE membership enjoyed by enterprise workers and cadres at the #1.

This was unacceptable to the overwhelming majority of workers and cadres, especially because the sale would effectively lay off, without responsibility for severance payments, all workers under the age of 35. As a result, in April 1992, the workers gathered at the factory and made known their dissatisfaction with the proposal and adamant refusal to accept it. The workers and cadres put forth a counterdemand—namely, democratic management of the factory with the goal of breathing new life into the #1 as an SOE. Soon thereafter, after meetings were held between the city government and #1 cadres, a public meeting of the #1 WRC was held, at which a respected shop floor manager was chosen by the workers as the new factory director. Changes were made in managers and Party representative, new management styles were adapted, and within a short space of time productivity had revived and the SOE was profitable and paying wages once again.

The #1 factory did apparently manage to turn around its productivity and profitability in a short time. The 1,300-odd workers contributed out-of-pocket loans to the company to revive an investment fund base. The new leaders instituted a fresh management policy based on developing products such as fashionable dungaree and flannel wears that would win purchase orders from foreign companies. Also a new management style was developed around the principle of rewarding management based on performance, which resulted in a reduction of administrative units from 24 to 10 and cuts in management cadres from 140 to 54. In 1993, a Hong Kong investor visited the factory and was, the story goes, so moved by the enthusiastic energy in the factory that he established a joint venture with #1 and imported dyed fabric machinery from Hong Kong.

Remuneration was reorganized around the principle of piece work, which was determined according to a collective contract. Shop floor managers' pay and bonuses were also tied explicitly to modern measurements of efficiency and product quality, which resulted in increases of piece-wage rates by 40 percent at #1. In addition, according to official documents, some 6 million RMB were invested by the company in the construction of new housing units for workers.

As Zhao and Nichols' (1996) field interviews with workers and managers in textile SOEs in Henan province found, classically capitalist devices of speedup, increases in work hours, intensified forms of labor control, and the like are frequently legitimated by the language of SOE enterprise reform. Likewise, in the case of 'democratic management' reform, official documents and media stories reflected a trend of employing concepts such as 'enterprise transparency,' 'worker investment,' 'election of managers,' and so on to legitimate the labor discipline necessary to attract purchase orders from foreign companies.

Interviews with the #1 union chief and three WRC members revealed that, in the case of #1, 'democratic management' was a discourse that was appropriated by managers and cadres to justify the severing of the government ministries' direct obligations to the reproduction of the SOE. WRC members explained to me that one of their important jobs was ideological work, which consisted of persuading workers to accept piece-wage rates and work speed rules because the SOE now relied almost entirely on foreign purchase orders for its economic survival. When asked if that did not contradict state-socialist principles, I was told:

> In a manner of speaking, you're right. But then again, if we don't do what appears to you as "unsocialist," there are no wages, no social security, and no jobs for the workers. There is no WRC, there is no union, and there is nothing outside of scanty unemployment insurance payments. (WRC representative no. 3, July 1999)

In any event, in 1997, the #1 encountered major difficulties yet again. When the AFC struck, it had a devastating effect on many textiles enterprises in China that were dependent on the revenue from foreign purchase orders that enabled them to maintain payments on new machinery necessary to compete in international markets. The #1 was no exception because many of its products were sent in the direction of Southeast Asia.

The union chief related the unfortunate set of circumstances as such:

> It's really unfortunate, most of our trade is with Southeast Asian partners. Once the Asian Financial Crisis hit, all of a sudden our orders dried up. We had some very extensive purchase order agreements that just went belly up. It's not really something that we can blame the government policy for in any way, it's really just a matter of bad luck. The workers didn't blame us, they realized that the fate of the enterprise had nothing to do with how it was managed or with their workers representatives. (Union Chief, July 1999)

On top of this misfortune, the enterprise could no longer profitably accept purchase orders because the provincial government, in response to the problem of declining competitiveness that stemmed from devalued currencies in Southeast Asia, lowered the amount of tax rebates returned on each purchase order. This effectively made it impossible for the #1 to reproduce the social costs built into the SOE modus operandi. By the end of 1998, the #1's main workshop had closed down. To make matters worse, the factory was ordered to stop production until it had overhauled its drainage system to meet environmental standards not met by its antiquated and polluting technologies. For the #1, this meant having to search for an 'environmental protection loan.' However, new lending policies made conditions for loans more strictly based on profitability potential and the existence of a guarantor.

Finding a guarantor in 2000 was the problem that most vexed the #1 management and made it unable to revive production in the main plant. Instead, the #1 laid off the workers at the main factory. A Hong Kong-based firm that originally invested in the company formed a partnership with the #1 in a factory outside the main factory's premises. Under this shareholding corporate arrangement, the #1 supplied labor and took care of the management, whereas the Hong Kong investor supplied the machinery and capital. At this factory, there also existed a WRC and 'democratic management,' although its role was even further compromised by the decidedly advantageous position of the foreign investor given the situation of both enterprise debt and unemployment at the #1. When asked about this, the responses from the WRC members and the union chief revealed the limits of what discourse of workers' democracy can offer workers, as it was framed by Party leaders and enterprise cadres:

> The fact remains that as long as we have the foreign investor working with us we still have a WRC. The WRC can negotiate with the company

about the terms of production, investment, and the like. If the workers are unhappy, we can go and negotiate with the investors on behalf of the workers. As well, as long as there is the WRC as an SOE entity, we can negotiate through the city government as well on the terms of invest-ment and production. (Union Chief, October 2000)

When I pressed a WRC representative on what the terms of negotiation would be like in a situation like this given the crisis that faced the #1, she conceded that democratic management faced no small challenge:

> Of course we would prefer that we could negotiate from a stronger bargaining position. However, what matters really is getting a factory productive so that we can help workers get their wages. If we can't do that, then we cannot be a WRC anyhow. But I don't think we have a negotiating strength issue in any event, the foreign investor knows us and respects us. That is enough for us. If production needs to be sped up, workers also understand. They will do what is necessary. What is important is they keep the faith of the investors and they can maintain their wages. And we are here to help with that and to com-municate workers concerns to the investors. (WRC representative #2, October 2000)

In the course of interviews, I asked the union chief whether he had given any consideration to broader possibilities of democratic management beyond the individual factory because the #1 was part of a provincial and national policy. Was it possible, instead of relying solely on private inves-tors to save the company, to coordinate with other companies that were successful models of democratic management?

> You know, you have a real point there. That would be great actually; we could help each other out in moments of crisis. But that's not what the policy of the government is, it is to get companies back on their feet and let them fend for themselves. I'm a member of the Party of course and that's not our Party policy. Would I like it? I think it would be a good thing, but it's not possible or realistic under our circumstances of reform. (Union Chief, October 2000).

In the end, the majority of the #1's workers faced a fate of being laid off and having to find private factory work if young and skilled or tem-porary low-paying jobs if unskilled and older. In any event, by the time of the interviews, the likelihood of being able to strengthen the #1's integrity as an SOE through the state-sponsored policy of democratic management had been exhausted because the #1 had only become more dependent on capital, especially from abroad, to make up for what the #1 union chief informed me was its biggest obstacle to survival, the lack of capital.

THE CASE OF ANYANG CHEMICAL FIBER TEXTILE ENTERPRISE: THE OFFICIAL VERSION

The Anyang[13] Chemical Fiber Textile Factory case (hereafter Anyang Textile) was cited in field interviews with its senior managers and the general secretary of the Anyang ACFTU as one of Anyang's best examples of democratic management 'in action.' In the fall of 2000, the factory had 4,318 workers, of whom 518 were retired,[14] making it Anyang's third largest SOE. Officials and enterprise administrators stated that, in September 1995, the company carried out a democratic election of the factory director because Anyang Textile was laden with heavy debt and losses.[15] In addition to lost wages, the company also had not paid back workers for loans they had made collectively to help finance Anyang Textile. Almost two thirds of workers had been laid off. Some 400 workers and cadres applied for transfers, just one of many signs of lost faith. Enterprise leaders were caught engaging in corruption, which led to their arrest and the decision to democratically elect a new factory director.

It was agreed that assignment of a factory director by the city government was not desirable because the last factory leaders it chose were such failures. Therefore, a democratic election was seen as a better formula to resolve the leadership crisis, although the city leaders still played a formative role in the process. The city set up an enterprise administrator democratic election organizing committee, consisting of relevant governmental department leaders, factory directors from successful large enterprises, accountants, and economists. This committee then placed ads in newspapers for potential candidates. They received 60 applications, narrowed that number down to 30, and then selected 10 from that group's written statements. After conducting job interviews, five remained for consideration. Groups representing company leaders, city government leadership, and workers' representatives from the WRC interviewed the five and chose a director of a small-textile SOE in Anyang.

According to these cadres, within a month of being elected, the new director turned the company around. One matter that was resolved quickly was the problem of funds turning up in private accounts before the new leader was democratically chosen. Those funds were returned and monitored more carefully because of the new policy of enterprise transparency, which bolstered the democratic credentials of the new director. Enterprise cadres who before the election of the new leader had not contributed to the collective financing fund were required to pay in their share.[16] Enterprise leaders were also required to subject their use of company phones to WRC monitoring. As a result of these reforms, confidence in the WRC was restored and, consequently, productivity at Anyang Textile improved greatly. Although management became stricter on the work floor, cadres told us workers had no objections because they once again received wages. Wages remained relatively evenly distributed, with the director only receiving double the wages of workers.

Anyang Textile invested almost 9 million Yuan in high-technology machinery. According to the enterprise union chief, after democratic management became policy, the government interfered in production much less. Worker surveys reported almost 90 percent levels of satisfaction. In the past, approaching workers for company loans was much more difficult because workers were in a state of poverty. Now they had wages, and when the company lacked capital, workers responded positively to loan requests. All the cadres we talked to were excited about the prospects of entry into the WTO because the textiles sector stood to gain from lower tariffs in the United States. This they also believed would strengthen the position of the company and thereby benefit workers. In this sense, one cadre told me, WTO entry would 'add to the benefits the company enjoyed from *minzhu guanli's* contribution to increased efficiency and worker motivation.'

ANYANG TEXTILE WORKERS INTERVIEWS

In September 2000, I conducted five private interviews with Anyang Textile workers. These interviews were conducted via contacts in Anyang who knew the enterprise and its workers. I conducted all the interviews, most consisting of one- to two-hour periods, separately. Interviews required a day in advance to schedule. In all, I interviewed three women production workers, one machine repair worker, and one maintenance worker.

The workers' assessment of the changes that Anyang Textile had undergone in the past few years was quite different from what company leaders and Anyang trade union officials related. The company apparently had changed its name, using the director's name, and a subcontracted franchise company likewise changed its name in a similar fashion. In the eyes of the workers, the company was essentially the director's possession:

> Actually, this is something that we joked about among ourselves. Here is this state owned company and now it's no longer China's company, it's the director's company. But we're still a state owned enterprise? So we call it a state owned enterprise in name, that is, in the director's name! (Anyang Textile worker 3, November 11, 2000)

As for the collective investment in shares of company stock (*zhigong rugu*) called for by administrators, workers, who were expected to contribute 3,000 Yuan,[17] were quite ambivalent about the idea. The machine repair worker told us it was forced on workers, a common phenomenon in companies in trouble or about to undergo shareholding conversions. The company was slated to become a shareholding company in a month at the time our interviews were conducted. Workers interviewed stated that most Anyang Textile workers were unconvinced that the company would be able to pay out dividends on their 'investment shares,' thus their tendency to not strongly support investing in shares. Of course, the company had a high debt level, owing the banks some ¥ 2 million in interest. Nonetheless, a worker explained that she intended to 'invest' in shares of the shareholding company when it was formed:

> Well, look at it like this. As I told you already, there isn't much choice in the matter. Let's say I don't invest in the company. Well, probably I'd protect myself from a bad investment, but there'd be a more immediate downside to consider. You know what that is? It's simple actually. I'd be out of my job and that is something that is not desirable for obvious reasons. (Anyang Textile worker 2, November 13, 2000)

Inquiries about democratic management were met with derision from interviewees. Only a month prior to the interviews in November 2000, some 100 workers had gathered and sought out the director, demanding overtime pay, and were met with punishment for doing so and had to write 'apologies' for their actions. Workers were assigned task classifications (i.e., heavy vs. light lifting) according to how well they got along with the factory director. Levels of work intensity only increased since the new director took over. Favoritism was cited in every interview, in addition to inappropriate use of company funds for auto purchases and dinners for friends of the director. The two male workers who had worked on the shop floor for longer periods contended that the old factory director was more concerned about workers' needs, especially social security. One of them related his perspective of the conflict like this:

> You know, they say all this stuff about democratic management? But this is not what they must mean. In China workers are supposed to be in charge. But now basically our feelings don't matter. That's bad enough, but if you leave this factory, where else can you go? In the old days at least it was possible to have a job or to go somewhere else if you had the right connections. What is this all about? (Anyang Textile machine worker, November 13, 2000)

Regarding the WRC's role, the machine worker told us that it was something that shop managers chose, and in any event workers' representatives didn't speak out that much. The representatives did cast ballots for this director, but they really knew little about him. These accounts were basically confirmed by three women workers, in their early to mid-20s, who worked on the production line. They contended that work intensity had increased with the new director. Some several hundred workers were led by a worker surnamed Gao to demand overtime pay for work performed on National Founding Day (October 1), but were told the director was not present. The workers were offered the choice of two additional days off during the Spring Festival, but they countered that the law allows for seven additional days off as compensation. The workers were dispersed, and Gao was demoted.

> That Gao was just unlucky. You say democracy? How can there be democracy if they do that? This is not the way it was before, even if things in the old days weren't perfect, you know? All we know now is we can lose our job for any reason and then what? (Anyang Textile machine worker, November 13, 2000)

Although these SOE workers were openly cynical and dismissive about the way managers used the language of workers' democracy, this did not mean that the workers regarded the concept as one that had no meaning. At one point in a discussion, I asked a machine worker whether he thought the whole concept was meaningless, except as an ideology that enterprise administrators used to rationalize the power they enjoyed as China restructured its economy. This machine worker engaged a discourse of workers' democracy also, only quite different from the one deployed by managers and cadres interviewed in the same factory. The problem for the worker was not just how much reality diverged from the managers' narratives of workplace democracy at Anyang Textile:

> No, I think democracy in our enterprise would be a great thing if we could use it to deal with our main problems. And ask any worker right now, they'll tell you without blinking an eye: our main struggle is keeping our jobs. I've been here how many years and I have to "hope" that the manager lets me keep my job? That's not democracy for the workers. If we had democracy in our workplaces, this would not be a problem to begin with. No workers would say the way to solve the problems our enterprises face in China is to lay off workers when they didn't cause the debt crises in the first place! So no, I'm not saying at all that democracy or democratically managing our enterprises is a meaningless concept. It *should* happen, only not like this, (Anyang Textile machine worker 2, November 2000)

Democracy at the point of production was only valuable to them if it guaranteed certain basic rights that socialism had always promised SOE workers in China. With or without workers' democracy, that was a fundamental obligation of the SOE to SOE workers in China.

The women workers I interviewed recalled the election of the director, but stated that he only lasted a year. Thereupon, they explained, the factory encountered more losses and production stoppages. The company lacked inputs like cotton because of capital shortages, which was closely related to the problem of corruption in the enterprise. When the most recent director took over, the government made a series of special loans to buy raw materials, which accounted for the subsequent turnaround of the company. Without the loans, the women believed there was little likelihood of a revival.

With respect to the functioning of the WRC, the women production workers expressed satisfaction in a sense. Representatives do try to represent workers' interests and relay workers' sentiments to enterprise cadres; however, they are generally ineffective. On minor production-related issues, such as eating schedules, the WRC can occasionally make some impact. However, in areas of real power-related matters (i.e., important production strategies, management approaches, work pace, etc.), they have little capacity to make changes.

In any event, they noted that WRC meetings are only once a year, and workers do not know much about the content. Production-related issues are all decided on by senior managers and cadres; the WRC has little to say about such matters. "There doesn't seem to be much need for a WRC," one female line worker exclaimed at one point. "It has no real relationship to the workers. It's just a formality" (Interview with Anyang Textile women worker 3, October 2000). The attitude of these women workers confirmed the findings of Zhang (2001) that I discussed in the previous chapter. Workers have a sense that democratic management would be about something that should protect workers, and in this sense it falls far short:

> What's the point of their democratic management or even saying they have that? It's not that great a concern to me, but I know for other workers who are facing layoffs (*xiagang*), it's a really unfair situation. I don't think workers should have to worry about being laid off, not if they really are serious about their so-called democracy. I just think it's a real problem and they deserve better. I wish there was a way out of the situation; it just seems unfair. Luckily I'm young; I can leave, so many can't. (Anyang Textile women worker 1, November 12, 2000)

YELLOW TIGER WIRE TUBING FACTORY IN XINXIANG

Managers at Yellow Tiger Wire Tubing Factory (hereafter called Yellow Tiger) stated in interviews that their enterprise was a producer of spare parts for refrigerators and air conditioners in the small city of Xinxiang, located roughly 60 miles from Zhengzhou.[18] Its workers were highly skilled, and many even had college degrees. Its products were regarded as some of the best in the country, and the company was also said to be well known in Asia. Yellow Tiger exported to foreign markets and was, at the time of interviews, the second largest payer of taxes in Xinxiang. Yellow Tiger was a small enterprise that employed only 200 to 300 workers when it began operations in 1974. At the time of the interviews in late 2000, the company employed about 1,300 workers. A manager explained that in the early 1990s the company began to experience debt problems and was having trouble paying workers' wages:

> The fact is this director Cao was in a lousy relationship with the workers. They didn't trust him and the problem of the debt didn't do anything to increase their faith in him or his decisions. Morale was going downhill and fast. This is when the idea for a change in the leadership was needed and that the new leader should be democratically elected. Something had to be done in any event and this way seemed to work best. (Yellow Tiger manager, September 4, 2000)

It was widely felt that an election, with guidance from city leaders, would be the best way to restore worker confidence and improve the company's competitiveness. According to officials and managers, in 1994, the factory director (subsequently known as the CEO after conversion to shareholding corporation status) was 'democratically elected.' One senior manager declared during an interview quite excitedly,

> Now that we have democratically reformed our management system and there are new markets coming to China as soon as we sign the WTO agreement, we're quite optimistic about our future opportunities to expand and increase our production. (Yellow Tiger manager 3, September 5, 2000)

INTERVIEWS WITH YELLOW TIGER WORKERS

Mr. Yang, a 36-year-old electrical worker, stated that in a period of high unemployment in SOEs, he felt lucky to work and bring in 500 to 600 Yuan a month.[19] Yang stated that his impression of the Yellow Tiger history differed from those provided by managers. He contended that the enterprise never was in high debt in the 1990s. If it was experiencing losses, it was still able to pay out wages to workers. Yang claimed that the then factory director, surnamed Cao, was not removed because his relationship with workers was bad, but rather because officials no longer supported him. This was more than likely tied to his youth and lower level of education, which reflected badly on an enterprise that was performing well and increasing in its stature among competitors. When the company organized a 'selection committee,' consisting of company cadre, city cadres, and representatives from the Yellow Tiger WRC, they narrowed down the field to three candidates and then workers chose the new director from that list.

Yang did agree that Yellow Tiger's productivity and competitiveness improved quickly when the new manager instituted reforms to make the company more transparent. A new management system was devised that emphasized efficiency and input from workers, modeled on the Japanese lean management philosophy. The practice of frequently treating cadres and visitors to lavish dinners and gifts was ended. Workers responded positively to both the new style and the increase in company productivity.

When pressed to describe the democratic election process, Yang responded that he actually knew little about the 'democratic election' of the company director and was a bit surprised to hear of such an event. He stated that the present director, surnamed Li, was basically appointed by local officials. Although the managers claimed that a 'democratic policy decision committee' had been formed, this worker recalled that shop floor or mid-level managers chose most representatives.

Yang seemed to possess a somewhat contradictory ambivalence toward this process, which I asked him to clarify. He rejected the claim that democratic management had much to do with the productivity of the company. More likely, he countered, the quality of the commodities the enterprise produced explained the enterprise's condition, which itself is related to the good foundation that the company had for many years before 'democratic elections.' As for worker participation in management, Yang's response was now markedly cynical; it was here he was most explicit about his suspicions about the way managers and the director had explained the impact of democratic management on Yellow Tiger:

> I guess what I'm trying to say is that we workers have no demands and no enthusiasm for participation in any event and why should we? Even if they wanted to concern themselves, there's nothing they could change. Under the present economic conditions, with things around the country not going too well for SOE workers, workers' demands are fewer, only concerning themselves with getting wages. By that I don't mean better wages, I just mean, very simply, any wages! (Yellow Tiger worker 1, September 27, 2000)

He went on to elaborate, asserting that if conflicts ever occurred between managers and workers, workers would never turn to the union because 'all they do is send little gifts out during Chinese new year to us and not much else.' Then when asked if the problem of democracy in China's SOEs was shaped by the ongoing plague of corruption by directors and cadres, Yang opined with nary a hint of sarcasm:

> We pray the director is treating many clients to dinner! All we care about is getting our salary, and if that helps, then so be it! Indeed, a director who is able to keep the enterprise running because of his skills of wining and dining those who invest, by all means may he be as skilled in the art of corruption as possible! (Interview with Yellow Tiger Worker Yang, October 2000)

Mr. Yang provided a fascinating view into the mindset of a Chinese SOE worker at the start of the 21st century. On the one hand, he seemed almost complacent. However, his words are laden with contempt that only came out slowly as the conversation moved forward into the early morning, one that pointed an accusing finger at the official discourse of workers' democracy in China. As he put it just before we finished our interview:

> Democratic management, fine. What about the democratic right to a job? That's what we're supposed to have first and foremost, no? This is a socialist state owned enterprise with Chinese characteristics, no? If we don't have that, the democracy in the enterprise is not one that has much relevance to us as SOE workers. For now all we can do is get by and hope to make it to retirement with a pension. (Interview with Yellow Tiger Worker Yang, October 2000)

Another production worker, Mr. Zhao, a 38-year-old male assembly line worker who had worked at Yellow Tiger for 15 years, was optimistic about the prospects of shareholding, noting that if workers were called on to buy stock in the company, they usually did so and earned dividends. However, he felt that he and his coworkers were not inclined to think about democratic participation as something that had great relevance to their most pressing needs as SOE workers. The factory had a pretty good record taking workers' suggestions and besides:

> As long as the company is able to pay wages, we're not concerned about much else. Whether or not our suggestions are implemented isn't something that matters to us. Workers are most concerned about whether or not the company is going to go bankrupt. At present, democratic management can't guarantee that the company won't go broke in the future. Obviously that is what it should do. Our factory continues to produce these days because it still has the support of the city government and the banks. We work hard because we're afraid the enterprise might go broke otherwise, not because we have any more say in our enterprise's affairs than another SOE or even a privately owned company! (Interview with Yellow Tiger Worker Zhao, October 2000)

On the face of it, it would appear that workers such as Zhao display classic traits of apathy, with little or no trace of any of the discourse of democracy. However, looked at through a slightly different frame, implied throughout his discussion was a conviction that democratic management only has meaning if it can guarantee an SOE worker's right to a job. Here, then, democratic management actually is a notion that is deeply socialist in meaning and used, even when it appears rejected as farcical, to reject the dominant and core expectations of workers in the period of transition from state socialism—namely, that they give up their claims to the right to a job by virtue of working in an SOE. When I asked Zhao whether he thought it was possible to have democratic management and layoffs, he looked at me with a look of little more than bemusement.

XINXIANG WIRELESS ELECTRONICS FACTORY ADMINISTRATIVE CADRES ON DEMOCRATIC MANAGEMENT AND SHAREHOLDER CONVERSION

Two senior managers and a union chief informed me in separate interviews that the Xinxiang Wireless Electronics Factory, a producer of wireless communication products that employed about 1,500 workers, had carried out a democratic election of the company director in 1994 (Interviews with manager Yao and Liu, Xinxiang Wireless Electronics Factory, October 2000). The company carried out this election due to heavy economic losses that it suffered throughout the 1990s. These losses were caused by the practices of the then director and his team of managers, who were too interested in maintaining good political relationships and not concerned enough with production in competitive markets. Although the company experienced losses, it was able to keep up payments of wages, but this was a precarious situation that could not be tolerated for much longer due to the threat of losing access to credit. He also was blindly investing company funds in new areas that had nothing to do with the factory's production, but promised quick profits. Actually, he was investing in products that had little future, but provided him with opportunities to profiteer.

The union chief explained that workers wanted to have the chance to elect their own factory director and put the factory on a new road to becoming competitive (Interview with union chief Hao, Xinxiang Wireless Electronics Factory, October, 2000). After electing a new factory director in 1994, the factory turned around rather quickly, with investments in appropriate products that ensured profitability. This worked to stimulate workers' interest in productivity, which in turn spurred a desire to convert the company to shareholding corporation form. Workers and managers, Hao explained, both enthusiastically invested in stocks since profits created the basis for dividends. Workers now had a chance to vote through their stock purchases in addition to benefitting from the extended power their WRC won during final negotiations for the shareholder conversion plan. (Interviews with manager Yao and Liu, Xinxiang Wireless Electronics Factory, October 2000)

INTERVIEWS WITH WORKERS ON
DEMOCRATIC MANAGEMENT AT XINXIANG
WIRELESS ELECTRONICS FACTORY

A 48-year-old sales division worker, Mr. Li, with 32 years seniority claimed that, in fact, the director who was 'democratically elected' was not elected through the WRC. Instead, he was basically selected through a process that was dominated by the city government. From that point until 1998, when the company became a shareholding corporation, there were no more 'elections.' In 1998, the company leadership passed a resolution whereby stockholders' representatives voted for the board of trustees, which then organizes the enterprise leadership. This maneuver was what was referred to at the beginning of this chapter as the 'Employees—Director—Supervision' system, created for SOEs that became subject to shareholder control.

Since the democratic selection, Li agreed that the company's performance improved: New products were developed with better market potential, and workers' level of motivation increased as a result. The WRC was now selected and reelected every three years. Since the democratic selection, Li felt that the company had become much more transparent, the quality of management was improved, and the enterprise had performed much better in sales.

However, the system of stock ownership has certain weaknesses, especially for the smaller investors, because there is no security, which Mr. Li explained:

> If bad decisions are made, the small investor can lose quite a bit. There should be small investors' representatives on the board of trustees. Of course the system has certain advantages for workers, since they can receive dividends at the end of the year in addition to their wages. But that's not why workers invested, if they did; they were more motivated by their tendency to do what the government says they should do. If it were only workers of their own accord demanding shareholding conversion, the government wouldn't approve it actually. (Interview with Worker Li, Xinxiang Wireless Electronics Factory, October 2000)

Mr. Li's view was critical of the idea that shareholding could bring workers greater power:

> Oh yes, I'd love to have more say through the WRC or the investors' representative on the WRC, are you kidding? We should have that. We aren't just investors after all. We're workers in this SOE and they shouldn't forget that. But actually I don't expect that will happen. After all, ok, we have a representative on the board. Great, but they can still fire us maybe. Or lay us off even worse. So, what power do we have really? If we have democratic management as they say, why can't we

protect our job? That's what I want, otherwise, this shareholding is just a share of a private company in which I have no rights whatsoever. (Interview with Worker Li, Xinxiang Wireless Electronics Factory, October 2000)

In this passage, note how Mr. Li takes the discourse of workers' democracy in China and engages it like other workers in a way that is rich with the socialist idea that a job is not merely a mechanism to secure a wage or a dividend share, but a fundamental right, his core identity as an SOE worker. He takes the official discourse of workers' democracy and uses it against itself even as he embraces the dividends he might earn from a 'shareholding' company.

A 51-year-old production worker with 31 years seniority, surnamed Zhou, stated that the 1994 selection was not direct democracy. He contended instead that it was a matter of the city government evaluating several candidates. In the end, the vice-director was *chosen*, not elected, and the WRC was not involved. In 1998, the director became the CEO, and the enterprise was transformed into a shareholding corporation without an election. Thereupon he explained the factory only produced one good, which was both marketable and the basis of the company's success. He continued,

And, of course, the companies that make our product are not that many in number, so we dominate the markets. But the older workers have mostly been forced to quit or been laid off. Now we mostly employ younger temporary workers (*lingshigong*). The result is a company culture of looking out for yourself if you're a worker and concentrated authority in the hands of the factory director. The director frequently threatens workers who complain to him, "If I can't take care of you, I'll deal with your wife." Older workers are kept from working, whether they have issues with him or not. The factory has basically become his factory. (Interview with Worker Zhou, Xinxiang Wireless Factory, October 2000)

The notion, inherent in state-socialist transition in 1990s China—namely, that enterprise directors should have more power like their counterparts in capitalist economies—was greatly resented by Mr. Zhou. As the conversation turned to the matter of democratic management, he first told me that the company was more transparent now, and that the WRC elections played a role in that. However, as with other interviews, I found that as the discussion carried on, Zhou revealed attitudes that showed him to be deeply critical of the lack of substance in the process that is referred to as democratic management by cadres. Toward the end of our conversation, he was a little more forthcoming on his attitude toward the WRC:

The WRC is basically chosen at the whim of the managers and some are chosen by workers, though not by secret ballot. So workers don't

really think it's something important and don't really care who is chosen as representative. So the quality of representation is pretty per-
functory. (Interview with Worker Zhou, Xinxiang Wireless Factory,
October 2000)

When the Xinxiang Wireless was converted into a shareholding corporation, the company leaders were the same as before. The shareholders selected the CEO. Most workers did not buy shares; the majority were
bought up by leaders. It seemed to Mr. Zhou that conversion to shareholding should bring about some kind of benefits, like starting a new product
line or dividends to the workers. But because workers did not buy in, there
were no real benefits to mention. Mr. Zhou was retired early, so his life has
no security and he could not find a new unit to take him:

> That left me with no choice but to turn my labor relationship over to
> the employment center, since the city government wants to make our
> company take responsibility for its own losses and gains, so the com-
> pany doesn't care about what happens to me, nor the city government.
> And the union doesn't speak out on behalf of workers—how can it
> since it's representing the Party's policies in any event? In my opinion,
> the enterprise's operations should be transparent and major decisions
> should have to be approved by workers' representatives. Now it's just
> a matter of the director having complete control. The present leader-
> ship is more like a mafia group. The conversion was just a policy to
> transfer power to the director. The workers have no security or power
> and the future is bleak. Our biggest concern is our rights, especially
> livelihood security. Only when there is true democratic management
> can the workers have security and the ability to exercise rights and
> protect them.

Again the linkage between the enterprise's duty to workers to provide
work and social security stands in contrast to the perspective required of
a wage worker who accepts that, no matter how great the remuneration,
one's fate as a laborer is invariably up to the market. A wage worker might
have the right to organize in a union and fight politically for certain protections from markets, but, as no less than Adam Smith put it in the Wealth
of Nations, wage workers must simply accept that capitalists in markets
have a far greater capacity to influence the outcome of struggles over the
character of capitalist labor markets. In these cases, we hear workers like
Mr. Zhou rejecting the idea that investors should have the lion's share of
say in the enterprise. Workers' representatives, even in shareholding corporations that are still SOEs juridically, should retain power vis-'a-vis matters
concerning workers' fates. He could be no less clear about what he meant
by 'fate,' a direct reference to what the government no longer cares about in
his opinion—namely, whether SOE workers have work.

PATTERNS IN INTERVIEWS WITH HENAN SOE
WORKERS ABOUT WORKERS' DEMOCRACY

It might be tempting to take away from these interviews the impression that SOE workers have little interest in workers' democracy or that it does not inform the way they think about the changing relations of production that transition from state socialism is imposing on them. Indeed, the workers I interviewed in these companies seemed far more interested in hanging onto their jobs long enough to be able to access pensions when they retire. However, there is reason to doubt such a conclusion and to regard it as jumping the gun. In fact, embedded in these interviews with Henan SOE workers was a sense of what workers' democracy should be, and that sense was quite different from what enterprise cadres hold. For the latter, it was a means to rationalize the Party's attempt to sever its fiscal and social responsibilities for the fate of both the SOE as an institution and those persons who produced the SOE's surpluses that were used to develop Chinese state socialism for decades—its workers. For these workers, transition or no transition, markets or no markets, an SOE had an obligation to workers to provide jobs; workers' democracy, be it in whatever form, was something they believed should be intimately linked to that principle. That is, workers' democracy was about far more than simply elections; it was about a social contract that once broken renders the concept of workers' democracy glaringly lacking in substance. On the one hand, SOE workers whom I interviewed expressed great pessimism toward the way workers' democracy performed as an institution in the period of transition, offering comments like, 'What good would it do?' Yet if one scratches beneath the surface, one finds that they do not reject the concept. Indeed, what one finds is the potential for the utilization of a discourse of workers' democracy by SOE workers as a tool to do something they did not have to do in China for nearly the past half a century: fight to save jobs. As I try to show in Chapter 7, SOE workers in China drew on that potential when faced with bankruptcies and fraudulent 'privatizations' in the mid- to late 1990s.

6 Workers' Democracy versus Fraudulent Privatizations

INTRODUCTION

Throughout the 1990s, the discourse of workers' democracy was a resource that China's SOE workers who collectively and actively resisted the terms of small- and medium-sized SOE privatization could and did employ widely. As one labor activist put it to me, this was "immediately evident insofar as the institution through which SOE workers challenged privatization was their WRC."[1] It seemed apparent that the SOE workers whom I interviewed believed that workers' democracy could help them resolve their crises under the right conditions. However, they advocated for a workers' democracy that was truly a product of workers' discussions and elections, independent of and/or in opposition to the Party or capitalists' interests in privatization in China.

The literature on SOE workers' collective organization in response to privatization in China tends to suggest that their resistance is held back by an underdeveloped appreciation of liberal citizenship rights as a basis to fight for the redress of their core grievances as they confront the deleterious impacts of privatization. However, I found something different from my interviews with SOE workers who protested privatization in China at the turn of the new century. These workers' ideas about workers' democracy and resistance to SOE privatization extended beyond the interpretive framework of citizenship rights. This was the case because, even if implemented, such liberal concepts of citizenship rights are insufficient to resolve the crises in the SOEs, which workers face as structurally determined price tags of China's transition from state socialism.

The cases in this study also show that, in the moment of resistance to privatization in the Chinese SOEs, the discourse of workers' democracy provided (at least in these instances) a terrain on which workers could battle assumptions that have provided the ideological justification for the social relations of China's transition from state socialism. That is, this discourse was not merely one that China's ruling cadre elites used to impose a new set of class relations of domination on China's workers; it was also one that China's SOE workers have used to attempt to resist and supersede those relations. The contending interpretations of workers' democracy that are evident in this chapter also throw into relief the uncertainty of the Chinese transition from state socialism. They further suggest the sources of SOE workers' failure, since the 1990s, to develop a powerful and more coordinated SOE workers' movement, which is discussed in Chapter 7.

The data in this chapter are based on interviews I conducted in November 2000 with SOE workers who became protest leaders in the moment of fraudulent SOE privatizations in Zhengzhou, the capital city of Henan Province. These interviews reveal that, in the moment of collective protest against privatization, workers made use of central concepts and institutions that constituted the discourse of workers' democracy in China. As they did so, they not only used this discourse to justify their right to job security, but also the right of workers to democratically control state-owned factory assets.

SOE WORKERS' CRISES AND THE PROBLEM OF CITIZENSHIP RIGHTS

Starting in the mid- to late 1990s, the problems faced by China's SOE workers became too intensely volatile (and violent) to ignore. To the surprise of some, in contrast to the Tiananmen Square protests, which were organized by students and an emerging urban middle class, now it was China's SOE workers who were frequently demonstrating the highest levels of collective protest as the new millennium approached. A spate of articles and books in both academia and the media energetically addressed and expressed a rapidly growing interest in Chinese SOE workers' resistance to the excesses of neoliberalism (Blecher 2003, 2005; Chan 2001; Chen 2003, 2006, 2007; Hurst 2004; Lee 1999, 2000a, 2000b, 2002, 2007; Philion 2005; 2007; Tong 2005; Unger and Chan 2004). It is safe to say that the East Asian Financial Crisis (EAFC), which began in late 1997, alerted social scientists to the ongoing crisis of China's SOE workers. This led to a reconsideration of something that had largely been overlooked until the crisis—namely, the contribution that SOE workers might make in shaping China's future policy directions for economic development.[2]

As this literature evolved, a focus formed on the problem of 'rights,' especially the ways in which SOE workers made use of liberal legalistic understandings of rights, which seemed to accompany the prominent role assigned to private capitalist investment in the Chinese economy. In this view, China's SOE workers' resistance to coercive production relations could occur with greater effectiveness because workers could now put forth citizenship and autonomously based rights demands. These demands could only be effectively articulated as Chinese workers came to identify themselves as possessing individual and collective interests that diverged from enterprise administrators. Such an interest-based framework of labor-management's relations implicitly moved away from social obligation-based ideologies of labor-management harmony embedded in the Maoist period state-socialist enterprise labor relations (Gallagher 2005).

However, SOE workers' protests, despite their dramatic frequency and militancy, remained characterized as 'nostalgic,' 'desperate,' 'survival oriented,' and, simultaneously, operating with forms of consciousness that 'reproduced the ideologies of capitalism.' China's SOE workers were regarded as only weakly assimilating market-embedded notions of legal citizenship rights that could strengthen workers' organizational capacity (Lee 2000a). Furthermore, Blecher (2002) contended that Chinese workers' protests lacked a militant character because they essentially submitted to the logic of capitalist markets. Once state workers received some form of compensation as a means to redress grievances, their protests and challenges to neoliberal policies were neutralized.[3]

Ching Kwan Lee (2007, 9) took the lead as the most prolific sociologist to document and analyze the transition of consciousness among China's SOE workers:

> In the rustbelt, I have found "protests of desperation," in which veteran state workers, staking their claims on moral and legal grounds, primarily take their grievances to the street, leveraging a strategy of political bargaining by shaming local officials and disrupting traffic and public order, and make only occasional and individual forays into the legal system. Rhetorically, workers' insurgent claims draw on political discourses of class, Maoism, legality, and citizenship. Such protests coexist with a survival strategy that relies on the remnants of socialist entitlements, primarily allocated welfare housing, and on informal employment. (x).

Lee's field interview-based research contrasts SOE workers in the north with those in the south, a large number of whom migrated from rural regions to private-sector work in the cities. The latter, she argues, more naturally and aggressively resort to discourses that stress legally bound citizenship rights. For migrant workers in southern China, conditions of work are shaped more directly by for-profit markets, which it is argued gives rise to a different type of consciousness from northern SOE workers, one that is more citizenship oriented. Throughout Lee's work is a theoretical frame that conceptualizes state workers as being less likely to possess a consciousness that can substantively challenge the new and distinctly uneven balance of power between labor and capital under China's neoliberal turn from state socialism. Lee contends that, although China's SOE workers also engage a rights-oriented rhetoric, their actions are more rear guard in nature than private-sector workers in the south. As a result, she conceptualizes the former as seeking not so much to transform labor relations as much as to salvage severance payments from a government they expect to fulfill its socialist 'duty' to help workers cope with unemployment. Despite their passionate levels of anger, one has to conclude from this analysis that SOE workers lack a sense of interests that are distinct from their employer, thus their underdeveloped assertion of rights. Or even when China's SOE workers *do* engage legal rights, their faith in such rights are weak because of their (quite accurate) belief that the law in China is not taken seriously by judicial officials who hear cases that workers bring to court.

Chen Feng (2007) has also provided important and rich research on the state of Chinese SOE workers' fights against forced and unpopular privatizations in the past decade. He likewise chooses the problem of rights as the key theoretical prism through which to interpret the sociological significance of China's SOE protests. Chen stresses how individual rights are overvalorized at the expense of collective rights in Chinese labor law in the post-Mao period. Chen meticulously delineates the protection of individuals' bargaining rights that Chinese labor law currently accords workers and finds that they are far greater than rights Chinese workers enjoy at the collective level:

> (W)hile Chinese labor legislation stipulates workers' individual rights regarding contracts, wages, working conditions, pensions, and so on, it fails to provide them with collective rights, namely, the rights to organize, to strike, and to bargain collectively in a meaningful sense. The exercise of collective rights, of course, does not necessarily change the basic structural disadvantage of labor in a capitalist economy where employers determine the nature and availability of jobs, but as labor history in other social contexts shows, it is crucial for the development of "class institutions" . . . that can countervail managerial as well as state power for workers' interests. Labor rights in China are defective in that they contain no constitutive laws that enable workers to assert themselves as a collective power capable of effecting labor relations and effectively safeguarding their individual rights. (60)

Chen's cautionary note about structural advantages enjoyed by capital that do not necessarily change, even with the assertion of collective rights by workers, is one I take up later. The theoretical point of reference for Chen is Marshall's (1992) conceptualization of citizenship rights, whose component civil, social, and political categories all play a role in the historical development of 'industrial' citizenship (Chen 2007). The critical means through which industrial citizenship (in the form of political representation by parties that could advance welfare-state protections) were won by working classes was through the collective rights won by trade unions to organize and represent workers' interests (Chen 2007). SOE workers in Maoist China enjoyed many social rights and protections, in the best cases even beyond welfare-state protections in most advanced capitalist societies (Li 1994).

However, Chen notes that Chinese workers lacked any developed sense of their collective rights to self-organize during the Maoist period of state socialism. When faced with crises brought on by the privatization wave that began in the mid- to late 1990s, SOE workers found themselves in a quandary. SOE workers had constitutional rights accorded workers in privately invested enterprises to individually bargain over the conditions of their work. However, when faced with crises of mass unemployment that hit the SOE sector in the mid- to late 1990s, such individual bargaining rights provided state workers with little legally guaranteed collective means to fight the kinds of corruption and outright theft of state property by China's new class of 'gangster capitalists' (Holmstrom and Smith 2000). Likewise, due to low levels of collective organization, the level of promised state forms of relief for SOE workers faced with crises of unemployment are either minimal or minimally implemented (Chen 2007).

At the same time, Chen (2007) notes, there do exist collective rights encoded by Chinese labor law that give SOE workers rights that state or private-sector workers in most advanced capitalist states would envy:

> Workers' lack of collective rights is a crucial factor that contributes to their powerlessness in the face of the force of the market. Collective rights are not totally absent from China's labor legislation. Both the Labor Law and the Trade Union Law, for example, contain clauses on the rights to organize although defined vaguely and abstractly. There are also administrative decrees on collective bargaining. *The government also stipulates that SOEs' restructuring scheme must be approved by Staff and Worker Congresses (SWCs).* But all these rights are circumscribed by various political and institutional factors that have made them either unenforceable or hollow. (65–66; italics added)[4]

Chen (2006, 2007) and Philion (2007) have argued that the role of the WRCs have been prominent in SOE workers' protests against fraudulent privatizations in China. However, Chen notes that such institutions remain weak, lacking strong governmental support as a means to fight privatization-associated forms of primitive accumulation. Chen's argument is twofold: (1) labor law provides little in the way of protection of workers' rights to fight perceived injustices associated with privatization and neoliberal developmental policies more generally, and (2) the laws that already exist to collectively empower SOE workers are minimally enforced by China's Party state.

WHAT RIGHTS? WHOSE CITIZENSHIP?

Both levels of argumentation are needed. However, is either level sufficient at cracking open contradictions that exist throughout the literature on China's state workers' protest consciousness? For example, it appears taken for granted that, with either a greater appreciation of liberal notions of legally codified rights and self-interests or greater structural (i.e., legally encoded) guarantees and enforcement of collective rights, China's SOE workers would necessarily be able to advance their class interests in a period of neoliberal economic overhaul. However, the stress on citizenship rights, which is prevalent in so much of the literature on China's working class today, has come under criticism from theorists of globalization and neoliberalism (Bartholomew 2006; Lin 2006; Harvey 2006). These theorists argue that the emphasis on diverse bundles of citizenship rights in a period of global neoliberal restructuring has resulted in an undertheorization of the balance of class power embedded in another fundamental right that is married to citizenship rights and that reigns supreme—namely, the right of property.

The argument on the nature and value of rights for the working class is not a new one and has been of concern since the origins of capitalism. Marx's *On the Jewish Question* posed one of the most forceful critiques of 'rights' under capitalism as long as the right to property remained supreme.[5] Often misinterpreted as an outright denial of the value of bourgeois rights won by workers in the transition from feudalism, Marx was in fact pointing out that a comprehensive analysis of the political-economic dynamics of capitalism would indicate that rights won by workers remain insufficient for actualizing the working class movement's goal of emancipation from the specifically coercive wage-labor relation. Laws cannot, given the structurally (i.e., juridically and militarily) enforced and sacrosanct character of private property, alter the built-in ruthless competition that devalues and punishes alternatives to private capital as the basis for fiscal growth (Harvey 2006). The same law that giveth with one hand can well taketh with the other.[6]

The problem at hand is not merely the imbalance of power between capital and labor, now generalized in the global arena. What Marx called 'bourgeois rights' or, in the modern vernacular, 'citizenship rights' do not address adequately the necessarily ruthless dynamic of capitalist competition and its impact on fiscal choices of either national or global bodies. This is the case despite the potential for universalizing labor law through globally negotiated trade treaties that involve global institutions that represent and advocate for the rights of workers (e.g., ILO, ICFTU) (Greenfield 1997, 1999). Under conditions of what have been terribly inexactly classified as 'globalization,'[7] in exchange for opening economies to global capitalist investment and markets, working classes in 'developing' countries are told they will reap the benefits of legally codified rights that did not exist under regimes that actively closed off markets with the aid of political authoritarianism. These rights are, then, to be engaged by workers who no longer have to submit to corrupt political bosses who monopolize both access to markets (including labor markets) and the means of physical violence.

However, as Habermas (1989) argued in *The Structural Transformation of the Public Sphere*, markets progressively deracinate the power of the public in the transition to capitalism and how so retains a particular relevance to societies in transition from noncapitalist modes of production:

> ... (T)he "unifying" system of mercantilism already established the beginnings of a privatization of the process of social reproduction in the positive sense: the latter might gradually evolve autonomously, that is, in accord with the laws intrinsic to the market. For in proportion to the increasing prevalence of the capitalist mode of production, social relationships assumed the form of exchange relationships. With the expansion and liberation of this sphere of the market, commodity owners gained private autonomy; the positive meaning of "private" emerged precisely in reference to the concept of free control over property that functioned in capitalist fashion. (74)

Harvey (2006) contends that the current enthusiasm about liberal citizenship rights as the ameliorative mechanism to redress the types of economic inequality and political injustice that global neoliberalism spawns undertheorizes the dynamic and systemic character of dominant social processes of capitalism:

> The positive sense of justice as a right has . . . been a powerful provocateur in political movements: struggles against injustice have powerfully animated movements for social change. The problem, of course, is that there are innumerable concepts of social justice to which we may appeal. But analysis shows that certain dominant social processes throw up and rest upon certain conceptions of justice and rights. To challenge those particular rights is to challenge the social process in which they inhere. Conversely, it proves impossible to wean society away from some dominant social processes (such as that of capital accumulation through market exchange) to another (such as political democracy and collective action) without simultaneously shifting allegiance from one dominant conception of rights and of justice to another. The difficulty with all idealist specifications of rights and of justice is that they hide this connection. (54–55)

It is exactly the nature of emancipation SOE workers can derive from primarily focusing on and struggling for legally bound citizenship rights, given the structurally shaped dominant processes of China's political economy of transition in the current period, which I critically interrogate in the case of Chinese SOE workers' struggles in Zhengzhou. I argue that, when tested, the 'citizenship rights' frame only partially addresses the source of the new social relations of coercion and dispossession that SOE workers faced during the 1990s as their enterprises were faced with privatization.

CASES OF RESISTANCE TO
PRIVATIZATION IN ZHENGZHOU

The case studies for this chapter bear certain similarities to the ones discussed in Chapter 5, in that they all are small- and medium-sized SOEs in Henan Province. These SOEs were likewise struggling to maintain production in the face of growing debt and layoffs. They were all located in the city of Zhengzhou, only a one- to two-hour train ride from the enterprises discussed in Chapter 5. However, the SOEs in this chapter experienced far more volatility and conflict, which resulted from choices that enterprise and Zhengzhou city cadres made as they sought to benefit from the CCP's national SOE policy of 'grasping the big and letting go of the small.'

Before assessing their significance, I first provide a brief exposition of three cases of what can only be loosely called 'privatization.' These served as the sources of interviews with workers' leaders of protests against the terms of restructuring in individual small- and medium-sized SOEs in Zhengzhou City in the late 1990s and early 2000s.

THE ZHENGZHOU PAPER FACTORY,
ZHENGZHOU, HENAN

The Zhengzhou Paper (ZZP) factory's decline is a story that is known throughout Zhengzhou City, not only because the level of collective protest that it attracted was so high, but because the circumstances of its degeneration have been experienced by SOE workers city wide.[8] From the mid-1990s, in line with the Party's policy toward SOEs of 'taking a firm grip on the large, letting go of small,' the Zhengzhou city government encouraged small- and medium-sized SOEs to resolve their manifold debt problems by finding a merger partner with whom to form share-based cooperative enterprises (*gufen hezuozhi*). Outwardly, this policy was supposed to head off the debt problem and its source—namely, inefficient management—by injecting fresh capital into the SOE and subjecting it to modern management techniques to revive profitability. Workers were guaranteed by law to be able to have final say in the matter of such transfers of ownership rights. They were also to be able to retain rights to the factories' assets in the event promises made in the process of the transfer were not kept. The reality, however, was a quite different matter.

The ZZP was established in 1958 as a producer of print paper. As of the 1990s, it employed 860 workers, of whom 171 were retired.[9] Its crisis began in 1995 when the factory, due to debt and the existence of one workshop that violated environmental regulations, was ordered to temporarily halt production. By the end of 1997, ZZP had endured almost three years of plant closure, except for three workshops that were rented out to private businesses, with over 80 percent of the original workforce out of work.

When workers' representatives received word that there were several companies who were willing to merge with ZZP, they expressed enthusiastic interest in any company that could save their SOE. On November 26, 1997, the WRC held a special meeting to meet with four merger candidates. Of the four, Fenhua Inc. attracted the WRC members' interest and unanimous approval choice as merger partner. Fenhua's leaders made a merger offer that promised to revive production and restore all employment positions, back pay, and pension obligations. ZZP workers proceeded to await the implementation of the merger agreement, which, after 8 months of waiting, was finally approved by the Light Industry Ministry, officially transferring registration of ZZP assets to Fenhua Inc., making ZZP now one of Fenhua's subsidiary companies.

However, Fenhua failed to live up to its side of the contract, especially provisions calling for it to contribute to a circulating capital fund, revive production, reemploy all workers, construct new workshops, and purchase new machinery and new warehouses. To make matters worse, Fenhua likewise reneged on its obligations to pay its share of subsistence relief and health fund contributions. As months of waiting for Fenhua to fulfill its end of the agreement dragged on, it became increasingly transparent that the merger was simply a device for Fenhua to absorb SOE assets at a cheap price. Only 20 percent of workers were reemployed in a workshop of the factory that was rented out to a private business. Finally, only two months after the merger was officially approved, Fenhua, with the cooperation of the original ZZP director, applied for and secured a loan using the factory's land as collateral without securing the approval of the WRC.

After waiting almost a year to see whether the situation would improve, anger with Fenhua drove workers to take new actions to defend the SOE. After trying unsuccessfully to secure a meeting with the Fenhua subsidiary director, 50 workers gathered and marched to the city government and Light Industry Ministry offices to present their grievances and petition officials for a resolution. As a result, Fenhua leaders and ZZP WRC representatives signed an agreement which stipulated that Fenhua not make any changes in its implementation of the merger agreement without consulting the ZZP WRC, consult the WRC for approval of any plans to sell or develop company land, abide by principles of democratic management in line with laws regulating SOE shareholding cooperatives, and allot subsistence relief to the workers. Soon thereafter, the Fenhua director declared at a mid-level management meeting, "This agreement is null and void. What was once known as ZZP is now Fenhua Inc., whatever I say goes!" Thereupon, Fenhua devised a number of rationalizations to fine workers involved in the petitioning activity that brought about the city government-brokered agreement, only sharpening the terms of the conflict.

After an unsuccessful attempt to meet with Fenhua management one more time, workers' leaders, now having completely lost any trust in Fenhua's intentions, proceeded to take up the task of investigating the origins of this merger partner. They discovered that the company was essentially slapped together just prior to the merger. Indeed, the Henan Provincial Commerce Ministry actually granted Fenhua a business license on the same day that the merger agreement with the ZZP WRC was signed. Suffice it to say, upon further investigation, it became clear to the WRC representatives that almost everything the workers were told about Fenhua from the get go was the product of invention. On October 19, faced with the reality that the WRC and ZZP workers had uncovered the truth about the merger's fraudulent basis, the Henan Light Industry Ministry organized an arbitration meeting between workers' leaders and Fenhua management, at which the Fenhua CEO refused to appear, sending instead the original ZZP factory director (now 'Fenhua general manager'); after four days of negotiations, talks broke off.

Fenhua then sent five board members to meet with and negotiate a new agreement with the ZZP WRC. The end product of this several-day meeting involving both workers' representatives and rank-and-file workers was a resolution passed overwhelmingly by the WRC on October 28, calling for the nullification of the merger and return of authority for ZZP operations to the ZZP WRC. However, on October 29, one of the Fenhua board members managed to secure a copy of the ZZP land ownership certificate, which alerted the WRC to the Fenhua board's interest in taking out a mortgage on the ZZP property. The WRC leaders sought out the Fenhua leaders and demanded an explanation, giving them a deadline to respond to their demands, at which time if unmet would result in defiant acts on the part of the workers. On November 3, police showed up at the factory in a standoff with workers whom Fenhua claimed were threatening to engage in terrorist acts against the city's electrical and water supply systems, which only further enraged the ZZP WRC and rank and file.

In May 2000, Fenhua, after many months at a time denying workers' subsistence payments, retirement pensions, and health insurance contributions, insisted that the only hope for workers to receive what was owed them in back payments and wages was to accept the selling of ZZP land. By June 2000, the stakes were clear in the eyes of the WRC and rank and file. There was little reason to believe Fenhua's claim that selling off the land would result in the workers retrieving lost payments or the revival of profit-making productive activities. Indeed, it was transparent that Fenhua's intention was to bankrupt the factory, thereby legitimizing the death of the ZZP as a SOE unit altogether and profiting from the sale of the land to real estate developers. The WRC and rank and file had already, by this point, petitioned government ministry officials in small and large groups over 30 times since the merger, with no change in the situation. On June 7, the WRC held a mass meeting and declared its intention to occupy the factory until the city forced Fenhua to return ownership of the ZZP back to the WRC. From this date until August 8, ZZP workers kicked out Fenhua representatives from the factory and collected rent payments from the one workshop that was still in production.

The occupation lasted a little over two months. When workers' leaders approached the Working Committee formed by the city government to seek a resolution to the standoff, they were told the committee was unable to resolve the workers' problem, that their action was illegal, and, in any event, that they were just taking orders from superiors. On August 7, two workers' leaders were detained and subsequently arrested by the police. On August 8, a force of some 500 police officers was amassed at the factory gates, forming a human wall leading to the factory, dispersing those inside, and surrounding the factory, thus enabling Fenhua representatives to retrieve locked files and damaging documentary evidence of wrong doing since the merger. Thereafter, some 40 workers were detained and questioned. In September, the Working Committee then ordered the ZZP workers to reelect its WRC. The workers elected the two worker leaders who were now in jail. The WRC continued to put out resolutions calling for the immediate release of the two leaders and for ownership of the factory to be turned over to the WRC. By March 2001, the city agreed to turn over ownership rights to the WRC, nullifying Fenhua's relationship with the ZZP.

YIBIAO AIR CONDITIONER FACTORY (YAF)

Aside from the commodity produced, the stories of YAF and the ZZP are strikingly similar. An employer of 300 workers, the YAF ran into problems of debt starting from the beginning of the 1990s that required a solution. The resolution would be merging with a company called Guotong Technologies Development Ltd. (Guotong), with whom a merger agreement was signed on February 27, 1997. Although a Singaporean company had made a bid for merger with Yibiao, a small private company that engaged in buying and selling of technologies aggressively sold itself to the Yibiao WRC by topping every condition of merger that the Singaporean company offered, making it irresistible in the eyes of the WRC. In return for merging with and securing control of YAF's assets valued at 40 million Yuan, Guotong agreed to pay off YAF's debt and reemploy workers. However, this company had a history of employing false estimates of its own assets to secure licenses, ownership certificates, and government approvals for mergers with other factories. This knowledge was possessed by a group of workers and lower level cadres; nonetheless, the factory director proceeded to accommodate Guotong by arranging to transfer and/or sell off machinery, parts, and remaining company possessions to ensure a low-assets appraisal. As a result, the factory lost its capacity to produce. Guotong proceeded to go back on its promise to invest 5 million Yuan in new production lines, rented out two office buildings near the factory to outside companies, forced workers to 'resign,' terminated labor contracts with 28 workers, and sent another 51 workers on vacation leave without salary.

In January 1999, YAF workers held a mass meeting to carry out a 'Democratic Evaluation.' At this meeting, the general sentiment was that Guotong lacked the means necessary to revive the SOE and that, aside from the factory director who became a Guotong general manager, Guotong was the only real beneficiary of the merger, almost overnight able to nab for itself a chunk of state assets. However, the workers at YAF, except for a small number who were 'reemployed' in odd jobs by Guotong (e.g., restaurant dishwashing, piecework clothing production), were transformed into 'orphans' presented with the constant threat of factory asset liquidation. Workers began making their objections known to Guotong by forming a 'Save the Factory Committee,' whose main duty was preventing the further sell-off of the company. Appeals to the Light Industry Ministry were to no avail; officials asserted that the factory no longer belonged to the ministry and that, in any event, there was no road back. In 2003, the WRC won its battle to annul the merger agreement with Guotong. At that point, the leadership was trying to figure out how to devise a workers' cooperative that can produce enough in value to make the enterprise's contribution to the retired workers' pension fund. However, the likelihood of that project reaching fruition was quite low because the leadership had been compelled to accept the debt that had accumulated since the mid-1990s, leaving them unable to find new sources of credit to fund any cooperative projects.

ZHENGZHOU POWER SUPPLY GENERATOR FACTORY (PSG)

The PSG, founded in 1956, had 1,725 employees, active and retired, and was at one point one of the largest tax contributors in Zhengzhou. The factory was a well-known supplier of medium-sized power supply generators to oil fields, machinery, and parts, with a workforce of 1,750 workers, of whom 600 were retired. In 1993, the Mayor of Zhengzhou appointed a new factory director (Shi) who managed to turn the originally quite successful SOE supplier to Chinese oil fields into a company torn apart by unprecedented debt. According to workers' leaders, the debt was artificially created[10] through a number of activities, including the disappearance of large bank loans intended for machinery investment, raising funds from worker 'investment' schemes designated for workers' housing construction that were siphoned off to unknown accounts, the selling off of materials and machinery at cheap rates, and the apportioning of production line management positions and profits to relatives. When workers petitioned Chen to audit Shi's performance record as factory director, as required by SOE law, he refused. Shi was instead automatically reassigned (and promoted) to a post in the city government. The situation with the next two directors followed this pattern, and by the end of 1996, under the direction of the mayor, the factory director declared the factory bankrupt. In early 1997, Chen had arranged for the factory to be 'purchased' by the Sida 'corporate group' at no cost. The deal was brokered on the condition that Sida take responsibility for the employment situation of all employees.

Similar to the ZZG and the YAF situations, workers at the PSG SOE also experienced a sharp decline in standards of living during this 'transitional period' starting from 1995 onward. However, unlike the case in ZZG and YAF, when Sida took over the factory, production did not shut down altogether. Although a sizable proportion of the original workforce was rendered redundant through a variety of mechanisms, including forced early retirements and layoffs, some 400 workers remained at work in the factory by 2000. However, by 1999, Sida was also making clear its intention to follow through on the city government's directive to carry out the selling off of the company property and land. Sida warned the remaining active workers that if it did not carry out its plan, they would lose their jobs and any chance for future security.

One key move on the part of Sida to facilitate the complete sell-off of factory property was the relocation of machinery to a smaller cross-town factory that also belonged to the PGS. With the 'relocation' of the factory, all that would remain was the finalization of the sell-off of the factory land to real estate developers. To Sida's disappointment, this plan would not proceed as smoothly as expected. Although Sida was able to coerce active workers into not resisting directly the relocation of plant property, it could not do the same with retired workers or preretirement age workers who had been laid off. From early 2000 on, there were numerous incidents of workers organizing in bands and making it impossible for Sida to go through with relocation of the machinery and materials used in the main plants. Critically, due to the large-scale nature of the PGS factory and machinery used to make power generator suppliers, moving machinery was not the kind of activity that could take place in a short period or in secret. As a result, mobilization took place to disrupt any attempts to 'set up camp' on the part of movers.

In March 2000, workers' leaders hung three banners from the factory gates stating, respectively, 'Steadfastly Stand by Mao Zedong Thought,' 'We Will Never Go the Way of Privatization,' and 'Long Live Jiang Zemin!' In June 2000, the mayor organized a 'working committee' to meet with the WRC to negotiate. Although the spirit of negotiations seemed serious, no follow-up action took place that changed the situation at PSG. Instead, Sida brought in Public Security Bureau (PSB) police to intimidate workers' leaders, telling workers they were operating at the behest of the working committee. In July, another working committee put together by the City Heavy Industry Bureau arrived on three separate occasions with PSB offices to inform workers' leaders that their actions were both wrongheaded and illegal, that the property of PSG belonged to the Sida 'Corporate Group' to which workers had no claims, and that the banners should be taken down immediately or the workers would face imminent arrest.

On July 27, Sida's 'general secretary' met with a mass meeting of PSG workers and relayed an announcement from the Vice Mayor (who sent additional PSB officers to be 'new working committee members' present at this meeting), stating that the government stood entirely by the Sida Corporate Group. Finally, in late August 2000, two workers' leaders were arrested. By mid-November, they were released. Thereafter, the conflict of PGS workers against Sida and the city government's attempt to remove factory machinery and materials from the main factory site in order to facilitate the sale of PGS land continued without resolution and sometimes turned violent as Sida remained determined to carry out the 'transfer' of factory machinery.[11]

SOE WORKER' STRUGGLES IN HENAN AND THE DISCOURSE OF WORKERS' DEMOCRACY

During interviews in Zhengzhou on the background and strategies of their protests, workers' leaders at these three embroiled SOEs defined the terms of struggle in harsh and polarizing language. These leaders made frequent reference to the need for challenges to privatization with every tool available to the 'democratically elected WRC', a phrase repeated and emphasized again and again:

> As long as we have the support of the workers in this struggle, there is no way that those thieves can take our factory away from us forever. The one thing we have in this battle is our right to this factory. And if those who promised us so much can't deliver on their promises, then we have a right to democratically run this factory ourselves and the government has an obligation to let us try. This factory is the workers' factory and no-one else's. (Air Conditioner Factory Leader 4, November 15, 2000)

However, the workers in the Zhengzhou cases were not at all enthusiastic about the official discourse, which featured endless calls for 'democratic management' in SOE factories that were in the process of undergoing restructuring throughout China. From their vantage, the official system of WRCs, 'democratic management,' and 'production control' were part of a general policy designed to rationalize the toppling of the SOE and the rights of SOE workers. Another leader from the PSG declared that, although democratic management was not something the Party took seriously, it was something that the SOE workers at PSG had to insist on to protect their interests as SOE workers:

> Our factory is a very prestigious one and we've supplied the whole country with our products. Now all that is forgotten? We have to do

something to make sure that the power of the SOE workers is recognized and respected as it once was. If we don't unite and do something about controlling this factory's future, no one else will. You can say you're supporting "democratic management" until you're blue in the face, but when it comes down to it this kind of democratic management isn't any more real than what is done in privately owned companies. So until you have a commitment to workers' security, we can't take their calls for democratic management seriously. But we *can and must* organize workers and let them decide how the factory should be run and keep outside interests from speculating on the assets we've built these many years. That's real democracy for workers. (PGS Workers' Leader #2, November 11, 2000)

Furthermore, incorporating ideas that had been popularized in the 1990s that plainly were borrowed from the Cultural Revolution days, workers' leaders espoused the need to revive production through the mechanism of 'democratic management/production control.' Ironically, the move toward privatization perhaps was necessary to create the space for that possibility. An exchange between a former cultural revolutionary and a workers' leader at the YAF showed that skepticism toward the official institutions of workers' democracy in China's SOEs could be grounds for developing a counterhegemonic understanding of the core concepts found in the official discourse of workers' democracy in China:

Mr. Jiang: All along they've been able to do as they want regardless of what the WRC said.

Mr. Yang: Well, isn't that the point? It's your factory. How can it be run in workers interests if workers can't even speak what they think, control what happens when managers make decisions? Who's factory is it anyhow?

Mr. Jiang: God Damnit! This is what it all comes down too, what we are doing *now* is what we should have been doing years ago, organizing a real WRC that is actively involved in factory matters, the whole factory. This we must do better in the future, our lives, our jobs hinge on our abilities to do so. (Interview with worker leader #2, YAF, Henan, September 2000)

Consistent with Lee's (1999, 2000a, 2000b, 2002) findings in the case of SOE conflicts in Liaoning Province, workers in the Zhengzhou cases became virtual experts in labor and enterprise law. In the process of challenging (and continuing to challenge) the illegal machinations of factory directors and government cadres, workers' leaders frequently employed the set of concepts that constitute workers' democracy. The use of legal frameworks has a dual function in these cases. On the one hand, it provides workers' leaders with a mechanism to challenge Party-based corruption in the period of transition, an obvious plus as Lee points out. At the same time, the law also provides the state with a device to channel workers' protests and to exhaust them because legal routes require long periods of time to reach a verdict and then verdicts are often only minimally enforced. Indeed, this was the trend in the three Zhengzhou cases, where workers' leaders chose to rely more on legal battles in the aftermath of collective protests.

In certain senses, it could be argued that the workers' leaders professed attitudes that, consistent with Blechers' (2003) research on disgruntled joint-venture workers in Tianjin, seemed to identify with official ideologies. Although they virulently resisted SOE restructuring in China, workers' leaders in Zhengzhou were also prone to express a discourse of workers' democracy that, at times reproduced the official interpretation of that concept in China.

Another instance, detailed in my field notes, reveals the link between levels of consciousness and strategies. My initial presumptions were that the workers' leaders were unaware or unwilling to let go of their faith in the Central Party, despite considerable evidence that the Party was not supportive of the respective struggles they led. While discussing strategies for protests with two workers' leaders at the air conditioner factory and three activist supporters about the plans to go it slowly, as opposed to pursuing more radical protests that might link up with other factories in similar predicaments, the following exchange took place:

Q.: You're making appeals to the central government leaders for help, what about combining forces with other factories?

Mr. Liu: That's not a good idea right now.

Q.: What makes you believe that?

Mr. Liu: It's not realistic.

Q.: Is it realistic to expect the central authorities to help out in your case since their privatization policies are what led to your troubles?

Mr. Liu: Probably not.

Q.: You mean you agree that the Central Party is not likely to help out or be sympathetic?

Mr. Liu: That's fair to expect, right.

Q.: I'm not clear then, what is the reason for appealing, then, to the Central Party? I don't mean to disagree necessarily, I'm just not sure what the point is of that if you're agreeing that it's not likely to elicit results.

Mr. Liu: It's like this, we know the limits, but workers aren't at the stage to recognize them or to raise the ante in terms of collective struggle.

Q.: You mean they don't understand their situation is as desperate as it is?

Mr. Liu: It's not that, you see. It's more a matter of working to the point of collective strategy means first removing other options. If they haven't been tested, workers see no reason to exclude them, number one. Number two, while we know well enough that the Party is not a friend of this struggle at the national level, association between different factories will occur only when workers really feel that the Party, at local and national levels, has nothing to offer their individual factories. Then they will respond in a way that would conform with that recognition. The best we can do at the moment is work with what we have ideologically and slowly lay bare the realities.

Q.: How do you account for it not being clear already?

Mr. Liu: The Party has the capacity to deal with individual factories with temporary solutions designed to mollify the anger state workers feel. Here some pension payments, there some severance payments for several months, and here again crackdowns against the leaders when needed. So it's a step by step process you see.

Often what was regarded as 'practical' won out over 'unfeasible' alternatives. This was not the case in the #1 Dyed Fabric Factory discussed in Chapter 5, where workers' leaders plainly were only able to play the role of aiding outside private investors in the establishment of a new labor discipline based on the priorities of world markets. In the Zhengzhou cases, where workers' leaders were much more confrontational with factory and government cadres, this also occurred. Even the ZZP leaders, probably the most radicalized of the three factories studied, saw no viable alternative to forming a shareholding corporation (*gufenzhi*) once they got the factory back from the Fenhua 'company.' Although the move to privatize initially was carried out through this mechanism, which they could see would lead to a redistribution of the assets into the hands of a small number of shareholders, they held, nonetheless, that this was the only route to go if they were to accomplish the goal of bringing the factory under the democratic control of the workers. When the contradiction was pointed out, leaders acknowledged that it was possible that workers could end up losing the capacity to democratically control the factory, but believed that there was little other choice given the realities that blocked opportunities to secure a loan from a state bank.

In the YAF case, workers' leaders were keen on how the lack of democratic management led to the collective state of crisis that YAF workers experienced beginning in the mid-1990s. Like their confreres at the ZZP, YAF workers' leaders were able, through their struggle, to secure back rights to the factory property. However, since winning back those rights, they were basically not able to do much with that victory, in large part, because, along with the property, they also won the problem of the factory's debt. Although YAF leaders recognized the link between the corrupt pilfering of their factory and the lack of involvement of workers in the factory's management, they were not nearly as likely to rely on the active participation of workers in the battle to win back their property. They instead organized a 'Save the Factory' committee, filling the role of the WRC in abstentia, which depended on the pledge of a small core of older skilled intellectual workers to carry out the campaign against Guotong.

We've organized, but we have to have a core group of workers like ourselves who have the means and skills to read enterprise documents, find out how we Guotong has lied to the workers and translate that into the basis for mobilizing against Guotong. We continue doing what the WRC would do if the enterprise were still in production. But we can't organize elections and organize on a mass basis, as much as we might like to do that.

As a result, their bargaining capacity never matched up to that enjoyed by the ZZP leaders, who relied on a newly formed elected union and WRC to develop a more mass-based strategy to pressure the city government to return possession of factory property rights to ZZP workers.

Finally, PPG workers' leaders at times appeared to be as militant as workers in the ZZP, yet they did not win nearly as much. Indeed, their face-offs with the police were the most violent. Nonetheless, they did not win back their collective right to their enterprise. In interviews, they were deeply bitter toward the city government for its betrayal of the rights of the PPG workers and its corrupt interest in selling off the company to speculators, which they contended was only a means to prevent workers' winning democratic control of the workplace.

This should be the workers' factory, they have put their lifeblood into this enterprise and it's an important one in this country! Look at how this company has failed. In China, aren't those intellectuals and corrupt cadres always calling for reforms? And who do they blame for the state enterprises failures, thus leading to their need to be "reformed"? The workers! Again, I ask you, look at how this enterprise has declined. All the evidence tells any reasonable person we did not cause the problems here. And we have all these 'reforms' to make enterprises democratic, how has this led to anything that looks like democracy in our workplace? They only want the democracy of the markets. If democracy doesn't call for workers direct involvement, it's a worthless reform and we want real reform, democracy that we SOE workers control. We're supposed to run this factory, not markets and corrupt cadres. And we'll fight for that. (Interview with Mr. Yao, PPG worker, November 2000)

However, in terms of organization, the leaders' strategy was primarily one of relying on leftist Party cadres in Beijing to pressure the central Party to intervene in their situation. This strategy was quite a natural one because, compared with all the other cases, the potential for mass mobilization of workers at the PPG was lowest due to the ability of the Sida 'company' to continue to provide some form of employment to a substantial fraction of PPG workers. About half of the active workforce was transferred to office-related jobs that paid lower but reliable wages for the interim. PPG workers' leaders found it least practical to focus on the problem of workers' democracy because, until they secured repossession of factory property rights, such matters remained abstract. In interviews, they were also the most likely to concede that they were primarily interested in winning compensation for retired workers as the price for transferring ownership of the land on which the factory sat.

It is not an accident that Chinese workers took so long to attempt to use a discourse of workers' democracy that radically challenged the official discourse of democracy. One of the leaders at the ZZP explained to me, when I remarked that the workers seemed to have waited quite long, that workers in China were traditionally passive and trusting of their leaders. I asked why this would be the case when ZZP workers as an example had a tradition of electing their WRC and involvement in production decisions. He replied,

> Well, in a sense that is true; but not enough so. During the 1980s they were taken care of, which was their main concern. As long as things were well, they just left management matters to representatives and authorities. They had little real motivation to become more involved in the affairs of managing the company. So really the WRC was not that active in representing workers' interests as much as helping out cadres with management related issues. Therefore, it was not until it was really very late that workers realized that relying on the company leaders was not a viable option, even though the leaders had already abused them for years through layoffs and corruption. Now we have a lot of 'catching up' to do and we can't do it if we don't sustain the power of our WRC as one that this time is truly controlled independently by the workers with freely elected representatives. (Interview with ZZP leader He, ZZP, Zhengzhou, September 2000)

Mr. He's comments indicate that a discernible development had taken place in the attitudes of these workers and their leaders toward workers' democracy in the late 1990s, in response to the conditions of production that the transition from state socialism imposed on them. That they chose this more radical discourse of workers' democracy is not the only noteworthy phenomenon here. It is just as noteworthy that the way Zhengzhou workers used the discourse shows a dramatically different understanding of the concept from those who hoped it would produce a new class of wage workers who surrendered to markets the right to decide what their role (if any) they should play in SOE production or national development for that matter. No longer, in these instances, were SOE workers in Zhengzhou using the WRC merely to curry the favor of directors. Instead, they engaged the discourse in attempts to save what they steadfastly believed was their core right as SOE workers in a socialist society—namely, a job.

THE ZHENGZHOU STRUGGLES AND SOURCES
OF CHINESE WORKING-CLASS WEAKNESS

However, the ideals of workers' leaders who led battles against privatization in Zhengzhou rarely developed to the point of formulating a plan for democratically administering production to sustain workers' livelihoods. To the contrary, workers' leaders at Zhengzhou Paper seemed to view both the ideal and the concrete practice of workers' democracy as part of their struggle against privatization. During interviews, workers' leaders laid out an idea they had come up with in the course of their struggles with Fenhua in order to ultimately secure severance or pension payments and even wages; workers' direct control of management of whatever future production took place in the factory could also contribute to employing workers. From their vantage, neither subordination to state ministries nor submission to capitalist markets were necessary or inevitable outcomes of their battle with Fenhua and city government officials, so long as principles of workers' democracy—through collective ownership and control—were the foundation of future enterprise activity. An interview with a WRC leader of the 2000–2002 battle for repossession of factory property rights underscored the importance of reinvigorating production with workers' democracy as the alternative to corruption:

> We know that the only way we can remain strong is to keep our WRC independent *and* responsible to the workers. We only have power if they are active in the decision making in the future. That is what we have that those who want to take away our factory don't enjoy. If we don't keep that as our fundamental means for fighting for our rights, we will have nothing. That means this factory is truly the workers' factory and what they decide is what goes, end of story. We don't just want to be told we we have rights to make our grievances known; we want control of this factory. (Interview with Workers' Leader Lin, Zhengzhou Paper, November 2000)

This belief in the WRC's role as both an independent organization and one that would actively enable workers was, according to workers' leaders, a means to preserve socialist values against market-dominant ones. That such thinking could be found in the Zhengzhou Paper case indicates that Blecher's (2005) and Lee's (2007) skepticism as to the consciousness of this sector of the Chinese working class might require some rethinking.[12] Nevertheless, the workers encountered a serious structural barrier to their strategy—namely, assumption of the enterprise debt that years of factory managerial and municipal corruption engendered. In a nutshell, the lack of state support put Zhengzhou Paper workers' leaders in a position of not knowing where to find the capital necessary to invest in production in order to provide state enterprise workers with social and job security.[13]

This pushed some leaders[14] in the direction of consigning their futures to restructuring along lines of corporate shareholding once rights to factory assets and land were restored to the WRCs:

> We'd like to convert the company to a shareholding form to receive financing for the enterprise once we've revived production. Of course we would like to secure funding from the state, but we recognize that there is no way we will be a candidate for that given our size and past history of debt. Our main obstacle right now is that we can't claim the factory as ours, therefore little progress can be made in protecting the workers' rights to subsist. (Interview with Zhengzhou Paper WRC chair, November 2000)

Unfortunately, the idea of seeking private stock purchasers as a means to save the factory contributed to undermining the WRC that had led the struggle for repossession of the factory for almost five years after the 2000 factory takeover. Because the debt problem would not be forgiven by the government banks, WRC leaders' confidence in their original plans for direct worker ownership and control diminished with every passing day. 'Realism' began to set in, as did the tendency to engage in factional blame games within the WRC. A marked turn away from their earlier ideals was revealed in the frenzied attempt by WRC representatives to find outside private investors to resolve their debt problems, in lieu of relying on workers' collective shareholding and investment as a means kick start production at the factory.[15] Interviews conducted in August 2005 reveal that a labor activist from Beijing frequently met with the Zhengzhou Paper WRC in 2002 to persuade them to stick to their plan to rely on worker control of the factory through equal ownership of stock and democratic management:

> This is what was most frustrating because this inclination to look to private investors for investments in the factory after the WRC retained its property rights to the factory is what undermined their solidarity. Many regarded the WRC's internal battles as a result of personality clashes. That certainly had something to do with it. But there was more to it than met the eye. Instead of turning to the workers to debate and decide on different options, they took it upon themselves to find outside sources of capital and invariably that led to WRC representatives identifying with the goal of bringing in private investors instead of strengthening their bond with workers. While I advocated strongly for making the issues known to the workers and letting them debate what route to go, in the end the representatives went each their own way frantically trying to win outsiders' interest in the factory and not involving workers in that process. This is what really led to the failure of the WRC to carry through their original plan to implement worker control of the factory after taking it back from the fraudulent "private

capitalists" who stole it from them. (Interview with activist Lai, Beijing, August 2005)

There was one other factor that added to the detour from the WRC's road to worker-controlled production after the battle to win back factory property rights was won—namely, the politicized orientation of older local[16] cultural revolutionaries who were interested in establishing a relationship with the various SOE workers' leaders who organized collective actions against fraudulent privatization in Zhengzhou from 1999 onward. However, their involvement, although most welcome from workers seeking outside support, added to the difficulties in developing the conditions needed to promote campaigns for worker-controlled factories:

Activist Lai: These older supporters who were activists in the Cultural Revolution have sought to rebuild a type of militant political atmosphere that they lived through 40 years ago. That's all well and good, but by not prioritizing what the workers' movement needed in Zhengzhou to grow through the establishment of real models of actual worker-controlled alternatives to privatization, they caused harm to the workers' leaders.

Question: How so?

Activist Lai: Their interests were in building their own social movement, primarily by encouraging workers' leaders to join their Mao Anniversary Movement.[17] There's no better gift to the police than to politicize the workers' movement in this fashion; it gives them the perfect excuse to round up workers' leaders. At a time when leaders are needed to develop the base of the workers' movement, their potential is wasted in jail *and* the general public comes to associate the workers' protests with taboo political causes, which they naturally fear. (Interview with activist Lai, Beijing, August 2005)[18]

The outcome of the struggle at Zhengzhou Paper had special significance because it was a guidepost for other SOE WRCs in Zhengzhou insofar as it had the greatest potential to create an alternative model to the general (nationwide) paradigm of workers' overall defeat or resigned acceptance of future privatization. The WRC is and remains a potential mechanism that, if organized independently of enterprise administrators or the Party, can be employed by Chinese workers to defend their interests (Chen 2006; Unger and Chan 2004). However, it meets a definite limit if a more thoroughgoing practice of workers' democracy that diverges from official ideology is not put into practice as a result. In cases where WRCs are saddled with old debts and ever-more competitive conditions for loan procurement, the possibility of defending the interests of Chinese SOE workers by unequal stockholding arrangements remained minimal at best.

Ultimately, the demands of the SOE workers in Zhengzhou, seen in the most militant form at the ZZP, were embedded in unofficial discourses of workers' democracy that were expressed during battles against privatization. Contra much of the literature on these kinds of protests that occurred in China in the late 1990s and early 2000s in small- and medium-sized SOEs, I contend that these demands were ones that access to greater citizenship rights would not necessarily make a great difference in securing. It is unlikely, given the political economy of transition in China at the moment, that even if laws were changed or bills passed by the People's Congress (even a freely elected one), such levels of reform could have resolved the economic crises that workers faced. States do not accede to such demands without the necessary resources to construct a comprehensive welfare state. However, if, through self-organization, SOE workers in Zhengzhou had developed a model of sustainable workers' democracy that could sustain itself, a base for such organization and coordinated self-support in the SOE part of China's labor movement might well have become a reality.

7 Conclusion
A Future Discourse of Workers' Democracy in China?

INTRODUCTION

The labor organizing and militancy that China's SOE sector experienced in the late 1990s continued into the first two to three years of the new millennium. However, since then, it has, for the moment at least, tapered out. In some ways, China's labor movement now appears to have returned to a similar state as the early 1990s. Chinese workers in the private sector are more likely to be found engaging in various forms of organizing in response to the specific conditions of exploitation that characterize their contribution to national development. In these battles, although China's private-sector workers today will fight for the right to organize freely elected unions, they do not fight for the kinds of workers' democracy that SOE workers demanded in the 1990s. Despite their determination to challenge their capitalist employers (be they foreign or Chinese) over issues of wages and scheduling, China's private-sector workers are far less likely to challenge the right of capital to monopolize ownership and control of enterprises.

There is no reason that private-sector workers around the world cannot challenge capitalists' property rights as privately held ones. Indeed, such a consciousness has on numerous occasions been achieved by private-sector workers around the world since the start of capitalism. Of course, private-sector workers in China are not faced with the abandonment of their enterprises, as in Argentina most recently, where in recent years workers have challenged the price of neoliberalism by taking control of enterprises from absentee owners and cooperatively managing factory production for markets (Klein 2007). If the sectors of China's working class would move in such a future direction, it would have to be SOE workers to do so. Yet is there any good reason to believe that a discourse of workers' democracy could reemerge among SOE sector worker? Would there be any point to developing such a renewed discourse among SOE workers, especially since it is a sector whose enterprises and workers are ostensibly in retreat if not essentially vanquished by the 'inevitable' rampage of globalization?

DISCOURSES OF WORKERS' DEMOCRACY IN CHINA'S SOES: HISTORICAL CONDITIONS AND PROCESSES

A key argument of this book has been that such questions cannot be answered without treating the discourse of workers' democracy as a historically conditioned process. The reason that it remains possible that SOE workers in China might yet deploy a discourse of workers' democracy is that the problem of the SOE remains unsolved. As a result, the SOE has the potential to be a site of future struggles over a central question of transition from state socialism: Who shall control state assets for which the state no longer intends to take fiscal or moral responsibility?

From the late 1970s, a dramatic reorientation in the CCP leadership occurred that reflected a sense of the limits placed on development by factional battles, a shift that called for subjecting enterprises gradually but surely to the imperatives of for-profit market-mediated competition. This strategy promised a dramatic investment in human and fixed capital combined with greater amounts of enterprise autonomy in the realm of production and investment decisions. The transition enjoyed a decided advantage over the effort in the neighboring Soviet Union. This was primarily due to the large number of surplus laborers available in the rural sector, which during the Maoist period had experienced a lower degree of collectivization than laborers in the urban industrial sector (Selden 1994). Therefore, the introduction of a market-based enterprise sector produced a far less intense threat to the heart of China's political economy and thereby the political survival of the CCP than was the case in the former Soviet Union.

That strategy appeared to affirm the prevailing view outside China in social science literature that a more gradual approach to transition to capitalism, one that created a more 'mixed' economy and that spared the more sensitive SOEs the far-reaching restructuring and exposure to competition seen in China's rural sector, would avoid the disastrous calamity called 'shock therapy' that was later applied to the heart of Russian industry. These forecasts tended toward a static conceptualization of the transition to capitalism, seeing capitalism in the existence of given 'factors.' Typically, mainstream analyses take for granted that bringing in new capitalist ideologies into the Chinese workplace culture will perforce play a role in making China able to more quickly and successfully integrate into international circuits of capitalist production. However, this approach is not limited to mainstream social sciences; it is practiced by Marxist and various radical schools as well, taking for granted the existence of capitalism in the form of increased marketization and the more deleterious outgrowths of inequality in the period of Chinese transition. Their respective methodologies are likewise problematic because they leave analysts with little more than subjective sentiment or positivist 'variables' to evaluate the impact of 'capitalism' in China.

The alternative to this weakness, offered in this book, is a theory of transition from state socialism that can historically account for the outcome of that transition without taking for granted the actualization of capitalist relations of production in a still critical sector of China's political economy—namely, the SOEs. Borrowing heavily from Simon Clarke's work on the Russian transition from state socialism, the theoretical approach engaged in this book has been to not presume that capitalist relations of production have been born as a system of production relations in China. Instead, I have looked at what was the heart of value production in Chinese state socialism and noted that enterprises in this sector continue not only to play their vital role in the reproduction of the Party's monopoly of political power in China, but they also have been largely protected from exposure to capitalist markets and retained noncapitalist priorities to guide production management and investment decisions. Even in the small- and medium-sized enterprises in China, it remains apparent, especially in the cases we looked at, that although there has been considerable enrichment on the part of enterprise leaders at the expense of workers, wealth has been typically procured through monopoly advantages and, critically, corruption.

Indeed, the cases from Zhengzhou that I analyzed in Chapter 6 revealed one of two noteworthy scenarios: (1) cadres scramble for corrupt avenues to secure profits because there does not exist capitalist investment in their companies as long as they are expected to carry the burden of laid off workers social security needs, and (2) even when there does exist a foreign buyer, cadres reject it because there is greater profit to be made from running down enterprises and selling their land off to speculators who have no interest in production. SOE workers, in contrast, do not recognize the power of the market as their ideological barometer; instead, they cling to traditional state-socialist ideologies that call for the SOE to provide their basic social welfare needs for life in return for labor participation in SOEs. Even when SOE workers embrace an ideology of transition like workers' democracy to resist the terms of privatization (or, more accurately in the Zhengzhou cases, corruption), interviewed SOE workers sought to recapture possession of their SOE and to compensate workers for their losses and, ideally (if unrealistically), to provide employment through production revival. Rarely do SOE workers interviewed display the belief that by accepting the end of their relationship with their work unit they have a future in labor markets as they exist in present-day China. Nor do these workers believe that workers' democracy is a tool that they can employ to make a transition to market dependence a worthwhile one. From the perspective of the SOE workers I interviewed, market dependence is, in fact, regarded as a barrier to the resolution of their crisis—and this view we see when they engage a discourse of workers democracy.

As I noted in Chapter 2, there has existed a contested discourse of workers' democracy circulating in China since the Yenan period. Workers' democracy ran a gamut of notions, including democratic election of managers and directors, workers' supervisory committees, FMCs, and (during the Cultural Revolution) workers' management teams, cadre participation in production floor labor, all the way to spontaneous rebellions and direct production control where necessary.

However, none of these reform efforts were able to address and resolve a fundamental reality of Chinese state socialism—namely, the lack of actual democratic participation that workers could exercise in the face of Party-assigned cadres' dominance of enterprise production, be they production-oriented ones or politically correct revolutionaries who put the social welfare needs of the unit first and foremost. This is reflected in the apparent tendency of Chinese SOE workers during these periods, despite higher levels of worker participation than in most Stalinist systems, to remain largely uninvolved in the affairs of production decisions. Even in the 1980s, when the most thoroughgoing implementation of *minzhu guanli* occurred in the Chinese SOE, after a period of excitement about electing factory directors, workers actually showed little interest in their revived WRC. Worker satisfaction was instead associated with increasing salaries, which were products of increased investments from central ministries in urban industry and new (and generally popular) piece-wage policies that had little to do with the role given to the WRC in the SOE (or capitalism for that matter).

In Chapter 4, I contended that the discourse of workers' democracy, as it circulated in official literature in the first decade of transition from state socialism in China, differed significantly from what was envisioned and practiced during the Maoist period, even while borrowing many core notions from that era. Critically, from the 1980s on, the dominant view of workers' democracy in official media organs regarded workers' democracy, especially constituent institutions such as the WRC and democratically elected managers, as a complement to decreased intervention of state ministries in the SOEs and greater exposure to competitive markets. This perspective was, as I noted in Chapter 5, not unique; it was instead picking up steam globally in an age of neoliberal restructuring of capitalist production and trade regimes across borders.

However, the official discourse of workers' democracy in the period of Chinese transition has not been terribly effective in terms of legitimating the Chinese state's policy of 'letting go' of its responsibility for the fate of failing SOEs, especially for the social welfare needs of Chinese SOE workers. Even more important, the official discourse has also not helped make Chinese SOE workers accept a key ideological premise of transition—namely, that SOE workers should shoulder the burden for the failure of the Chinese SOE. Put another way, SOE workers have not assimilated the idea that their value in labor markets alone should be the final determinant of their futures when an SOE experiences failure.

Explanations for this outcome found in the literature have tended to stress particular aspects of the policy that make it unlikely that workers will be able to use the institutions of workers' democracy (i.e., the WRC, supervisory committees, etc.) to exercise control over important production- and investment-related decisions. Additionally, the failure of SOEs to act more like capitalist companies free from external interference in the affairs of production and investment has been cited as a major hindrance to institutionalizing workers' democracy in Chinese SOEs. The argument goes, if there were more enterprise autonomy, institutions of workers' democracy such as the WRC and unions would have more clearly defined roles as representatives of workers' interests. The findings in this book throw such assumptions up to question, if not into considerable doubt.

I could likewise have opted for the position taken in much of the radical and Marxist alternative in the literature and declared China capitalist and that therefore China's workers cannot find alternatives outside of capitalist ones (e.g., independent unions) to the social relations of transition from state socialism. However, this is unsatisfactory at a number of levels, as Burawoy and Vedery (1999) argue:

> A focus on the day-to-day realities of postsocialism reveals a much more ambiguous account of the transformation announced with such fanfare by theories of modernization and of market and democratic transition. Each of these theories has a limited view of the interaction and interpenetration of system and life world, macro and micro, global and local; we need instead to attend much more to how the unfolding uncertainties of macro institutions affect practices within micro worlds and also to how family, work, and community are refashioning themselves—often in opposition to what governments intend. . . . [W]e find time and again that every step forward in the direction of the market produces forces opposed. In reaction to the iron law of market expansion, we discover the iron law of market resistance. (7).

Simplistic conclusions (e.g., China has become capitalist given the existence of markets, inequality, privatization, etc.) offer little in the way of explaining why capitalism does not offer Chinese workers the kind of empowerment promised by the advocates of Chinese capitalism, be it laissez faire or with a 'mixed' human face. The price of capitalist transition, with special attention to how the dynamics of capitalist development impact that price in particular spaces and temporal periods, needs to be carefully theorized before any analysis of how far transition from state socialism has come and to where it might lead (Clarke 1993b; Harvey 2006; Wood 1994, 1999).

THE LIMITS OF TRANSITION AND DISCOURSES OF WORKERS' DEMOCRACY IN HENAN DURING THE 1990S

It is within this theoretical framework that I have attempted to analyze the impact of the discourse of workers' democracy on Chinese SOE workers in Henan Province. In Chapters 5 and 6, this book's investigations into the small- and medium-sized enterprises where workers' democracy was being vigorously promoted as a component of SOE privatization suggested that almost anything but capitalist production had taken hold in that sector. The failures to convert SOEs to enterprises that were compelled to produce like capitalist enterprises in the 1980s continued on into the 1990s. Directors of small- and medium-sized companies that I investigated in Henan were losing privileged access to state-guaranteed investment, yet they were still able to find a whole host of noncapitalist mechanisms of coercion to maintain their privileged position of power. Because their 'labor relationship' (*laodong guanxi*) with the enterprise (and thereby the state) remained in effect in most instances, workers likewise were still able in many instances, despite the great price forced on them for the failure of the companies, to demand 'fair compensation' from the state when their economic crises became too severe. One of the most common ways a small- or medium-sized SOE slated as 'let go of' survives is through directors compelling workers to buy 'shares' in the SOE as a converted shareholding corporation, the implication being that a worker, regardless of productive value, can retain his or her labor relationship with the unit and the concomitant social welfare benefits (albeit in a severely hollowed-out form) integral to it.

The case studies would appear to affirm our theory of transition from state socialism in China; that is, capitalism is hardly systematically in motion as the arbiter of value in the SOE sector. They tell a story of a sector of the economy in stagnation that does not submit itself to market regulation even when planning ministries absolve themselves of their responsibilities to small- and medium-sized SOEs. It is in this context that the discourse of workers' democracy as a component of Chinese transition is best understood.

The relevance of these case studies is that they make it apparent that a transition to capitalism is not only about wages or the right to collectively bargain—as important as such matters are to the working class of any country. The future appears to point in another direction—namely, a transition that demands that SOE workers give up their claims to the social welfare promises of state socialism in return for capitalist investment that does not deliver their kind jobs or social security. This struggle has not even transpired with sufficient results in small and medium sized SOEs, which have undergone the deepest levels of exposure to capitalist competition. As a consequence, capital does not dominate the political economy of China's SOE sector to date.

The cases from Henan show a setting in which Chinese workers possess little faith in new market-driven relations of production that are transposed onto traditional state-socialist ones in the period of transition. In the process, SOE workers have not remained passive recipients of discourses like workers' democracy that Party leaders and enterprise cadres attempt to engage as part of their justification for the declining position of Chinese SOE workers in Chinese society. State workers have, the studies indicate here, retained, even when they appear to be cynically dismissive of the idea *in toto*, a firm belief that if there is such a thing as workers' democracy, it should be linked up to the basic social obligations of the state-owned enterprise to provide workers with employment and basic social welfare protections.

The practice, by Zhengzhou workers in the period of resistance to privatization, of reemploying the discourse of workers democracy against the intent of Party cadres and enterprise leaders to compel them to accept tying their fates to their performance in markets should not be surprising. This is the case, although in instances where conflicts have yet to emerge in SOEs Chinese workers display little interest in their official institutions of workers' democracy. What is significant here is that, in a moment of resistance, workers employ a discourse of democracy that is deeply informed by the logic of state-socialist production and that is deeply opposed to the capitalist one that confronts them today.[1] This is a new phenomenon inasmuch as, although in the half century of Chinese state socialism Chinese SOE workers engaged the discourse of workers' democracy for a variety of purposes, they have never had to engage this discourse for the purpose of protecting their right to a job or basic social welfare.

That this has occurred does not signify therefore that there is necessarily great hope for Chinese workers in the near term to develop strategies of resistance that might bring about workers' democracy. There are a number of reasons for this, presuming that our case studies have at least some indicative value. For the most part, the Zhengzhou workers elected as independent leaders in the moment of resistance were consistently better educated skilled workers or lower level cadres (i.e., workshop managers, engineers, skilled machinists, etc.), chosen for their experience collecting and writing materials used to advance the case against fraudulent 'privatizations.' Although their experiences had revealed to them the relationship between the lack of workers' democracy and their respective factories' fates, they nonetheless remained limited in their capacity to develop a counterstrategy to transcend the coercive relations of Maoist and post-Maoist workers' democracy. On the one hand, they aspired, upon retrieving the property rights to their factory, to create an alternative to the model of enterprise relations the Party offered workers in the guise of workers' democracy in the moment of transition. At the same time, workers' leaders were just as inclined to believe that the only way to accomplish that was through converting their factories into corporate shareholding companies that were subject to competition. They were acutely aware that there were real contradictions in such a plan because outside investors could quickly outweigh workers in the control of stock. However, this was seen as unproblematic because many workers' leaders, when pressed, conceded that they did not have great faith in production workers' role in production and investment decisions. When asked about this, they noted that, although they came to their primes in the Maoist era and appreciated the popular discourse of workers' control from that era, workers in China never really involved themselves in the affairs of production. They left that to cadres, whom they judged on their ability to deliver social welfare benefits and wages. Because those were guaranteed regardless of who was in power, workers rarely felt the need to make waves about how production decisions were made.

By the mid- to late 1990s, when SOE workers were in dire need of organization, they had little immediate sense of how to use institutions of workers' democracy that existed in China to take back control of their factories from corrupt cadres. That, combined with the assumption of superior knowledge on the part of elected workers' leaders, made it unlikely that the discourse of workers' democracy could be used as an effective weapon to supersede the relations of production that characterize Chinese transition from state socialism. What remains to be seen is how the playing out of the Chinese transition from state socialism will impact the level of struggle in the Chinese SOE and throughout the Chinese working class in general. This invariably remains a matter of whether Chinese workers are compelled to accept the logic of capitalist production as a system of class relations in China's future or whether stagnant but non-market type of coercive class relations that dominate the Chinese political economy continue, or whether workers can battle both such outcomes as the path of transition from Chinese state socialism and battle for a new path that supersedes state-socialist and capitalist relations of production. In this analysis, capitalism not only cannot be assumed to have arrived in China's SOEs, but whether its future arrival is desirable for China's workers remains a matter of ideological struggle.

CAN AND WILL THERE BE A NEW DISCOURSE OF WORKERS' DEMOCRACY IN CHINA?

To be sure, there is no way of predicting for certain what is going to happen in the future as concerns the Chinese labor movement and the role of SOE workers as a social force bearing a particular form of class consciousness. However, possible trends in the future can be imagined given what we know about the current state of China's transition from state socialism. SOE workers' experience deploying a discourse of workers' democracy in Zhengzhou also suggest what could be needed for that discourse to play a more dynamic role in enabling SOE workers to challenge the social relations of coercion that have attended privatization in China's SOEs.

Although the role of SOE workers in China's labor movement has subsided in the last few years, it would be wrong to regard the cases that I documented in Chapter 6 as only relevant to SOE workers' struggles that ended roughly five years ago. On the one hand, the significance of the SOE sector is not as great today as it was in the Maoist period or even the first two decades of economic restructuring since Mao's death in 1976. However, it remains influential, monopolizing key sectors and in control of 57 percent of industrial assets as of 2006 (Meng and Dollery 2006). SOEs continue to account for about one half of total employment in China (Meng and Dollery 2006). It is through this control that the Party state continues to exert control over and, arguably, dominate national economic development strategies:

> (D)espite twenty years of reforms in Chinese industry designed to promote greater enterprise autonomy, China's large SOEs are still subject to direct and indirect intervention by an array of state agencies, national and local, and are still constrained by the ideological and political principles and sensitivities of the ruling Chinese Communist Party (CCP) in their efforts to reform and restructure. While they are not to be "let go," like their small and medium-sized counterparts (many of which have been sold off, merged, or declared bankrupt), they are subject to conflicting demands and pressures, by no means all of which are pushing them in the direction of "corporatizing" or marketizing reform. (Hassard, Morris, Sheehan, and Xiao 2002, 115–116)

Still, because it became a signatory to the WTO, China has become more dependent on exports and foreign investment (Hart Landsberg and Burkett 2006). As I noted in Chapter 2, even larger SOEs now are constantly under domestic and international pressure to reorganize assets and production line priorities in line with the expectations of global and competitive markets (Hart Landsberg and Burkett 2007). The same kinds of neoliberal orientations that drove privatization efforts in China's small- and medium-sized SOEs in the 1990s show up in manifold fashions today when it comes to dealing with the current SOEs that remain, now typically larger and still receiving support and protections from the Party state. Nonetheless, they have survived the ravages of the market faced by the small- and medium-sized SOEs that were 'let go' of in the 1990s. Although it is certainly the case that these survivors react much more to market forces than their former selves, they nevertheless are hardly dominated by capitalist market logic:

> In September 1999 SOEs were encouraged to diversify their stock rights and to list abroad. As financial intermediaries, asset management companies (AMCs) have also been set up. To separate the role of government as administrator and owner, SASAC was established. These measures improved the performance of SOEs to some extent, but the outcomes are still not adequate. For instance, consider the operation of the shareholding system. According to Tam (1999), 74% of chairmen, 80% of directors and 90% of supervisors in listed SOEs claimed that they were elected to their appointments—the election occurring during the custodianship of the enterprise by central government ministries. As a result, private shareholders can do very little to improve corporate governance. (Meng and Dollery 2006, 10)

It would be misguided, then, to presume that larger scale SOEs have already been compelled to submit to the logic of capitalist markets (Meng and Dollery 2006). It would be equally unwise to presume that they will not be sites of struggle in the future as a result of greater integration into global markets. Indeed, the literature by economists lamenting large SOEs' failure to fully carry out market-based restructuring invariably cites managers' fears of facing the kinds of open forms of rebellion that characterized the period of small- and medium-sized SOE privatization as a key hurdle for capitalist transition in China's SOEs (Lardy 1998, 2002; Meng and Dollery 2006).

In any event, the remaining SOEs today are not only typically large scale; they are, like their small- and medium-sized counterparts, complex entities. These SOEs also see discourses of workers' democracy that workers engage to shape understandings of their current conditions, problems, and futures. Even in large SOEs that have restructured and received state support to compete in cutting-edge national and global capitalist markets, exposure to and success in these markets proceeds accompanied by discourses of workers' democracy. For example, data from a 2006 study of workers' reflections on their experiences in technology sector SOEs in Guangdong Province that have successfully restructured indicate the discourse remains even where the market has made its greatest inroads within such enterprises (Chiu 2006). Chiu finds continuity and change in SOE workers' perceptions because the shop floor has become both more dynamic and ruthless than in previous eras when markets played little role in shaping workplace relationships.

Given their greater vulnerability to competitive change, especially skills expectations, older workers in these SOEs are especially sensitive to such 'reforms.' However, they are not alone in their ambivalence, and, as Chiu argues, SOE workplace relations are, like all social processes, complex ones. Younger workers in these SOEs are more excited about the innovative approaches to and improvements in worker output, along with increased monetary rewards for contributing to enterprise profitability in competitive markets. At the same time, many workers, old and young, still express doubt about their role as masters of their enterprises, especially in comparison with the past. One worker declares that as long as managers have the power to do on-the-spot checks, workers will never have any real power to influence managers. Some workers, because they are part of a team and total quality management (TQM) requires more interaction between managers and workers, feel they are more able to participate in production meaningfully. Still other workers are not won over by TQM's call for consultation with workers. They declare in interviews that TQM and SOE restructuring has not delivered substantive consultation. This undermines SOE workers' belief that restructuring is about democratizing the workplace or giving workers a real voice in production. In that vein, a worker declares that he cannot express his real thoughts on anything substantive if it goes against what managers want because he dreads his three-year employment contract would not be renewed as a means to punish dissent.

Finally, one enduring feature of these successfully restructured SOEs that Chiu finds is their high level of welfare benefits, which attract workers who would otherwise be drawn to privately owned enterprises that pay higher wages:

> The workers had broken their dependence mentality, to an extent. Although they still relied on the SOEs for welfare provisions, the workers realized that the sustainability of the enterprises directly affected their livelihoods, and that the sustainability hinged on the marketability of their products. It should be added, though, that the older workers resented the lack of job security induced by compulsory 3- or 5-year contracts after the reform. These findings have two implications. First, should reform produce negative results that impinge on workers material benefits, they will not accept management autonomy, which will lead to industrial action. Second, as long as their livelihoods are taken good care of, workers in reformed SOEs welcome means of upgrading their skills, unleashing their potential and adding to the intrinsic values of their jobs. (695)

In many ways, these successful SOEs sound like their small- and medium-sized counterparts in the 1980s: They are able to provide welfare benefits, wage increases, and promises of more meaningful participation in the production process. Regardless of whether workers in today's SOEs would draw on the discourse of workers' democracy, which SOE workers drew on in the 1990s to defend their enterprises and their livelihoods from market 'failures,' remains an open question that only time will tell when the vagaries of competitive markets make themselves felt on these newly restructured, cutting-edge, and larger SOEs.

LESSONS TO BE DRAWN FROM RECENT DISCOURSES OF WORKERS' DEMOCRACY IN CHINESE SOES

Two investigations of SOE crisis in the recent past provide insight into the relevance of the discourse of workers' democracy for SOE workers today: Unger and Chan's (2004) qualitative study of how workers employed institutions of grassroots democracy to protect social rights in a relatively successful state-owned distillery and Lin's (2005) analysis of a case of Liaoyang Ferro Allay Factory workers' struggles against privatization and corruption that drew international attention in 2002 and 2003.

The distillery that Unger and Chan researched was a large SOE that, unlike the cases I studied in Zhengzhou, but like the SOEs that Chiu looked at, had not gone bankrupt and had held its own into the 2000s.

SOE workers at the distillery mobilized to resist a plan by the distillery's administrators, in response to declines in profits, to cut back in a number of areas, including its contribution to funds for cheap and subsidized housing provided to distillery workers. In the 1990s, distillery workers had already, via their WRC, challenged administrators' visions for housing allotments as the enterprise ended its direct ownership of workers' housing units. In 2002, although workers had no sense that privatization was slated for the near future, they reacted viscerally to the threat of losing enterprise support for something they regarded as a social obligation of the enterprise. Workers were irritated that administrators slapped together a 'management committee,' which would be responsible for collecting new housing management fees. The enterprise union became involved, organizing elections of 'homeowners committees' to replace the 'management committee.'

Despite their determination to engage a discourse of workers' democracy to fight to protect something that was recognized as a material issue, by 2004, on the matter of imminent privatization, Unger and Chan found less readiness to do the same—even as the bulk of shares of the enterprise's stock ended up belonging to senior administrators. Instead, the workers hoped for the best from their administrators. Unger and Chan note that at the time it was clearly unlikely that the enterprise could continue to provide the welfare benefits workers were accustomed to for much longer. Unger and Chan conclude that, although the distillery workers by 2004 had displayed, for over a decade, a potential for developing their fight for 'grass-roots democratic activity,' they nonetheless clung to a mentality that embraced enterprise paternalism. This ideological orientation is regarded by Unger and Chan as spelling 'doom' for the social rights embedded in the SOEs that remain in China because China's neoliberal orientation at the national level militates directly against preserving such social rights.

It is true that 'enterprise paternalism' has functioned as a real barrier to Chinese SOE workers' incapacity to engage a discourse of workers' democracy in a way that can effectively create an alternative to the neoliberal choice of privatization and the loss of social rights and security for workers that that policy commands. Yet if we can anticipate that the battle over the social relations of production in China's remaining large and tenuously 'secure' SOEs has yet to see a finish, social science interested in the condition of China's SOE workers needs to provide a sense of what can be learned from SOE struggles where direct challenges to the privatization policies have occurred since the failed SOE protests of the late 1990s and early 2000s.

A report written up by a student and labor activist in Beijing (Lin 2005) on the mass actions in 2002, which sprung from the struggles of Liaoyang Ferro Alloy Factory (FAF) workers antibankruptcy protests, suggests that how SOE workers in China organized in this instance determined the ease with which Chinese authorities could ultimately limit their protest effectiveness.[2]

These protests contained the same discourses of workers' democracy that were employed by workers at other SOE factories around China at the time. The FAF WRC passed numerous resolutions against bankruptcy proposals that enterprise administrators put forth, even when police intervened on the latter's behalf to ensure the 'correct vote' and despite the Liaoyang ACFTU chief's support for a bankruptcy as a 'means to solve the workers' crises. When key WRC representatives were arrested for their roles as individuals 'inciting' demonstrations and unrest, Lin cites a worker who insists that leaders never acted as individuals at any stage of the protests:

> The actions initiated by the workers at FAF have never been a product of any one individual's decisions. Before (Workers' Representative) Yao went to the march he had just been elected as a "family relative representative."[3] The FAF workers actions have always been a result of *collectively* made decisions. Every single time we encounter some big issue, a WRC meeting at which open discussion and voting on resolutions occurred, and this was required. Let's be clear, neither Yao nor Xiao (the other workers' representative arrested for his role in demonstrations) could have singlehandedly organized the FAF workers. (15)

The protesting SOE workers in Liaoyang achieved an exceptional amount of solidarity from other factory workers in similar crises nearby, resulting in multifactory actions and the arrest of key workers' representatives (Lee 2007). However, despite that level of mutual support, Lin's (2005) report asks a critical question about the limits of SOE workers' protests against privatization—namely, why, even when SOE workers in China displayed a discourse of workers' democracy that has proved to be an asset in their battles to protect the social rights promised by state socialism, did their organizing not result in a movement that could grow?

Lin (2005) argues that the Liaoyang case is a good case to draw important lessons for future organizing in the SOE sector if and when SOE workers in 'protected' sectors experience crises that attend greater exposure to the vagaries of competitive markets. As I noted in Chapter 6, the literature on crises that China's SOE workers faced in the late 1990s focused on workers' fatalism and the lack of citizenship rights as major barriers to their capacity to resist the price tag of privatization. SOE workers in China have certainly been hindered by old models of enterprise dependence; this is indisputable, and the cases in Chapters 5 and 6 more than demonstrate that reality. Nevertheless, Lin argues that the focus on workers 'ideological flaws' treats workers consciousness as stationary, when in fact it is in process. SOE workers in China, I have argued in this book, did show forms of consciousness that went well beyond paternalism, even if that consciousness was on display too late in the process.

In their discourses (and practices) of workers' democracy, China's SOE workers often presented a quite radical vision for reform in China that called for workers' direct control of the workplace. Lin (2005) contends that state repression was not the greatest obstacle to their capacity to execute such a program, nor would the attainment of citizenship rights necessarily help much—as desirable and needed as they remain for the outcomes of workers' self-organization forms of workers' democracy they could produce. The trouble spot, or stumbling block, for China's state workers, be it in the 1990s or 2000s, was what kind of organizing occurred once workers mobilized. Organizationally, the workers' leaders in the FAF battles adhered greatly to principles of democracy, and this showed in the extent to which workers' representatives made it a point to communicate and actively involve rank-and-file workers in all important decision-making processes. It was this type of organizational commitment to grassroots democracy that enhanced WRC leaders' capacities to negotiate with and put pressure on the state to take their fight against corruption and privatization seriously.

At the same time, too great a reliance was placed on a core group of disciplined (and elected) workers' leaders. When police arrested core leaders on the charge of conspiring with foreign organizations, organizationally the WRC was not ready to replace leaders—or groom 'leaderless' leaders. It is because of this organizational weakness that the state had a relatively easy time breaking down the capacity of Liaoyang's workers to defend their protests and advance greater demands on the government. Although their demands for compensation and access to social services for workers were met, privatization of the FAF could not be stopped, nor could workers gain back control of the FAF and run it as a worker-controlled cooperative, which workers' leaders told Lin was a goal of their organizing efforts. Ultimately, it was at the organizational level where the discourses of workers' democracy were self-limiting.

Because the outcome of the processes of restructuring China's large-sized SOEs remains unknown, there remains the potential for conflicts between SOE workers and the Party state. Given the crucial role such enterprises continue to play in the legitimacy of the Party and its monopoly on state power, such conflicts should remain a matter of sociological interest to researchers who focus on the fate of China's working class and how it is shaped by the direction of transition from state socialism. No less so should our interest in finding ways for China's SOE workers to successfully struggle for real workers' democracy as a means to raise the hope that there are alternatives to the specific forms of market- and nonmarket-based coercion that characterize China's transition from state socialism.

Notes

NOTES TO CHAPTER 1

1. It is often taken for granted that Gramsci, by asserting subjectivity over structure, eschewed examination of the role capitalist political-economy played in limiting the possible outcomes of actions based on one or another type of counterhegemonic consciousness. However, at the very least, the relationship between 'base' and 'superstructure' is a back and forth one in Gramsci. The dynamic of capitalist political-economy, now global and intensively competitive in form and content, even for Gramsci, shapes the limits of the possible change that one or another counterhegemonic or hegemonic consciousness can engender (Ahmad 2002).

2. Simon Clarke's (1992, 1993a, 1993b) work on the transition from state socialism in the former Soviet Union has greatly influenced how I conceptualize the problem of the same transition in present-day China. Clarke's voluminous work examines in detail how, despite the wish to restructure markets in the former Soviet Union, Russian SOEs, which constituted the 'commanding heights of production' in the Soviet era, continued to act in distinctly noncapitalist ways even after they were 'privatized' well into the late 1990s. Clarke's understanding of state socialism is informed by the work of Ticktin's (1973, 1992) similarly capacious research and analysis of the 'Soviet mode of production' as one that was distinctly not determined by the logic of capitalist markets at the point of production or exchange.

3. By neoliberalism I refer to global developmental strategies that call for elimination of national state and other nonmarket-based regulations of domestic and global markets combined with privatization as the means to economically develop poor and wealthy economies alike. Harvey (2007) appropriately labels China's development as "neoliberalism with Chinese characteristics."

4. Luoyang is a city in Henan Province, about 400 miles south of Beijing.

5. In English, the 'C' in WRC is usually translated as either 'committee,' 'council,' or 'congress.'

NOTES TO CHAPTER 2

1. During this period (1937–1945), when the CCP's base of revolutionary operations was centered in Shanxi Province, it developed and perfected its strategy of mass mobilization of peasants via "discovery of concrete methods for

linking popular participation in the guerrilla struggle with a wide ranging community attack on rural problems" (Selden 1971, 276).

2. The Anshan Constitution refers to the mission adopted by China's most advanced iron and steel works factory (Anshan Works) in 1960, which overturned its commitment to the Soviet one-man management model enacted throughout the 1950s. In its place, a new 'constitution' was drawn up, which emphasized (1) politics in command; (2) strengthening party leadership; (3) launching vigorous mass movements; (4) instituting the "two participations, one reform, and three combinations" (cadre participation in productive labor and worker participation in management; reform of irrational and outdated rules; cooperation between workers, cadres, and technicians); and (5) going full speed ahead with technical innovations. (Hoffman 1977, 295).

3. Andors used the spelling 'Kung Ching" for this writer's name. 'Gong Qing' is the spelling in Pinyin, which Chinese use today and is standard in the literature elsewhere.

4. It is a safe estimation that Bettelheim's reports, as valuable as they appeared at the time, were far too dependent on official cadre interviews, with little in the way of independent confirmation at the mass-based level where much of the reforms he relayed were putatively initiated. This is not to deny the value of such interviews outright, but to highlight the fact that cadres have their own interests in conforming to a dominant line regardless of the circumstances. It is apparent that, throughout the Chinese Revolution, various factions framed the discourse of workers' democracy in order to reflect positively on the current line.

NOTES TO CHAPTER 3

1. Selden (1994) shows clearly how the different patterns of agricultural production organization in China and the Soviet Union shaped the outcomes of rural restructuring efforts in both countries. In Russia, the attempt to impose market norms of exchange on Russian agricultural producers was much more difficult because they had long ago been incorporated into a mechanized and collectively based large-scale model of production. Long accustomed to working a standard work day with wages and social security benefits at roughly the level of industrial workers, they were resistant to new policies that demanded their giving up social security benefit guarantees and taking on the risks associated with independent rural market exchange. In contrast, Chinese rural producers were historically less tied to the centrally organized social security-based benefits and patterns of work assigned to the industrial proletariat under Chinese state socialism. Thus, Selden argues, from 1949 onward, Chinese rural producers, regardless of the period, experienced patterns of work for exchange in local markets, which made it much easier for *rural producers* to make the adjustment called for when markets were granted a larger role in agriculture from 1978 onward.

2. Within the enterprise, 'cadres' would encompass directors, upper level management, and Party and enterprise representatives.

3. On the continual flow of funds from the central ministries to the urban (SOE) sector during the 1980s, see Cheng (1995).

4. Often overlooked by market enthusiasts, Hinton (1990) argued that these increased subsidies that the government provided to farmers for agricultural products, especially staple grains, played as critical a role in stimulating agricultural productivity and income gains as did exchanges in private markets.

NOTES TO CHAPTER 4

1. Part of the iron rice bowl policy that was most directly confronted that year was one that allowed children of SOE workers an automatic job assignment in the same factory.

NOTES TO CHAPTER 5

1. My first such interview was at the No. 1 Dyed Fabric Factory in Luoyang in July 1999. In September 2000, on hearing that there were factories where workers in the nearby city of Zhengzhou City were fighting fraudulent privatizations *and* calling for the right of their WRCs to take control of production, supporters of these SOE workers' protests helped me arrange meetings with workers in the nearby cities of Xinxiang and Anyang. These two cities were only a one- and two-hour train ride from Zhengzhou. They also happened to be cities whose names popped up frequently as locations of 'model democratically managed SOEs' in Henan.
2. See Todd Crowell and David Hsieh, "As Zhu Rongji's honeymoon ends, his reforms attract growing criticism. But Jiang Zemin is on his side." Available from http://www.asiaweek.com/asiaweek/98/0821/nat_1_zhu.html .
3. Changchun is a city in the Northern Province of Jiling, about 500 miles north of Beijing.
4. *Shenchang* means production and *zijiu* means to save oneself. The Luoyang No. 1 Dyed Fabric Factory case, which is discussed next, is one such instance where workers were said to carry out a spontaneous and mass-based production control to save their factory. It was regarded as the most radical of means to resolve crises faced by workers in Chinese SOEs.
5. *The Forum* is published at both national and provincial levels. Thus, in addition to the national edition, every provincial and city branch of the ACFTU has its own version of *The Forum*.
6. *Jilin Workers' Forum*, March 1996.
7. *Guanyu Henanshen Shixing Gongkaiminzhu Xuanpin Jingyinzhe Shiguoyouqiye Niukui Zhengying* de *Diaochabaogao*
8. Interestingly, the author of this report highlights the stories of two factories that are discussed later in this and the next chapter, namely the No. 1 Luoyang Dyed Fabric and Zhengzhou Ceramics Factories.
9. *Minzhu Xuanping Qiye JinYingzhe: Congfen Tixian Zhigongqunzhong Dangjiazuozhude Quanli* ("Democratically Choosing Enterprise Administrators: Aggressively Embodying the Right of Workers as Masters of Their Enterprises"), *The Workers' Movement*, 8(128), 31–36.
10. The companies were those featured as models of democratic management in the Henan-based editions of *The Forum*.
11. The main obstacle to this interview project being richer was my colleague's provision of only about half of the initially anticipated interviews. In the Luoyang No. 1 Dyed Fabric case, for example, although I was able to conduct rich in-depth interviews with the union chief and WRC representatives, expected interviews with workers at the factory, which would have been helpful, were never conducted. Nonetheless, interviews that were provided did possess ample content for analytical purposes.
12. One example from an electronics factory in Xinxiang provided me with an interesting interview with a retired engineer who had some insightful commentary on official claims that democratic management had 'turned around' the company and made it productive again. In a nutshell, he argued that

market conditions alone were responsible and that democratic management had nothing to do with the fortunes of the company. However, as a retired engineer, he hardly represented an average worker's perspective. My contacts in Zhengzhou then followed up with interviews of production workers at this factory.

13. Anyang is a city in Henan province, about a four-hour train ride (south) from Beijing. Xinxiang, mentioned later, is about five hours from Beijing, and Zhengzhou is seven hours by train. Except for the #1, I have slightly changed the names of the factories to pseudonyms in this chapter.

14. In Chinese SOEs, retired workers count as part of the total workforce. The company is responsible, through its contributions to the social security funds, for the social welfare of retired workers. If a company wanted to buy out an SOE, it would be considered responsible for their social security funds and other needs such as housing, health care, and so on. The failure, thus far, to set up a reliable national pension system from government funds has frequently contributed to difficulties in persuading capitalists to buy out Chinese SOEs.

15. Unless I state otherwise, claims made in this section are by the cadres we interviewed about Anyang Textile.

16. This 'fund' was a means that many SOEs started up in order to stave off financial crises and to maintain investment in production when the government reduced or cut off credit due to their failures in competitive markets.

17. Roughly five to seven months of salary for a production line worker.

18. These interviews with managers and the enterprise director were conducted in the first week of September 2000 by a labor activist in Beijing who shared an interest in companies that were said to be model democratically managed enterprises in Henan. I conducted interviews with the workers at the factory in the last week of September 2000.

19. At the time, this was the equivalent of about $US 63. The name of this and other workers are not their actual names.

NOTES TO CHAPTER 6

1. Interview with Mr. Lai, a labor activist in Beijing, August 2005.

2. When I began my dissertation research on workers' consciousness in the SOE sector, my biggest barrier was not political. Instead, it took me the longest time to find intellectuals in China who had an interest in the struggles of SOE workers and any sense of the need to research their struggles (see Philion 2005).

3. On the Web, Blecher has advanced such arguments at www.zmag.org/content/showarticle.cfm?ItemID=8434.

4. The SWC referred to by Chen is what I have called the 'WRC' throughout this book.

5. See http://www.marxists.org/archive/marx/works/1844/jewish-question/

6. Marx put it even better in Capital Vol. 1 on the nature of capital labor-based power relations in the factory system: "Les Dises sont pipe!" (The dice are loaded).

7. I believe intensified international capitalist competition would probably cover the matter; see Wood (1997a) and Burnham (1997).

8. According to outside supporters of the factory struggles in Zhengzhou, some 48 factories have had experiences identical in substance to the ZZP.

9. Most of the information about the company comes from documents supplied by workers' representatives, often in the form of petitions to the city and provincial governments and/or directly from interviews.

10. Workers' leaders from the ZZP reported that the factory's debt was largely a product of similar activities on the part of managers, and that in fact the company was quite viable before the factory machinery was solf off bit by bit.

11. Workers' leaders also claimed that, as in many similar cases across China at that time, underground gangs were also employed to carry out the task and to intimidate factory defenders.

12. There is reason for such skepticism, and Blecher and Lee both make strong and documented arguments for their estimation of SOE workers' class consciousness in China. Indeed, in the remainder of this chapter, concerns about the limits of the Zhengzhou case are laid out. However, there remain possibilities for strategizing how to realize the hope of a more radical (if idealistic) version of workers' democracy as a means to fight privatization in China's SOEs. This would require more research in the future. For Blecher's general thoughts on the state of Chinese working-class consciousness, see his article, "Why China's Workers are Losing their World" at www.zmag.org/content/showarticle.cfm?ItemID=8434.

13. Similarities with Russian cases of SOEs studied by Clarke (1993a, 1993b) that have 'converted' to 'capitalist' markets only to face the quandary of lacking capital and needing to resort, therefore, to noncapitalist means to survive are striking. The Catch 22 that the factory debt put workers' leaders in is summed up well in an article in *Guangdong News*, "Zhengzhou Zaozhichang Daipojuede Gaizhi Nanti" (Restructuring the Zhengzhou Paper Factory: An Unresolved Saga), www.southcn.com/weekend/economic/200410280022.htm.

14. Indeed, the leader quoted previously was one of the more militant of the leaders interviewed in Zhengzhou. It should be noted that, as Kasmir (1996) argues quite persuasively about the Mondragon Cooperative example, democratic management models can quite effectively be hooked up to lean production-oriented 'team management' strategies by capital to subvert the potential of actual worker self-organization.

15. By this point (2002), the economic situation of the remaining workers available to 'invest' in their factory, equally or not, made such a plan barely an option.

16. By 'local,' I refer to those from Zhengzhou and nearby cities within a radius of about 40 miles.

17. This refers to activities in Zhengzhou every September 9 to commemorate Mao on his birthday by marching to one of the few remaining statues of him and handing out leaflets criticizing the Party for departing from his policies and becoming corrupted by capitalism.

NOTES TO CHAPTER 7

1. Again the similarity with what Clarke found on Russian attitudes toward capitalist transition is strikingly relevant to the findings here. Clarke (1993a) found that Russian citizens were not against capitalist markets as much as opposed to the capitalist markets that they faced in the period of transition. What mattered according to Clarke was that the latter is what defines capitalism and why transition to capitalism is one defined by struggles whose outcomes are impossible to predict.

2. Lin is the pseudonym of a student and labor activist whom I met in October 2000 and August 2005 on stays in Beijing. He was a member of a student group that took an active interest in and traveled around China investigating working-class conflicts. He wrote up a report based on his own knowledge

of the workers' leaders and workers involved in the Liaoyang protest demonstrations in 2002. It was published at the Chinese leftist *Utopia* website (www.wyzxwyzx.com)

3. Yao's wife had worked at the factory and was retired. Yao had worked in the past at another rolled-steel factory. Because his wife was a retired worker, he was elected as a 'family relative' representative.

Bibliography

Ahmad, Aijaz. 2002. *Lineages of the Present: Ideology and Politics in Contemporary South Asia*. London: Verso.

Andors, Stephen. 1977. *China's Industrial Revolution: Politics, Planning, and Management, 1949 to the Present*. New York: Pantheon Books.

Andreas, Joel, Rachel Core, and Shaohua Zhan. 2007, March. *"Mass Supervision" in Chinese Factories Before and During the Cultural Revolution*. Paper presented at the meeting of the Eastern Sociological Society, March 2007.

Balfour, Fredrick. 2002, April 8. "How Much Is China Cooking Its Numbers?" *Business Week*.

Bartholomew, Amy. 2006. *Empire's Law: The American Imperial Project and the "War to Remake the World."* Ann Arbor, MI: Pluto.

Bello, Walden. 2002. "The Crisis of Capitalism: Review of Robert Brenner's Boom and the Babble." Frontline (India) 19(22).

Bernard, Mitchell. 1999. "East Asia's Tumbling Dominoes: Financial Crisis and the Myth of the Regional Model." In *Socialist Register 1999*, edited by Leo Panitch and Colin Leys, 178–208. Halifax: Merlin Press.

Bettelheim, Charles. 1974. *Cultural Revolution and Industrial organization in China: Changes in Management and the Division of Labor*. New York: Monthly Review Press.

Bian, Yanjie. 1994. *Work and Inequality in Urban China*. Albany: State University of New York Press.

Biddulph, Sarah, and Sean Cooney. 1993. "Regulation of Trade Unions in the People's Republic of China." *Melbourne University Law Review* 19 (2): 253–292.

Black, George, and Robin Munro. 1993. *Black Hands of Beijing: Lives of Defiance in China's Democracy Movement*. New York: John Wiley.

Blecher, Marc. 1986. *China: Politics, Economics, and Society*. London: Pinter.

———. 2002. "Hegemony and Workers' Politics in China." *China Quarterly* (170): 283–303.

———. 2003. "Nonsocial Movements and Social Nonmovements in China." In *Egalitarian Politics in the Age of Globalization*, edited by Craig Murphy 124–144. London: Palgrave MacMillan.

———. 2005. "What—and How—Are Tianjin Workers Thinking?" In *China's Newly Emerging Systems of Politics and Economy*, edited by Katsuji Nakagane. Tokyo: Toyobunko.

Bottomore, Thomas. 1983. *A Dictionary of Marxist Thought*. Cambridge, MA: Harvard University Press.

Bramall, Chris, and Marion E. Jones. 1993. "Rural Income Inequality in China Since 1978." *Journal of Peasant Studies* 21 (1): 41–70.

Brenner, Robert. 1998. "The Economics of Global Turbulence." *New Left Review* 229: 1–264.

———. 2002. *The Boom and the Bubble: The U.S. in the World Economy*. New York: Verso.

Brugger, Bill. 1976. *Democracy & Organization in the Chinese Industrial Enterprise (1948–1953)*. New York: Cambridge University Press.

———. 1985. "Democracy and Organization in Chinese Industry: New Directions?" In *China: Dilemmas of Modernization*, edited by Graham Young, 61–99. Sydney: Croom Helm.

Burawoy, Michael. 1996. "The State and Economic Involution: Russia Through a China Lens." *World Development* 24 (6): 1105–1117.

———. 2001. "Neoclassical Sociology: From the End of Communism to the End of Classes." *American Journal of Sociology* 106 (4): 1099–1120.

———, and Janos Lukacs. 1992. *The Radiant Past: Ideology and Reality in Hungary's Road to Capitalism*. Chicago: University of Chicago Press.

———. and Katherine Verdery. 1999. *Uncertain Transition: Ethnographies of Change in the Postsocialist World*. Lanham: Rowman & Littlefield.

Burnham, Peter. 1997. "Globalization: States, Markets and Class Relations." *Historical Materialism* 1 (1): 150–160.

Cao, Yang, and Nee, Victor. 2000. "Controversies and Evidence in the Market Transition Debate." *American Journal of Sociology* 105 (4): 1175–1195.

Carchedi, Guglielmo. 1987. *Class Analysis and Social Research*. New York: Basil Blackwell.

Chan, Anita. 2001. *China's Workers Under Assault: the Exploitation of Labor in a Globalizing Economy*. Armonk, NY: M. E. Sharpe.

Chan, Cecilia, and Nelson Chow. 1992. *More Welfare After Economic Reform? Welfare Development in the People's Republic of China*. Hong Kong: Centre for Urban Planning and Environmental Management, University of Hong Kong.

Chen, An. 1995. "Democratic Reform of Management Structures in China's Industrial Enterprises." *Politics and Society* 23 (3): 369–410.

———.1999. *Restructuring Political Power in China: Alliances and Opposition, 1978–1998*. Boulder, CO: Lynne Rienner Publishers.

Chen, Feng. 2003. "Between the State and Labor: The Conflict of Chinese Trade Unions' Dual Institutional Identity." *The China Quarterly* (176): 1006–1028.

———. 2006. "Privatization and its Discontents in Chinese Factories." *The China Quarterly* (185): 42–60.

———. 2007. "Individual Rights and Collective Rights: Labor's Predicament in China." *Communist and Post-Communist Studies* 40 (1): 59–79.

Cheng, Xiaonong. 1995. "Weichi Wending Yu Shenhua Gaige: Zhongguo Mienling de Jueze" (Transition vs. Stability: China's Dilemma). *Dangdai Zhonggu Yanjiu (Modern China Studies)* (1/2): 84–106.

Chibber, Vivek. 1999. "Building a Developmental State: The Korean Case Reconsidered." *Politics & Society* 27 (3): 309–347.

China to lag behind in more competitive post-crisis Asia. 1999, June 27. *AFP*.

Chiu, Catherine H. 2006. "Changing Experiences of Work in Reformed State-Owned Enteprises in China." *Organization Studies* 27 (5): 677–697.

Choe, Chongwoo, and Xiangkang Yin. 2000. "Do China's State Owned Enterprises Maximze Profit?" *The Economic Record* 76 (234): 273–284.

Clarke, S. 1992. "Privatisation and the Transition to Capitalism in Russia." *New Left Review* (196): 3–28.

———. 1993a. "Popular Attitudes to the Transition to a Market Economy in the Soviet Union on the Eve of Reform." *Sociological Review* 41 (4): 619–652.

———. 1993b. *What about the Workers? Workers and the Transition to Capitalism in Russia*. New York: Verso.

———. 2002. "Globalisation and the Subsumption of the Soviet Mode of Production Under Capital." In *Anti-Capitalism: A Marxist Introduction*, edited by Alfredo Saad-Filho, 187–200. London: Pluto Press.

———, and Petr Biziukov. 1992. "Privatisation in Russia: The Road to a People's Capitalism?" *Monthly Review* 44 (November): 38–45.

———, and Veronika Kabalina. . 2000. "The New Private Sector in the Russian Labour Market." *Europe Asia Studies* 52 (1): 7–32.

Cliver, Robert. 2002. *Minzhu Guanli: The "Democratization" of Factory Management in the Chinese Revolution*. Paper presented at the China's Long Twentieth Century: Words, Images, Voices: Third Annual Graduate Symposium, University of Chicago, April.

Cooper Ramo, J. 1998. The Shanghai Bubble. *Foreign Policy* 111 (Summer): 64–75.

Cumings, Bruce. 1998. "The Korean Crisis and the End of 'Late' Development." *New Left Review* (231): 44–70.

Feng, Tongqing. 2005. "Social Transition and Positive Adjustments in the State Enterprise-Worker Relationship. A Case Study in Chinese Enterprise Worker Participation." *Chinese Sociology and Anthropology* 37 (4): 34–51.

Filtzer, Donald. A. 1994. *Soviet Workers and the Collapse of Perestroika: The Soviet Labour Process and Gorbachev's Reforms, 1985–1991*. New York: Cambridge University Press.

———. 2002. *Soviet Workers and De-Stalinization: The Consolidation of the Modern System of Soviet Production Relations 1953–1964*. Cambridge, UK: Cambridge University Press.

Frazier, Mark W. 2002. *The Making of the Chinese Workplace: State, Revolution, and Labor Management*. Cambridge, UK: Cambridge University Press.

Gallagher, Mary. 2005. "Use the Law as Your Weapon! Institutional Change and Legal Mobilization in China." In *Engaging the Law in China: State, Society, and Possibilities for Justice*, edited by Neil J. Diamant, Stanley Lubman, and Kevin J. O'Brien, 54–83. Stanford: Stanford University Press.

Gramsci, Antonio. 1971. *Selections from the Prison Notebooks of Antonio Gramsci*. London: Lawrence & Wishart.

Greenfield, Gerard. 1997, November 24. *Transnational Capital and Workers in China*. Paper delivered to the Second International Seminar on TNCs in East Asia, Tokyo, Japan.

———. 1999 "The WTO, the World Food System, and the Politics of Harmonised Destruction." *Asia Monitor Resource Center*. Available from http://www.amrc.org.hk/asian_labour_update_article/world_trade_organisation/the_wto_the_world_food_system_and_the_politics_

———, and Leong, Apo. 1997. "China's Communist Capitalism: The Real World of Market Socialism." In *Socialist Register 1997*, edited by Leo Panitch, 96–122. New York: Monthly Review Press.

Habermas, Jürgen. 1989. *The Structural Transformation of the Public Sphere: An Inquiry into a Category of Bourgeois Society*. Cambridge, MA: MIT Press.

Han, Deqiang. 2000. *Pengzhuang: Quanqiuhua Xianjing yu Zhongguo Xianshi Xuanze (Collision! The Trap of Globalization and China's Real Choice)*. Beijing Shi: Jingji Guanli Chubanshe (Economic Management Publishers).

Harris, Nigel. 1978. *The Mandate of Heave : Marx and Mao in Modern China*. New York: Quartet Books.

Hartford, Katherine. 1990. "The Political Economy Behind Beijing Spring." In *The Chinese People's Movement: Perspectives on Spring 1989*, edited by Tony Saich, 50–82. Armonk, NY: M. E. Sharpe.

Hart-Landsberg, Martin, and Paul Burkett. 2001. "Crisis and Recovery in East Asia: The Limits of Capitalist Development." *Historical Materialism* 8 (1): 3–47.

———. 2006. "China and the Dynamics of Transnational Accumulation: Causes and Consequences of Global Restructuring." *Historical Materialism* 14(3): 3–43.

———. . 2007. "China, Capitalist Accumulation, and Labor." *Monthly Review* 59 (2): 17–36.

Harvey, David. 1982. *The Limits to Capital*. Chicago: University of Chicago Press.

———. 2005. *The New Imperialism*. New York: Oxford University Press.

———. 2006 *Spaces of Global Capitalism: Towards a Theory of Uneven Geographical Development*. London: Verso.

———. 2007. *A Brief History of Neoliberalism*. New York: Oxford University Press.

Hassard, John, Jonathan Morris, Jackie Sheehan, and Yuxin Xiao. 2002. "Globalization, Economic Institutions, and Workplace Change: The Economic Reform Process in China." In *Globalization, Employment, and the Workplace: Diverse Impacts*, edited by Debrah Yaw, 115–129. New York: Routledge.

Hassard, John, Jackie Sheehan, Meixiang Zhuo, Jane Terposta-Tong, and Jonathan Mooris. 2007. *Chinese State Enterprise Reform: From Marx to Market*. New York: Routledge.

He, Qinglian. 2000. "China's Listing Social Structure." *New Left Review* (5): 69–99.

Hinton, William. 1990. *The Great Reversal: The Privatization of China, 1978–1989*. New York: Monthly Review Press.

Hoffman, Charles. 1977. "Worker Participation in Chinese Factories." *Modern China* 3 (3): 291–320.

Holmstrom, Nancy, and Richard Smith. 2000. "The Necessity of Gangster Capitalism Primitive Accumulation in Russia and China." *Monthly Review* 51: 9.

Howard, Pat. 1991. "Rice Bowls and Job Security: The Urban Contract Labour System." *Australian Journal of Chinese Affairs* 25: 93–114.

———, and Roger Howard. 1995. "The Campaign to Eliminate Job Security in China." *Journal of Contemporary Asia* 25 (3): 338–355.

Hsiao, Hsin-Huang Michael, and Alvin Y So. 1996. "The Taiwan-Mainland Economic Nexus: Sociopolitical Origins, State-Society Impacts, and Future Prospects." *Bulletin of Concerned Asian Scholars* 28 (1): 3–12.

Hurst, William. 2004. "Understanding Contentious Collective Action by Chinese Laid-Off Workers: The Importance of Regional Political Economy." *Studies in Comparative International Development* 39: 94–120.

Jiang, Xueqin. 2002. "Letter from China." *The Nation* 274 (8): 23–25.

Kaple, Deborah A. 1994. *Dream of a Red Factory: The Legacy of High Stalinism in China*. New York: Oxford University Press.

Kasmir, Sharryn. 1996. *The Myth of Mondragon: Cooperatives, Politics, and Working-Class Life in a Basque Town*. Albany, NY: SUNY Press.

Klein, Naomi. 2007. *Sin Patron: Stories from Argentina's Worker-Run Factories*. Chicago: Haymarket Books.

Korzec, Michael, and Christopher Howe. 1992. *Labour and the Failure of Reform in China*. New York: St. Martin's Press.

Kotz, David M., and Fred Weir. 1997a. *Revolution From Above: The Demise of the Soviet System*. New York: Routledge.

———. 1997b. "Why did the USSR Fail? The Party Elite, Not the Masses, Wanted Capitalism." *Dollars and Sense* (212).

Lardy, Nicholas R. 1998. *China's Unfinished Economic Revolution.* Washington, DC: Brookings Institution Press.

———. 2002. *Integrating China into the Global Economy.* Washington, DC: Brookings Institution Press.

Lau, Raymond W. K. 1996. "The Role of the Working Class in the 1989 Mass Movement in Beijing." *Journal of Communist Studies and Transition Politics* 12 (3): 343–373.

———. 1997. "China: Labour Reform and the Challenge Facing the Working Class." *Capital and Class* (61): 45–80.

———. 1999a. "Left and Right in China's Economic Reform in the 1990's and the Facade of Third Thought Liberation." *The Pacific Review* 12 (1): 79–102.

———. 1999b. "The 15th Congress of the Chinese Communist Party: Milestone in China's Privatization." *Capital and Class* (68) 51–87.

———. 2001a. "Economic Determinations in the Last Instance: China's Political-Economic Development Under the Impact of the Asian Financial Crisis." *Historical Materialism* 8: 215–251.

———. 2001b. "Socio-Political Control in Urban China: Changes and Crisis." *British Journal of Sociology* 52 (4): 605–620.

Lee, Ching Kwan. 1999. "Focus on Employment Issues—From Organized Dependence to Disorganized Despotism: Changing Labour Regimes in Chinese Factories." *The China Quarterly* (157): 44–71.

———. 2000a. "Pathways of Labor Insurgency." In *Chinese Society: Change, Conflict, and Resistance,* edited by Elizabeth. J. Perry and Mark Selden, 41–61. New York: Routledge.

———. 2000b. "The 'Revenge of History': Collective Memories and Labor Protests in Northeastern China." *Ethnography* 1 (2): 217–237.

———. 2002. "From the Specter of Mao to the Spirit of the Law: Labor Insurgency in China." *Theory and Society* 31 (2): 189–228.

———. 2007. *Against the Law: Labor Protests in China's Rustbelt and Sunbelt.* Berkeley: University of California Press.

Leung, Joe, C. B. 1994. "Dismantling the 'Iron Rice Bowl': Welfare Reforms in the People's Republic of China." *The Journal of Social Policy* 23 (3): 341–361.

Li, Minqi. 1994. "China: Six Years After Tiananmen." *Monthly Review* 47 (8): 1–13.

Li, Tan. 1994. "Population Flow in the Big Cities." *Beijing Review* (July): 15–19.

Lim,Timothy. 1998. "Rethinking the Politics of Development in South Korea." *Journal of Contemporary Asia* 28 (4): 457–483.

Lin, Chun. 2006. *The Transformation of Chinese Socialism.* Durham,, NC: Duke University Press.

Lin, Jialin. 2005. *The Process of Restructuring Liaoyang Ferro-Alloy Factory and Workers' Struggle against Corruption.* Unpublished paper posted at the *Wuyouzhixiang* Web site (www.wyzxwyzx.com).

Liu, Binyan, and Perry Link. 1998. "A Great Leap Backward? Review of China's Pitfall by He Qing Lian." *New York Review of Books* 45 (15).

Lo, Dic. 1999. "Re-Appraising the Performance of China's State-Owned Industrial Enterprises, 1980–96." *Cambridge Journal of Economics* 23 (6): 693–718.

———. 2001. "China after East Asian Developmentalism." *Historical Materialism* (8): 253–264.

———. 2002. "Explaining the Financial Performance of China's Industrial Enterprises: Beyond the Competition-Ownership Controversy." *The China Quarterly* (170): 413–440.

Lu, Ping. 1992. "The Pyramidal Structure of China's Working Class." *Tiananmen Review* (June): 162–178.

McMichael, Philip. 2000. *Development and Social Change: A Global Perspective, Second Edition*. Thousand Oaks, CA: Pine Forge Press.

Manicas, Peter. 2007. *A Realist Philosophy of Social Science: Explanation and Understanding*. Cambridge, UK: Cambridge University Press.

Marshall, T.H. 1992. *Citizenship and Social Class*. London, Pluto Press.

Marx, Karl, and Fredrick Engels. 1935/1847. *Wage-Labor and Capital*. Chicago: C. H. Kerr & Company.

Meng, Xianming, and Brian Dollery. 2006. "Institutional Constraints and Feasible Reform for State-Owned Enterprises in China." ICFAI Journal of Public Administration 11(4): 7–26.

Nakagane, Katsugi. 2000, November. *SOE Reform and Privatization in China: A Note on Several Theoretical and Empirical Issues*. Discussion paper, University of Tokyo. Available from http://www.e.u-tokyo.ac.jp/cirje/research/dp/2000/2000cf95.pdf

Nee, Victor. 1996. "The Emergence of a Market Society: Changing Mechanisms of Stratification in China." *American Journal of Sociology* 101 (4): 908–949.

———, David Stark, and Mark Selden. 1989. *Remaking the Economic Institutions of Socialism: China and Eastern Europe*. Stanford: Stanford University Press.

Ollman, Bertell. 1992. *Dialectical Investigations*. New York: Routledge.

Panitch, Leo. 1994. "Globalization and the State." In *Socialist Register*, edited by Leo Panitch and Ralph Miliband, 60–94. New York: Monthly Review Press.

———. 1998. "The State in a Changing World: Social-Democratizing Global Capitalism." *Monthly Review* 50 (5): 11–22.

Parker, David, and Weihwa Pan, 1996. "Reform of the State Owned Enterprises in China." *Communist Economies and Economic Transformation* 8 (1): 109–127.

Perry, Elizabeth. 1994. "Shanghai's Strike Wave of 1957." *China Quarterly* (137): 1–27.

———, and Xun Li. 1997. *Proletarian Power: Shanghai in the Cultural Revolution*. Boulder, CO: Westview Press.

Philion, Stephen. 1998. "Chinese Welfare State Regimes." *The Journal of Contemporary Asia* 28 (3): 518–536.

———. 2005. "Extending the Limits of Fieldwork: Encounters with Chinese Workers Protesting Privatization." *Humanity and Society* 29 (3&4): 305–326.

———. 2007. "Workers' Democracy Versus Privatization in China." *Socialism and Democracy* 21 (2): 37–55.

———. 2008. *The Stubbornness of Class: Workers' Resistance and China's Transition from State Socialism*. Paper presented at the annual conference of the Association of Asian Studies, Atlanta, GA.

Qian, Yingyi. 1996. "Enterprise Reform in China: Agency Problems and Political Control." *Economics of Transition* 4 (2): 427–447.

———, and Xu Chenggang. 1998. "Innovation and Bureaucracy under Soft and Hard Budget Constraints." *Review of Economic Studies* 65 (1): 151–164.

Rawski, Thomas. 2000. "Is China's State Enterprise Problem Still Important?" Available from http://www.pitt.edu/~tgrawski/papers2000/SKETCH.HTM.

———. 2002. *Where's the Growth?* Available from http://www.pitt.edu/~tgrawski/papers2002/oped.pdf .

Riskin, Carl. 1987. *China's Political Economy: The Search for Development*. Oxford: Oxford University Press.

Rust sets in on reform. (1999, June 10). *South China Morning Post*.

Sabin, Lora. 1994. "New Bosses in the Workers' State: The Growth of Non-State Employment in China." *The China Quarterly* (140): 944–970.

Saich, Tony. 1984. "Workers in the Workers' State: Urban Workers in the PRC." In *Groups and Politics in the People's Republic of China*, edited by David Goodman, 152–176. Cardiff, Wales: University College Cardiff Press.

Selden, Mark. 1971. *The Yenan Way in Revolutionary China*. Cambridge, MA: Harvard University Press.

———. 1993. *The Political Economy of Chinese Development*. Armonk, NY: M. E. Sharpe.

———. 1994. "Russia, China, and the Transformation of Collective Agriculture." *Contention* 3 (3): 73–93.

Sheehan, Jackie. 1998. *Chinese Workers: A New History*. New York: Routledge.

Singh, Surjit. 1995. Trends in the Chinese Economy. *China Report* 31 (4): 429–445.

Sirianni, Carmen. 1982. *Workers Control and Socialist Democracy: The Soviet Experience*. London: NLB.

Smith, Adam. 1993/1776. *An Inquiry into the Nature and Cause of the Wealth of Nations*. Oxford: Oxford University Press.

Smith, Richard. 1993. "The Chinese Road to Capitalism." *New Left Review* (199): 55–99.

So, Alvin, and Henghao Chang. 1998. "Powerful Communist Party, Robust Capitalist Economy: Interpreting the Chinese Puzzle." *Huboldt Journal of Social Relations* 24 (1–2): 101–127.

SOE sell-off prospects looming larger as Jiang again takes charge. (1999, August 23). *South China Morning Post*.

Solinger, Dorothy. 1995. "The Chinese Work Unit and Transient Labor in the Transition from Socialism." *Modern China* 21 (2): 155–183.

State-owned enterprise reform change sees SOEs swap one crisis for another. (1999, June 10). *South China Morning Post*.

Taylor, Bill, Kai Chang, and Qi Li. 2003. *Industrial relations in China*. Cheltenham, UK: E. Elgar Pub.

Ticktin, Hillel. 1973. Towards a Political Economy of the USSR. *Critique* 1(1): 20–41.

———. 1992. *Origins of the Crisis in the USSR: Essays on the Political Economy of a Disintegrating System*. Armonk, NY: M. E. Sharpe.

Tong, Xin. 2005. "The Cultural Basis of Workers' Collective Action in a Transitional State-Owned Enterprise During a Time of Transition." *Chinese Sociology and Anthropology* 38 (1): 42–70.

Unger, Jonathan, and Anita Chan. 1996. "Corporatism in China: A Developmental State in an East Asian Context." In *China After Socialism: In the Footsteps of Eastern Europe or East Asia?*, edited by Barret McCormick and Jonathan Unger, 95–129. Armonk, NY: M. E. Sharpe.

———. 2004. "The Internal Politics of an Urban Chinese Work Community: A Case Study of Employee Influence on Decision-Making at a State-Owned Factory." *The China Journal* (52): 1–24.

Wade, Robert, and Frank Veneroso. 1998. "The Asian Crisis: The High Debt Model Versus the Wall Street-Treasury-IMF Complex." *New Left Review* 228 (March/April): 3–23.

Walder, Andrew G. 1986. *Communist Neo-traditionalism: Work and Authority in Chinese Industry*. Berkeley: University of California Press.

———. 1989. "Factory and Manager in an Era of Reform." *China Quarterly* (118): 242–264.

———. 1991. Workers, Managers and the State: The Reform Era and the Political Crisis of 1989. *The China Quarterly* (127): 444–466.

———, and Xiaoxia Gong. 1993. "Workers in the Tiananmen Protests: The Politics of the Beijing Workers' Autonomous Federation." *The Australian Journal of Chinese Affairs* (29): 1–29.

Waldron, Arthur. 2002. "China's Disguised Failure." *Financial Times.*

Warner, Malcolm. 1987. "Industrial Relations in the Chinese Factory." *The Journal of Industrial Relations* 29: 217–232.

Watson, Andrew. 1978. "Industrial Management and Experiments in Mass Participation." In *China: The Impact of the Cultural Revolution*, edited by Bill Brugger, 171–202. London: Croom Helm.

Wilson, Jeanne. L. 1987. "The Institution of Democratic Reforms in the Chinese Enterprise Since 1978." In *Worker Participation and the Politics of Reform*, edited by Carmen Sirianni, 298–328. Philadelphia: Temple University Press.

Wong, Linda. 1996, April 11–15. *Funding Options for Enterprise Welfare-Realities and Constraints.* Paper presented at the Association for Asian Studies Conference, Honolulu, HI.

Workers' Forum, National Edition (October, 1996).

Wood, Ellen Meiskins. 1994. "From Opportunity to Imperative: The History of the Market." *Monthly Review* (July/August): 14–40.

———. 1997a. " 'Globalization' or 'Globaloney'?" *Monthly Review* 49 (February): 21–32.

———. 1997b. "Labor, the State, and Class Struggle." *Monthly Review* 49 (July–August): 1–17.

Wu, Yiching. 2005. "Rethinking 'Capitalist Restoration' in China." *Monthly Review* 57 (6): 44–63.

———. 2007. *Reinterpreting Shanghai's "January Revolution:"A Case for Unthinking and Rethinking the Chinese Cultural Revolution.* Unpublished manuscript presented at the annual conference of the Association for Asian Studies, Atlanta, GA.

Yan, Hairong. 2002. *Development, Contradictions and the Specter of Disposability: Rural Migrant Women in Search of Self-Development in Post-Mao China.* Unpublished doctoral disseration, University of Washington, Seattle.

Yuan, Mu, Deming Yang, and Xuewen Xun. 1998. *ZhenTan: Shijiede Yazhou Jingrong Weiji (Shaking up the World: The Asian Financial Crisis.)* Beijing: Dangdai.

Zhang, Jing. 2001. *Liyi Zhuzhihua Danwei: Qiye Zhidaihui Anlieyanjiu (The Unit of Organized Interests: A Case Study on Labor Congress at Factory).* Beijing: China Social Sciences Publishers.

Zhang, Qinde. 1999. *Yanjiuyu Tantao (Research and Exlporation).* Beijing: Renmin Chubanshe.

Zhao, Minghua, and Theo Nichols. 1996. "Management Control of Labour in State-Owned Enterprises: Cases from the Textile Industry." *The China Journal* (26): 1–21.

Zhu, Xiaoyang, and Anita Chan. 2005. "Staff and Workers' Representative Congress: An Institutionalized Channel for Expression of Employees' Interests?" *Chinese Sociology and Anthropology* 37 (4, Summer): 6–33.

Index

Printed in the United States
by Baker & Taylor Publisher Services